I0803224

POSTCARD HISTORY SERIES

St. Augustine in the 1930s and 1940s

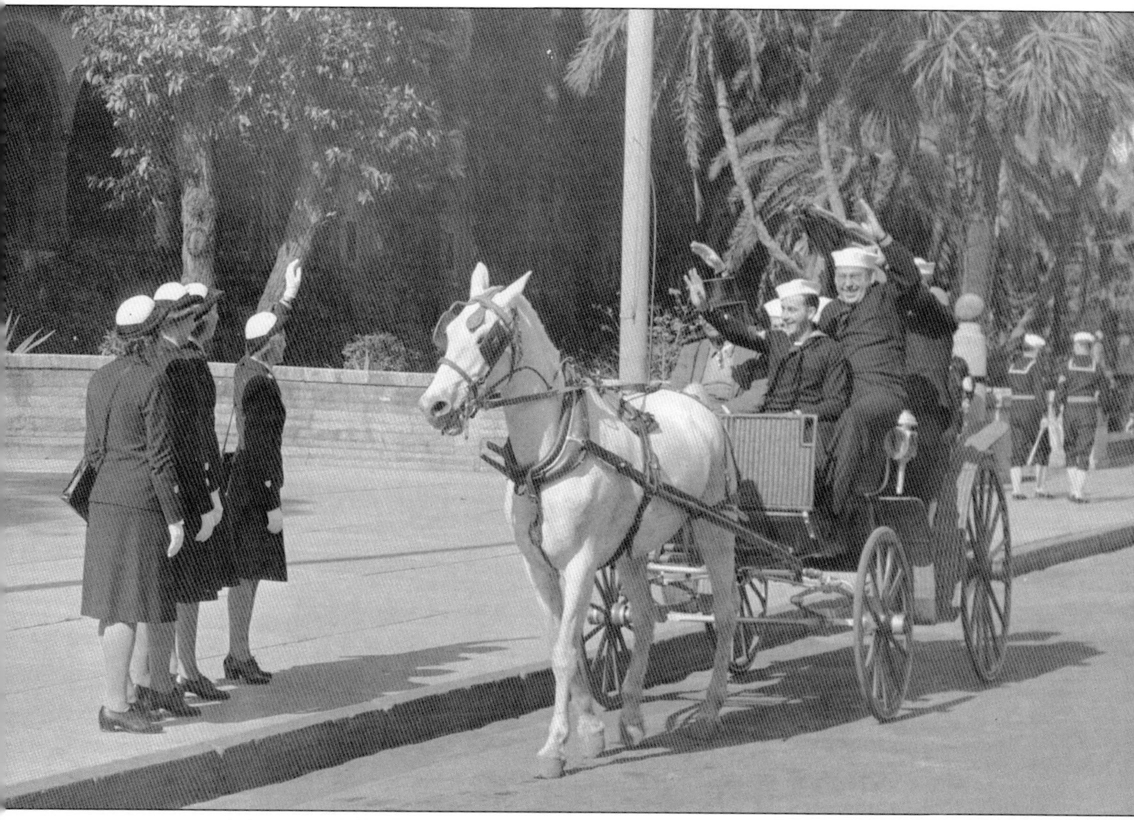

A group of SPARS (US Coast Guard Women's Reserve) waves to sailors in a sightseeing carriage in front of the Hotel Ponce de Leon. Several St. Augustine hotels, including the Ponce, were taken over during World War II to house male and female Coast Guard trainees. The influx of military personnel during the war years created an economic boom in the city. (St. Augustine Historical Society.)

On the Front Cover: Taken by local photographer Philip A. Wolfe, this postcard of Cathedral Place looks west toward the twin spires of the Hotel Ponce de Leon. At right, on the corner of St. George Street, is the Cathedral Rectory, surrounded by its unique concrete fence. When the cathedral was remodeled for St. Augustine's 400th anniversary in 1965, the rectory was razed and its fence relocated to a home at 262 St. George Street. (O'Neill Collection.)

On the Back Cover: Another Wolfe postcard shows one of St. Augustine's popular sightseeing carriages headed south through the City Gate. Owner Louis A. Colee began converting his St. Augustine Transfer Company to motorized vehicles in the mid-1920s and sold all his horse-drawn carriages. But he soon realized that tourists liked the nostalgic way of travel and began buying back the carriages, which remain a familiar sight in St. Augustine to this day. (Author's collection.)

Postcard History Series

St. Augustine in the 1930s and 1940s

Beth Rogero Bowen and the St. Augustine Historical Society

ARCADIA
PUBLISHING

ISBN 978-1-4671-0395-4

Published by Arcadia Publishing
Charleston, South Carolina

Printed in the United States of America

Library of Congress Control Number: 2019934177

For all general information contact Arcadia Publishing at:
Telephone 843-853-2070
Fax 843-853-0044
E-mail sales@arcadiapublishing.com
For customer service and orders:
Toll-Free 1-888-313-2665

Visit us on the Internet at www.arcadiapublishing.com

This book is dedicated to the author's cousins,
Betty Parkhill Bracken and Virginia Parkhill Danford,
whose photograph appears at the bottom of page 24.
Their fond memories of growing up in St. Augustine in the
1930s and 1940s were a great contribution to this book.

Contents

ACKNOWLEDGMENTS

I wish to thank Charles Tingley, senior research librarian at the St. Augustine Historical Society Research Library, for his help in gathering information for the book and proofreading the text. His knowledge of the people and places that shaped St. Augustine's history add many interesting details to the narrative. Also thanks to Bob Nawrocki, chief librarian, for proofreading the text and to Chad Germany, assistant librarian, for his help in gathering research material and technical advice in scanning the images.

I also thank Magen Wilson, executive director of the St. Augustine Historical Society, for her commitment to this project and proofreading the text. Also thanks to the former executive director, Dr. Susan R. Parker, for her help in providing information for the narrative.

I am extremely grateful to Lamona Brallier O'Neill for providing several images from her extensive postcard collection. Thanks for additional images go to Jack and Nadine Connahey, Henry Hird, Emily Alexander, Shelley Desvousges, Henry and Esther Whetstone, and Frank and Betty Usina.

Additional thanks for information used in the text go to Emily Alexander, John Brueggen, Marsha Chance, Merry Colee, Elaine Fraser, John Fraser, Dr. Thomas Graham, George Hellier, Anne Heymen, Marian Kimrey, Terran McGinnis, Margo Pope, Abby Preston, Tom Rahner, Penny Rolleston, Dr. Goodwin Seymour, Rob Sircy, Dr. Roger Smith, Sheila Stafford, Debbie Wicker, Anne Wolfe, and Bill Young.

And special thanks to my husband, Jerry Bowen, for his technical help with computer issues, along with his continual support and encouragement.

Unless otherwise noted, all postcards used in this book are from the author's collection, with images from the St. Augustine Historical Society noted as SAHS.

Introduction

The Great Depression came early to St. Augustine and the rest of the state with the collapse of the Florida land boom in late 1926. The town's major building project, Davis Shores, came to an abrupt halt with developer D.P. Davis's mysterious death at sea on October 12, 1926. The stock market failure in October 1929 only heightened the town's economic misery, and its major financial institution, the First National Bank, closed only a few years after completing its new six-story building on Cathedral Place. The city's largest employer, Henry Flagler's Florida East Coast Railway, declared bankruptcy and was in receivership by September 1931. The elaborate Ponce de Leon Celebration, held annually during the first week of April, was discontinued after the 1930 event. The Alcazar Hotel and its annex, the Cordova, closed in 1932, but the Ponce de Leon Hotel remained open, thanks to Flagler's brother-in-law William R. Kenan, now hotel president. Although the hotel began losing money in 1924, Kenan vowed that as long as he lived, the Ponce would carry on.

St. Augustine's citizens sought to adjust to this boom-to-bust economy. Many homes along San Marco Avenue and King Street, the route of US 1 through the city, were turned into rooming houses and tourist courts. The decline of the larger hotels with their own dining rooms created a demand for other eating places and several small restaurants, owned predominately by Greek families, opened in the downtown area. Prohibition ended with the ratification of the Twenty-First Amendment on December 5, 1933, and soon bars and package stores began opening in the city.

The city's economy began a slow recovery during the 1930s. On November 14, 1933, Jack Thompson and Harold Ryman acquired the bankrupt Davis Shores property at a receivership sale. They sold the subdivision's former sales office on Arredondo Avenue to the Knights of Columbus and began to sell the 1,500 remaining lots and acreage. The Florida East Coast (FEC) Railway came under the control of the feisty Edward Ball, whose older sister Jessie was married to Alfred I. DuPont. Through his control of the DuPont assets, Ball purchased the FEC's bonds and fended off a takeover attempt by the Atlantic Coast Line Railroad.

Public works projects, funded by Pres. Franklin Roosevelt's many "alphabet agencies," sought to provide work to local residents. The Civic Center, now the Visitor Information Center, was funded by the Federal Emergency Relief Administration and opened in 1935. The post office, today's Government House, was completely rebuilt and enlarged as a Works Progress Administration (WPA) project between 1936 and 1937. Another WPA project was the St. Augustine Beach pier and boardwalk, flanked by two commercial buildings and completed in 1939. In the late 1930s, the WPA rebuilt Fort Matanzas and constructed a combination visitor's center and ranger's residence on the east side of the Matanzas River. Construction for all of these projects required the use of native coquina stone, and former quarries along Old Beach Road were reopened.

One bright spot during the 1930s was the establishment of a winter art colony in St. Augustine, centered around picturesque Aviles Street. Local residents Celia Reid, Hildegarde Muller-Uri, and J. Dexter Phinney took the lead in establishing the Arts Club of St. Augustine in 1931 and soon were attracting prominent artists from several New England summer resorts. Local garden clubs sponsored a Day in Spain festival on Aviles Street, and the St. Augustine Historical Society created the Oglethorpe Battery Park and monument on Davis Shores in 1938.

Spurred by the Rockefeller-funded restoration of colonial Williamsburg in the early 1930s, city leaders felt that a similar effort should be undertaken to save St. Augustine's remaining colonial structures. Led by Mayor Walter B. Fraser, a local committee met with the Carnegie Institution of Washington, DC, on October 26, 1936. Its first step was a survey of the city's historical buildings, undertaken by Verne Chatelain, former historian with the National Park Service. Noted photographer Frances Benjamin Johnston received a $500 grant from the Carnegie Institution to photograph St. Augustine's historic buildings. The state legislature appropriated $50,000 for acquisition and preservation of historic buildings, but by 1940, only $5,000 had been received. World War II interrupted this ambitious project, and concerted restoration efforts did not resume until the formation of the St. Augustine Historical Restoration and Preservation Commission in 1959.

Marine Studios, the world's first oceanarium, opened on June 23, 1938. Located 18 miles south of St. Augustine on A1A, the oceanfront complex included a restaurant, motel, gas station, bus station, and marina. Visitors flocked to the attraction to observe sea life in two large tanks with viewing windows on three different levels. When wartime gas rationing affected travel and tourism, Marine Studios closed on June 30, 1942, and reopened June 1, 1946.

The decades of the 1930s and 1940s heralded the emergence of the shrimp industry in St. Augustine. Sicilian immigrant Sollecito "Mike" Salvador, together with his brothers-in-law Salvadore Versaggi and Antonio Poli, moved their shrimping operations from Fernandina to St. Augustine in the early 1920s. They established their businesses on the east bank of the San Sebastian River, just south of King Street, and were one of the town's largest employers by the 1940s.

World War II brought profound changes and economic recovery to the Ancient City. The Coast Guard took over the city's largest hotel, the Ponce de Leon, to house new recruits. Other hotels—the Bennett, Monson, Marion, and Ocean View—were also commandeered as training facilities. Coast Guardsmen watched for German submarines from the tower of the lighthouse and patrolled the beaches with dogs. Camp Blanding, near Starke, was expanded into a large infantry training center, and a naval air station was established at Green Cove Springs. Soldiers on leave from these facilities flooded St. Augustine, and a large tent city was built on the San Marco Lot (today's location of the city parking garage and events field) to house them. There was a huge demand for restaurants, lodging, bars, and entertainment, and city merchants were happy to comply and fill their coffers.

The burgeoning economy continued after World War II ended in August 1945. Many servicemen stationed here during the war were so charmed by the city that they returned to make it their home. The availability of VA loans under the Servicemen's Readjustment Act of 1944 created a postwar real estate and baby boom that also fueled a need for new furniture, appliance, and grocery stores. Widespread use of air-conditioning created a summer tourist season, and modern motels and restaurants soon opened on north San Marco Avenue and Anastasia Boulevard. Otto C. Lightner purchased the vacant Alcazar Hotel in 1947 and used it to house his extensive collection of Victorian antiques in his Museum of Hobbies. By the end of the decade, St. Augustine had fully recovered from the Great Depression and was riding an economic wave that continued into the 1950s.

One

Hotels

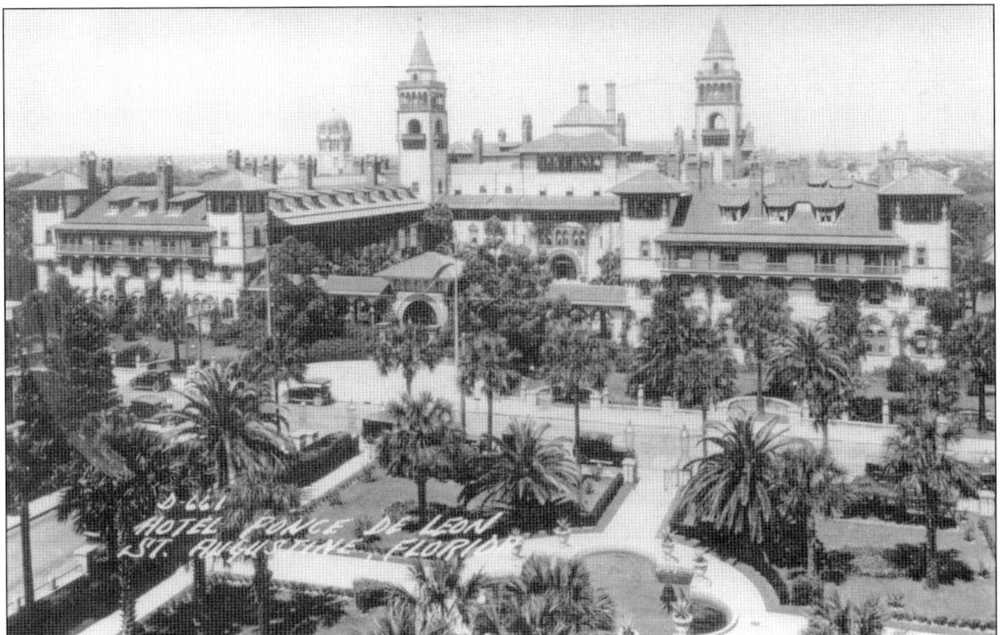

Henry Flagler's magnificent Ponce de Leon Hotel opened in January 1888. The Spanish Renaissance design of architects John Carrere and Thomas Hastings sparked the Mediterranean Revival style that soon became popular all over the state. Portland cement mixed with local coquina formed the hotel's poured concrete walls, and the Ponce's beautiful twin spires held large tanks that supplied the hotel's water.

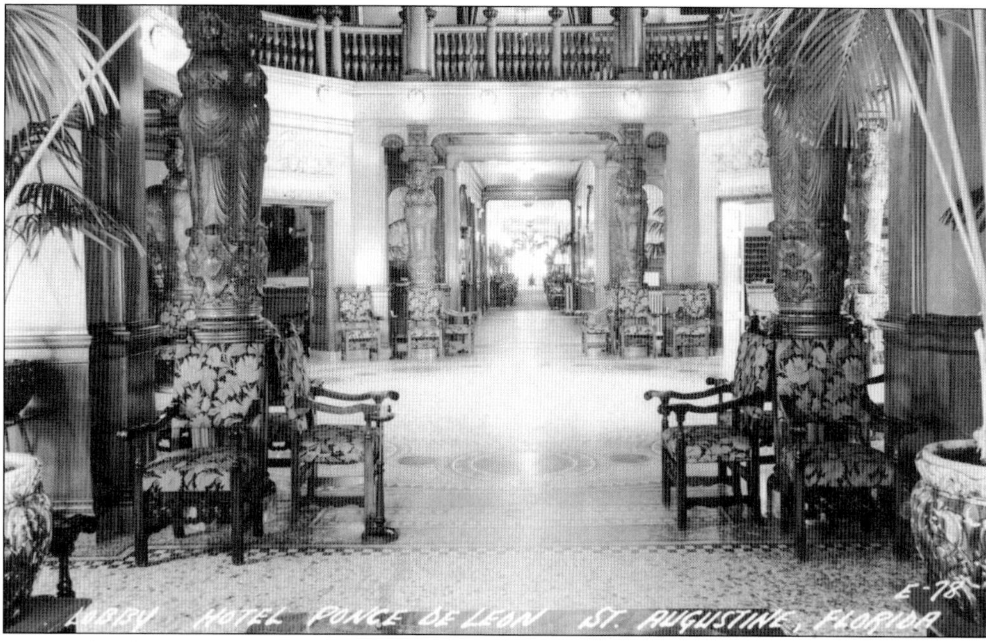

Framed by ornate oak columns, the Ponce's lobby opened into a soaring three-story rotunda, whose dome was adorned with murals by George W. Maynard. This view looks toward the hotel's entrance, with the reception desk at left. Construction of the Ponce de Leon Hotel was done by James A. McGuire and Joseph McDonald, who had built the San Marco Hotel.

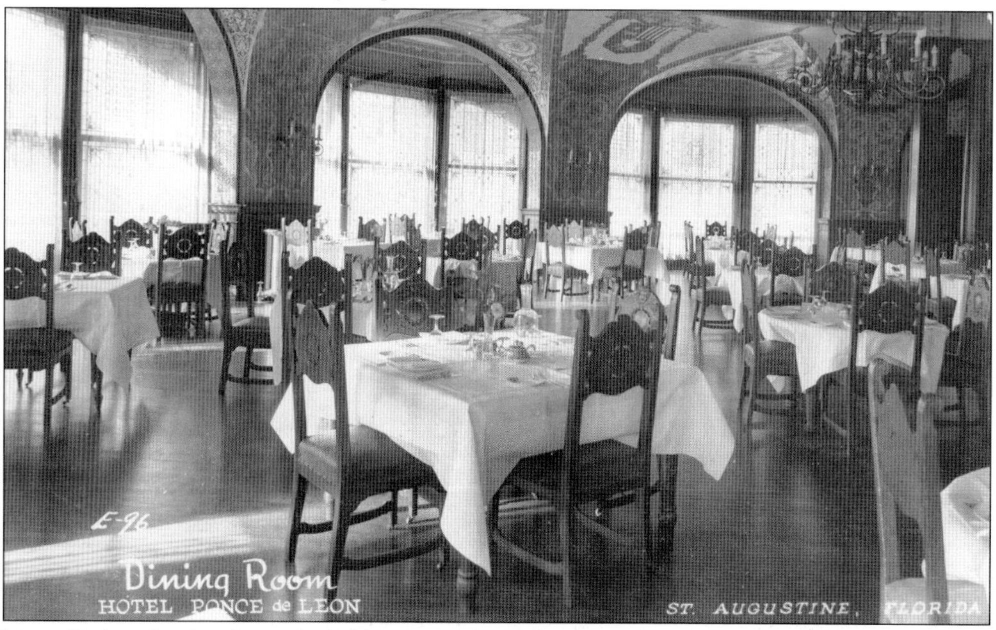

Up a flight of stairs from the lobby was the hotel's dining room. To make the room more intimate, it was divided into three sections, separated by two rows of oak columns. This postcard shows one of the side alcoves with its famous stained-glass windows by Louis Comfort Tiffany. Furniture for the hotel, including these unique chairs, came from Pottier and Stymus of New York City.

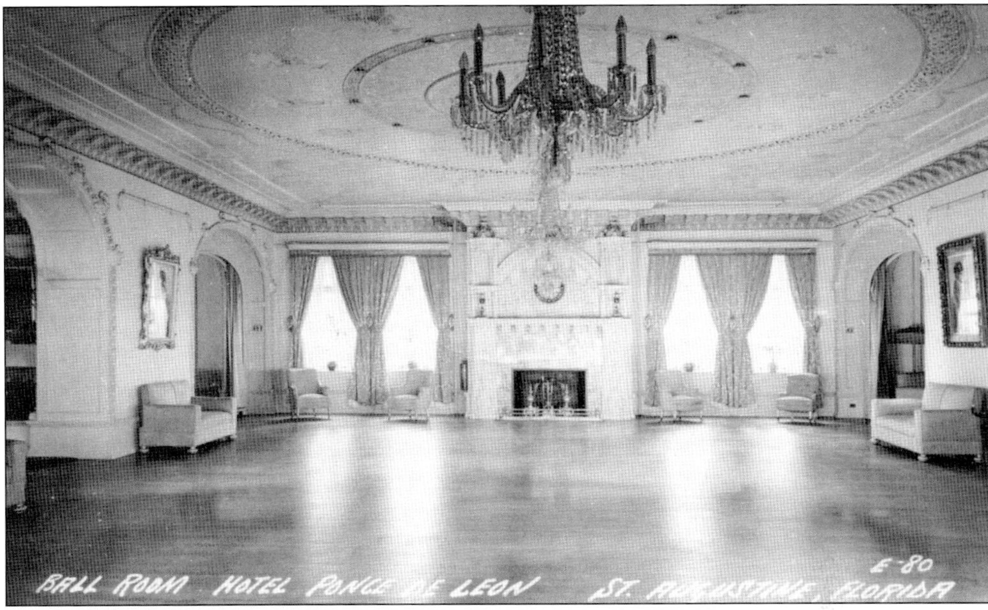

The lounge and ballroom are entered from a hallway leading west from the rotunda. The hotel's grand parlor, once filled with elegant furniture, had been converted to a sparsely furnished ballroom by the time of this 1940 postcard. The room features an elaborate fireplace with an onyx mantle, and the walls of the ballroom and lounge were hung with paintings by noted artists. St. Augustine's residents loved their "Ponce," and many local events and receptions were held in these rooms during the 1930s and 1940s. The Great Depression and the public's preference for motels after World War II brought fewer and fewer guests to the hotel, and it closed after the 1967 season, opening as Flagler College in September 1968. The college undertook a multimillion-dollar project to restore the building to its former glory and continues to preserve this unique place.

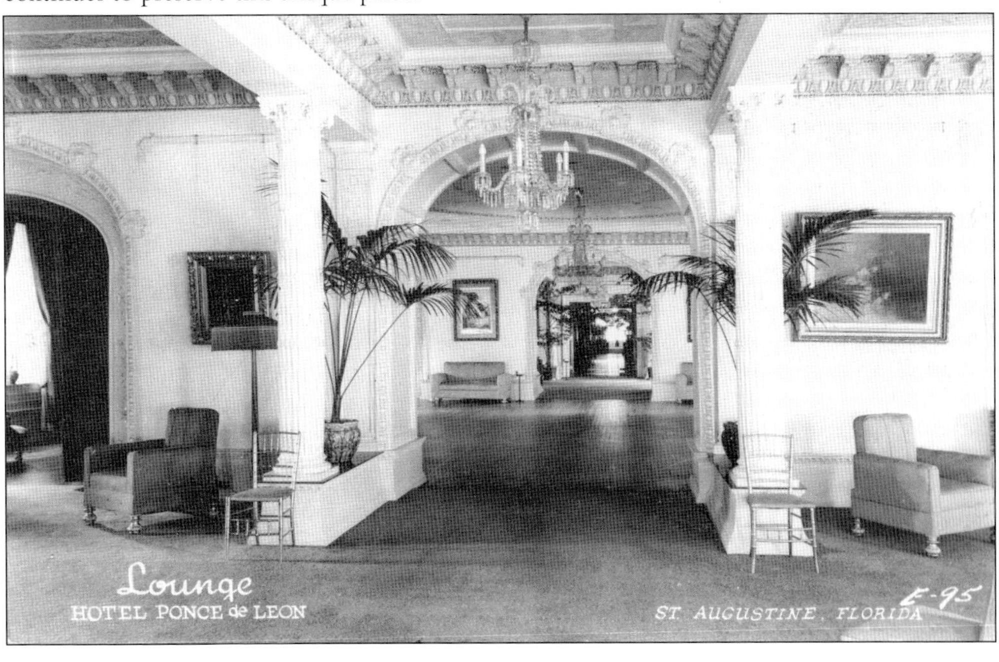

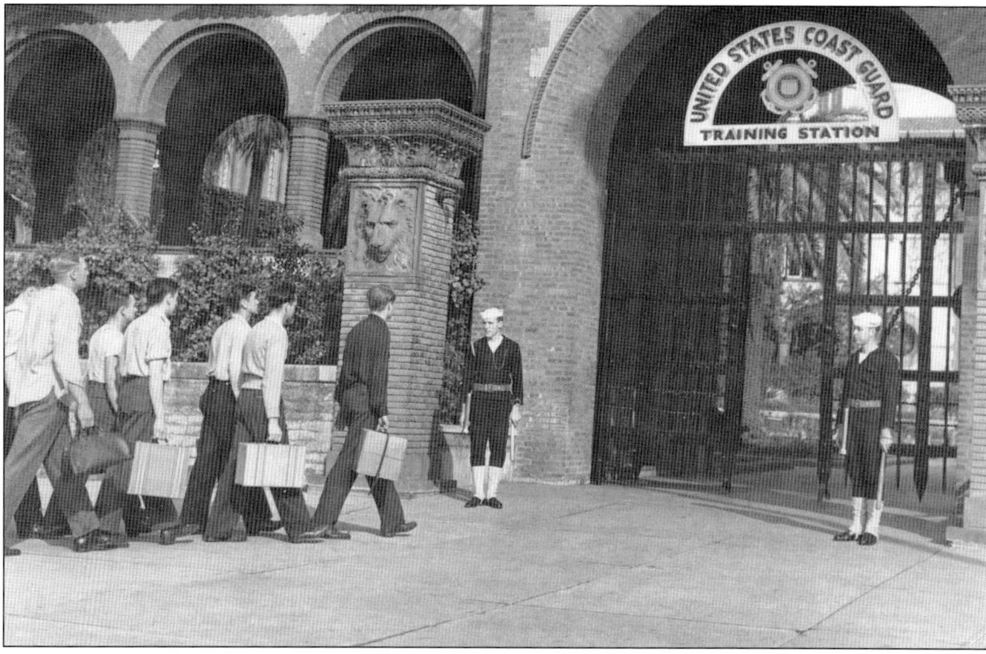

During World War II, the Ponce was taken over by the federal government and used as a Coast Guard Training Center. The hotel's furnishings were removed and stored across the street in the vacant Alcazar Hotel. From 1942 until the end of the war, thousands of young recruits received their basic and advanced training at the hotel, with up to 2,500 trainees living in the building at any one time. (SAHS.)

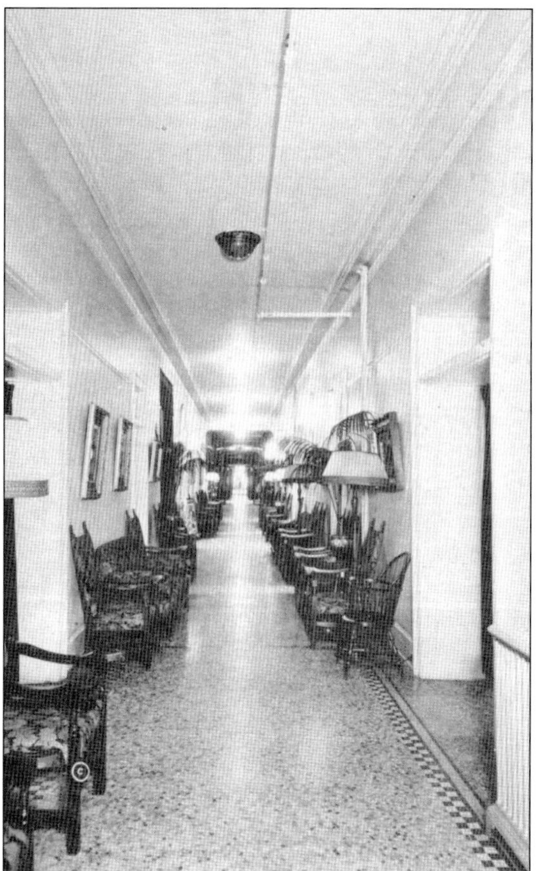

Peacock Alley was the name given to the hallway that ran east from the hotel's rotunda. The original Peacock Alley was in the Waldorf-Astoria in New York City, where the rich paraded for the admiration of others and themselves. Margaret Stancliff, whose husband managed the Doreta Hotel on Orange Street, produced this postcard and a series of other local scenes in the 1930s.

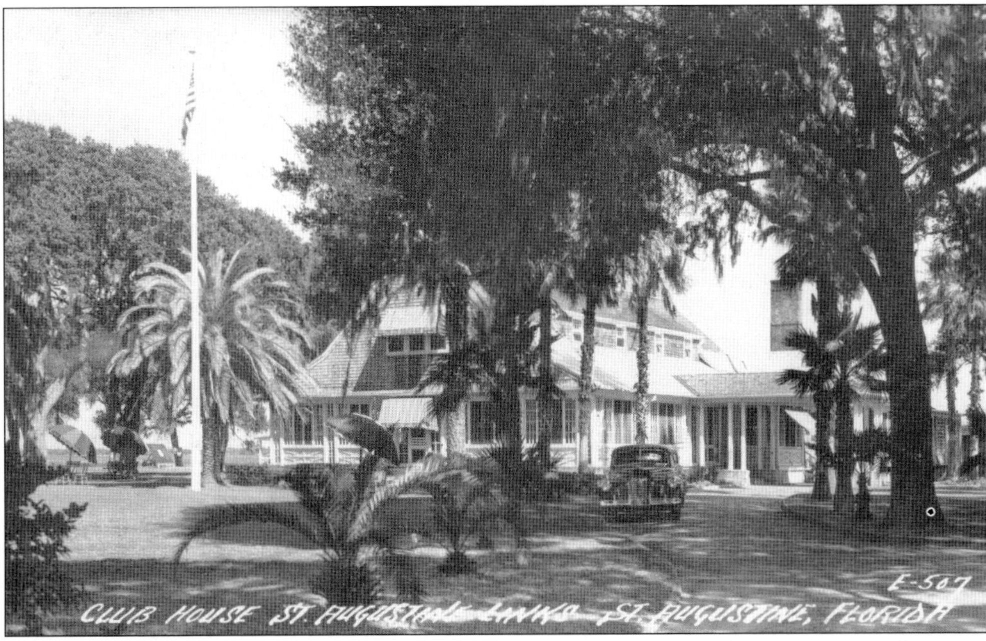

The Flagler System built the St. Augustine Links three miles north of St. Augustine adjacent to the marshes of the Tolomato River. The Donald Ross–designed course opened in January 1917 and featured this classic shingle-style clubhouse. The main room, surrounded by sun parlors, featured a large coquina fireplace and wicker furniture; it was a favorite spot for wedding receptions and other events. In the postcard below, a golfer practices a shot from the sand trap to the putting green located on the west side of the clubhouse. The course later became the Ponce de Leon Country Club but was closed in 2003 due to declining revenues. After an unsuccessful effort by locals to "Save Our Ponce," the property was sold to developer Chester Stokes and is now Madeira at St. Augustine.

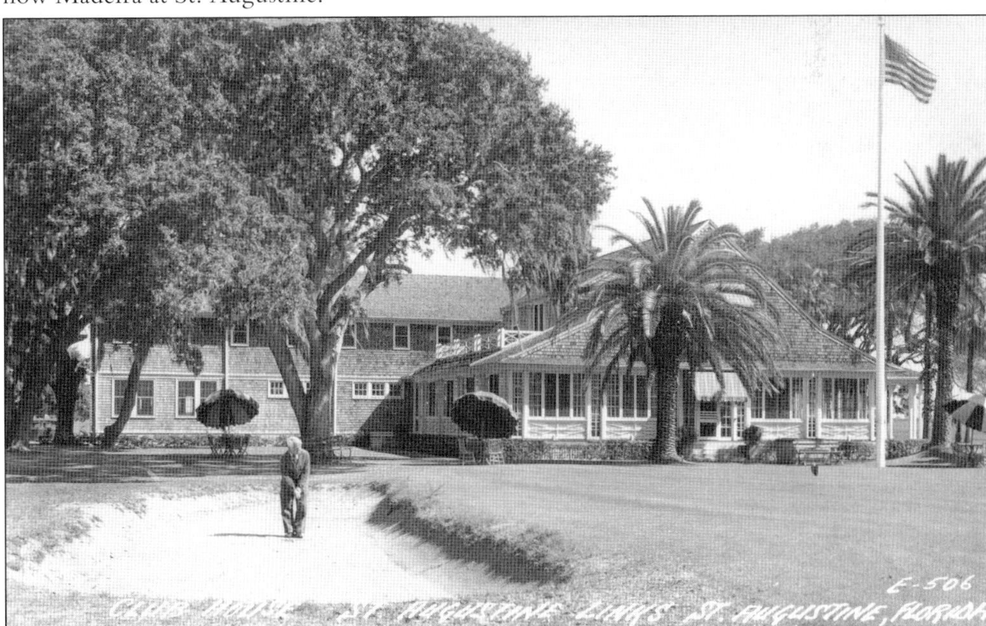

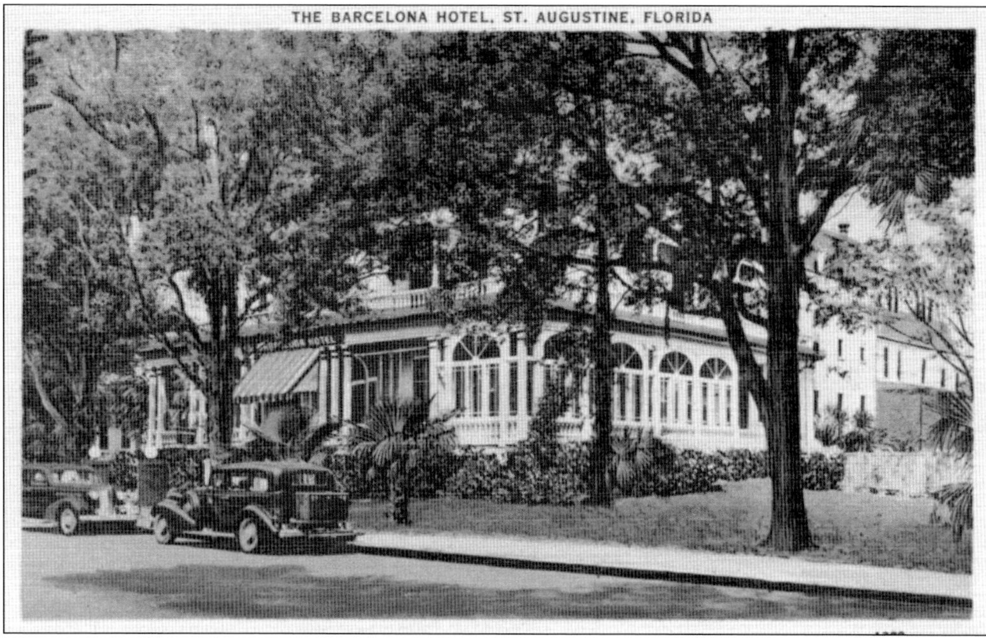

The Barcelona Hotel was originally the Ball Mansion, located on the future site of the Ponce de Leon Hotel. Henry Flagler purchased the home in 1885 and moved it to the northeast corner of Carrera and Sevilla Streets. During the 1930s and 1940s, the Barcelona was the headquarters of a winter baseball camp. Demolished in 1962, the site is now a parking lot for Ancient City Baptist Church. (SAHS.)

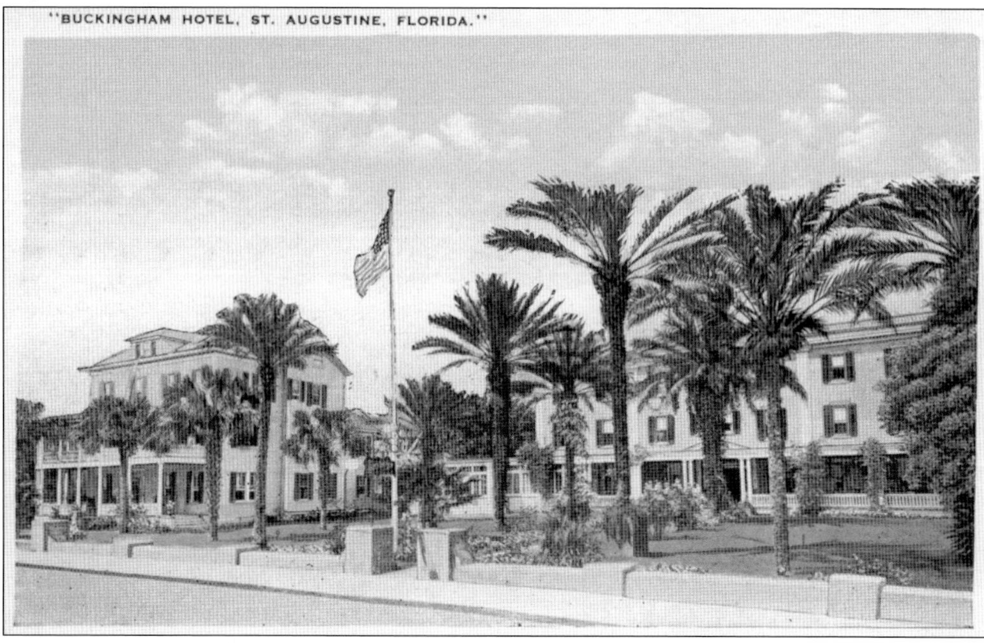

Located at 16 Granada Street, the original portion of the Buckingham Hotel, shown at right, was built in the 1870s as a nursing home for blacks, as a bequest from Buckingham Smith. In the 1920s, the home just to the south became the Buckingham Annex, connected by an enclosed porch. The hotel closed in 1964, and the site is now Flagler College's gymnasium. (SAHS.)

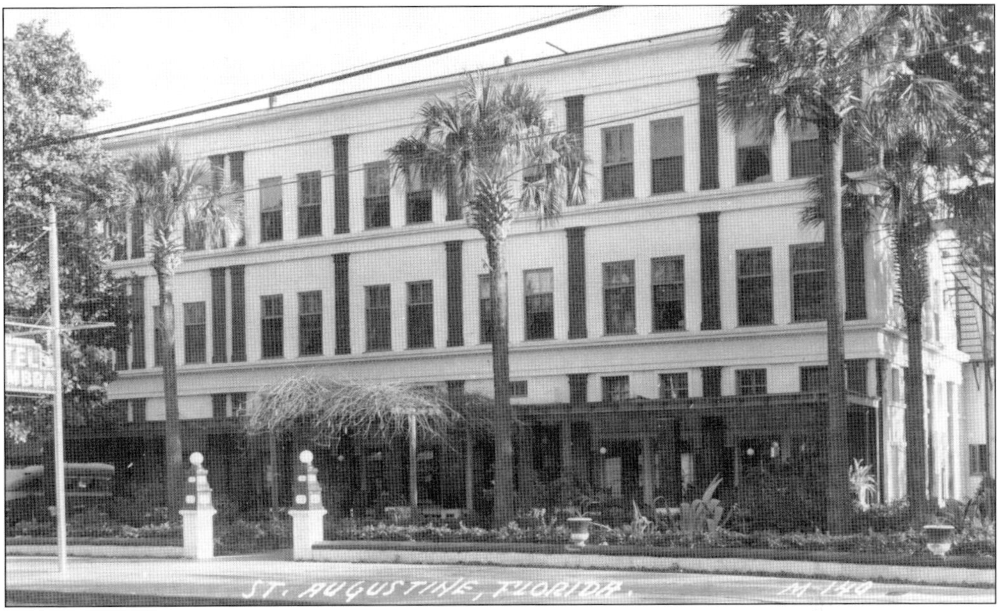

Built in 1895 by Franklin Smith, the Hotel Granada was on the southwest corner of King and Granada Streets. In 1913, Abraham S. Mussallem purchased the hotel and renamed it the Hotel Alhambra. Mussallem died in 1941, and his wife, Olga, continued to manage the popular hotel, which became the meeting place for the Kiwanis, Rotary, Lions, and Exchange Clubs during the 1940s. The hotel burned on September 21, 1954.

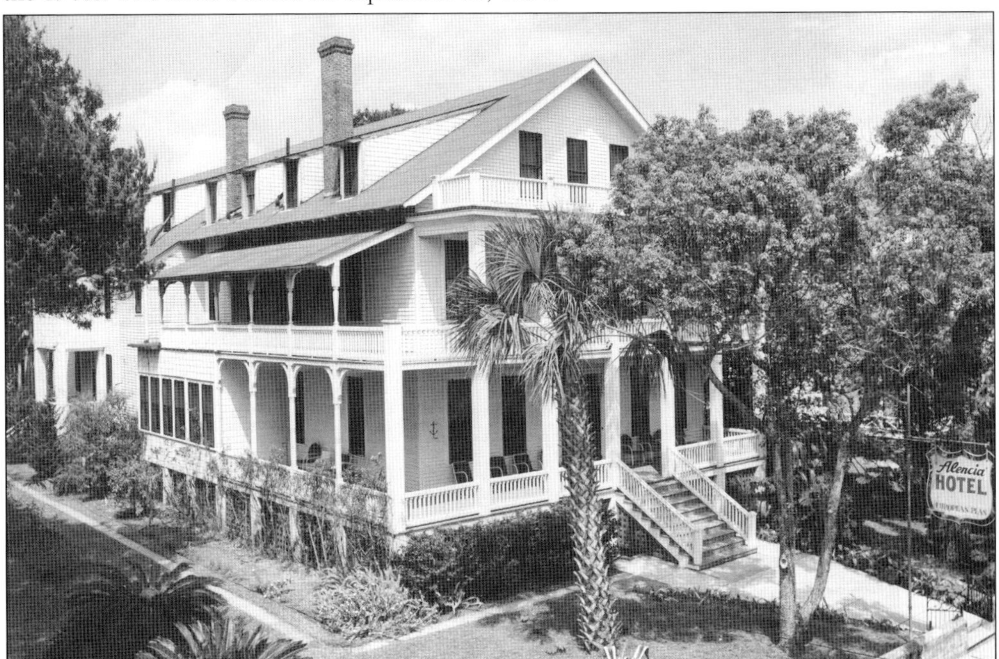

The Valencia Hotel at 276 St. George Street was built in 1892 by the Flagler Hotel Company as an annex to the Ponce de Leon. In the mid-1940s it was purchased by Howard B. Bonfield, who renamed it the Alencia Hotel to avoid confusion with the Valencia Apartments. The hotel was demolished in the late 1960s, and the site is now the parking lot for the St. Francis Inn. (SAHS.)

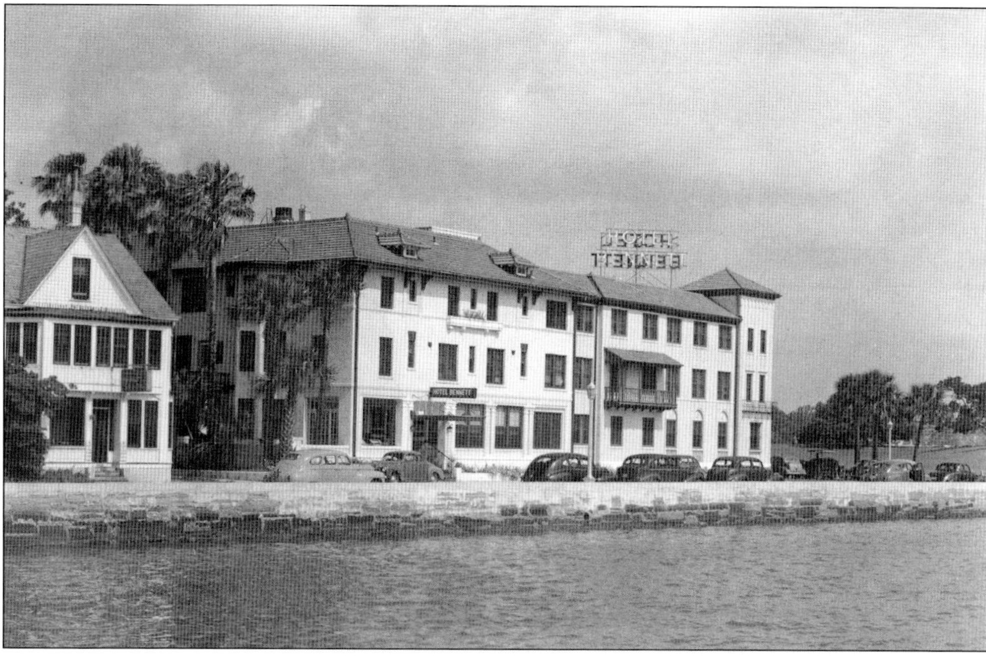

Stephen F. and Rosa Masters Bennett (Benet) opened the hotel at 10 Bay Street in the early 1900s. Stephen died in 1913, and his widow, who later married Paul A. McNally, continued to operate the hotel into the 1940s. During World War II, the Bennett housed the US Coast Guard Officer Candidate School. The hotel was demolished in 1961 when Fort Marion Circle was widened to become Castillo Drive. (SAHS.)

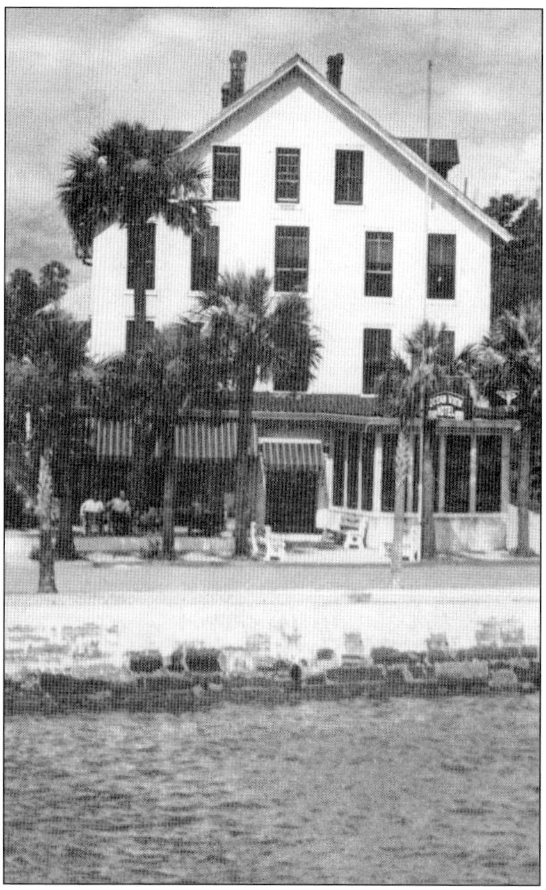

Henry E. Hernandez purchased the Ocean View Hotel at 132 Bay Street around 1911 from original owner W.S.M. Pinkham and owned the hotel throughout the 1930s and 1940s. During World War II, it was taken over by the SPARS, the women's branch of the US Coast Guard Reserve. The site is now a motel, the Bayfront Inn.

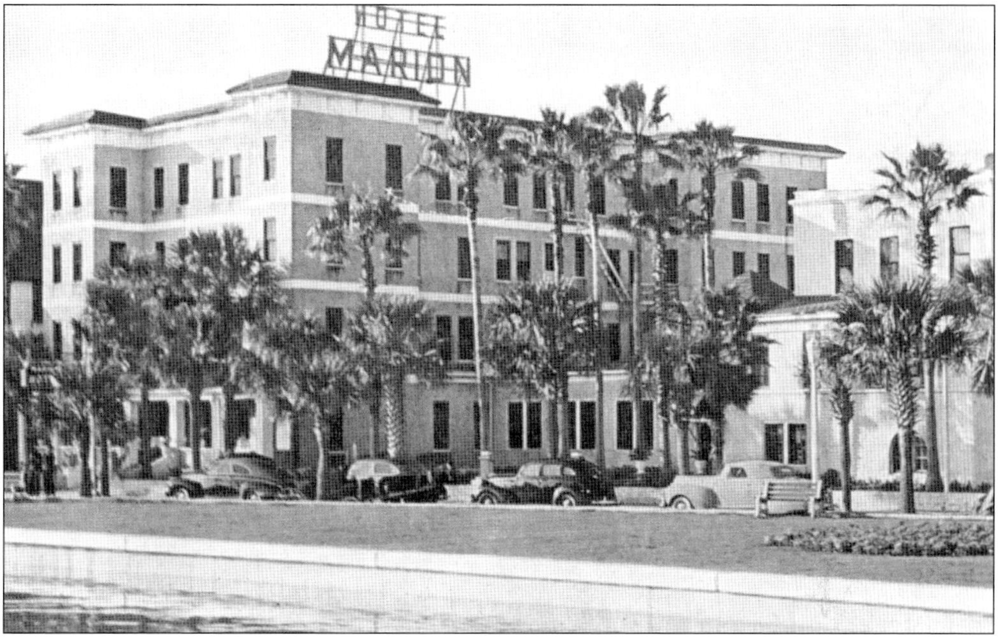

Swiss immigrant Henry S. Muller opened the Hotel Marion in the early 1900s. Located at 128 Bay Street, the popular hotel was remodeled several times and enlarged westward to Marine Street. The Hotel Marion was demolished in 1962 and replaced by the Marion Motor Lodge, owned by the Whetstone family, descendants of Muller's daughter Josephine.

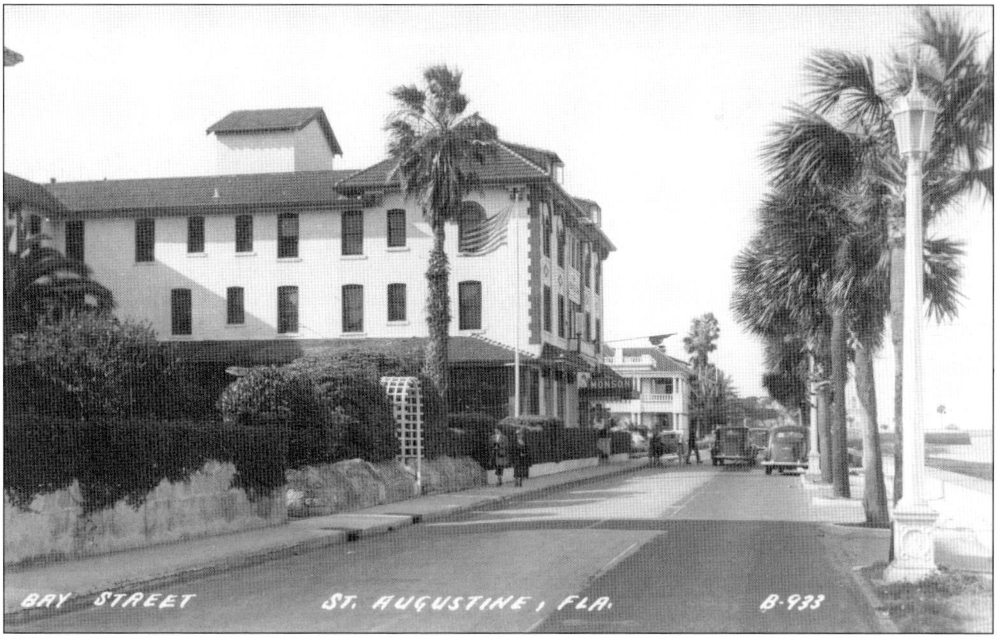

Anthony V. and Florence Young Monson opened the Monson House at 26 Bay Street in the late 1800s. Anthony died in 1915, and Florence's family took over ownership of the hotel, with Charles E. Young Jr. managing the hotel throughout the 1930s and 1940s. The Monson was razed in 1960 and replaced by the Monson Motor Lodge, scene of many civil rights demonstrations in 1964.

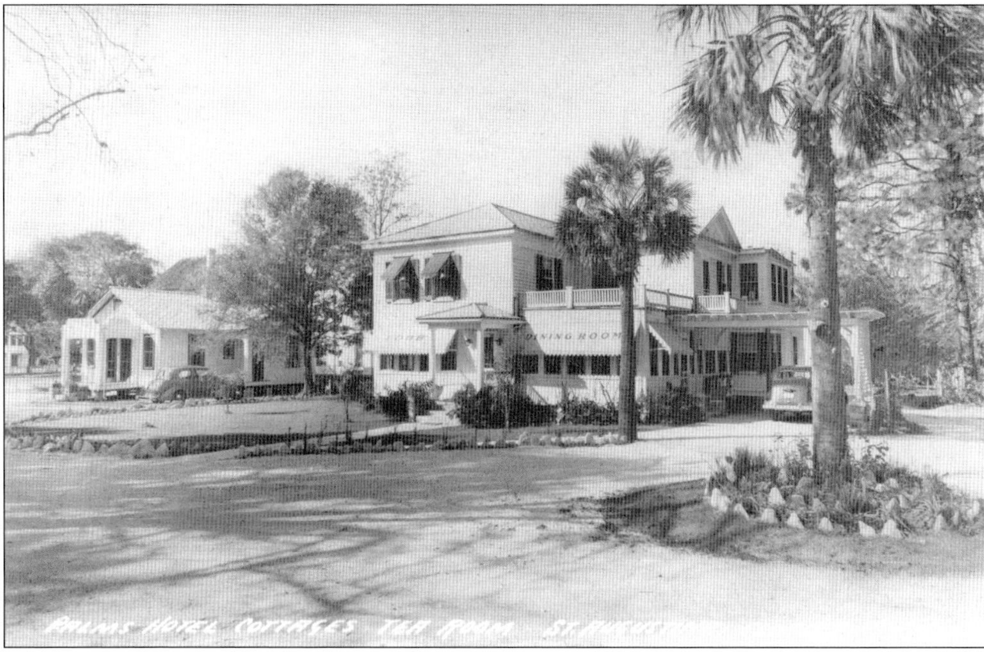

The Palms Hotel and Cottages is one of St. Augustine's oldest surviving motels. Located at 137 San Marco Avenue, it was started in the late 1930s by Owen D. Wolfe and his wife, Birdie. This view shows their original house, which became the dining room and lobby, with a rental cottage to the left.

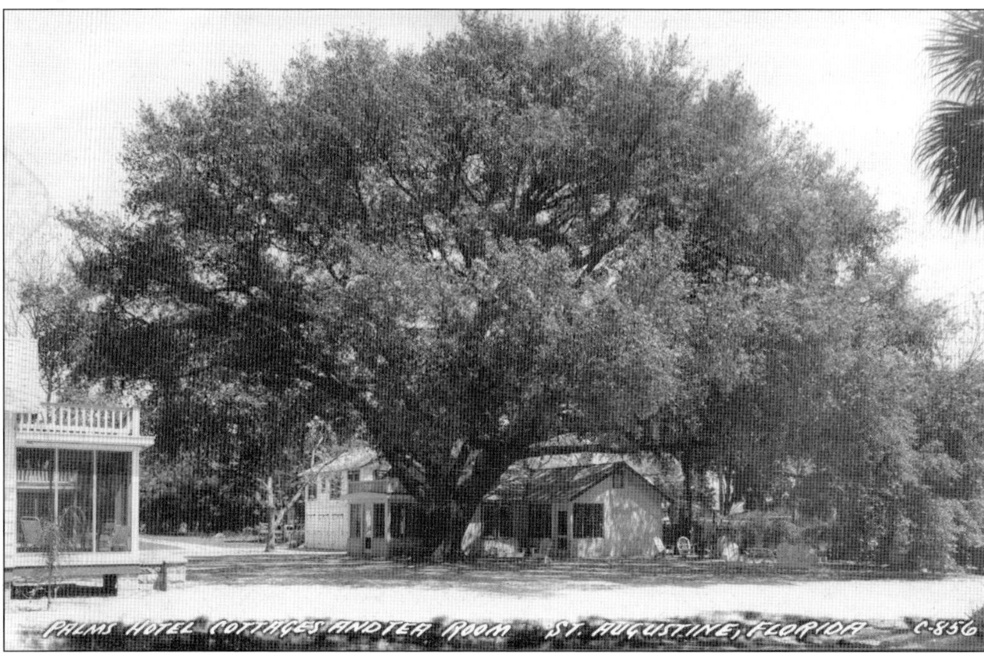

A landmark at the Palms is this magnificent live oak, The Senator, reported to be over 600 years old. Today, it is a stop for the sightseeing trains, and it recently lost one of its large limbs. Over the years, the Palms was rebuilt in various stages into a modern motel and is now a Howard Johnson by Wyndam.

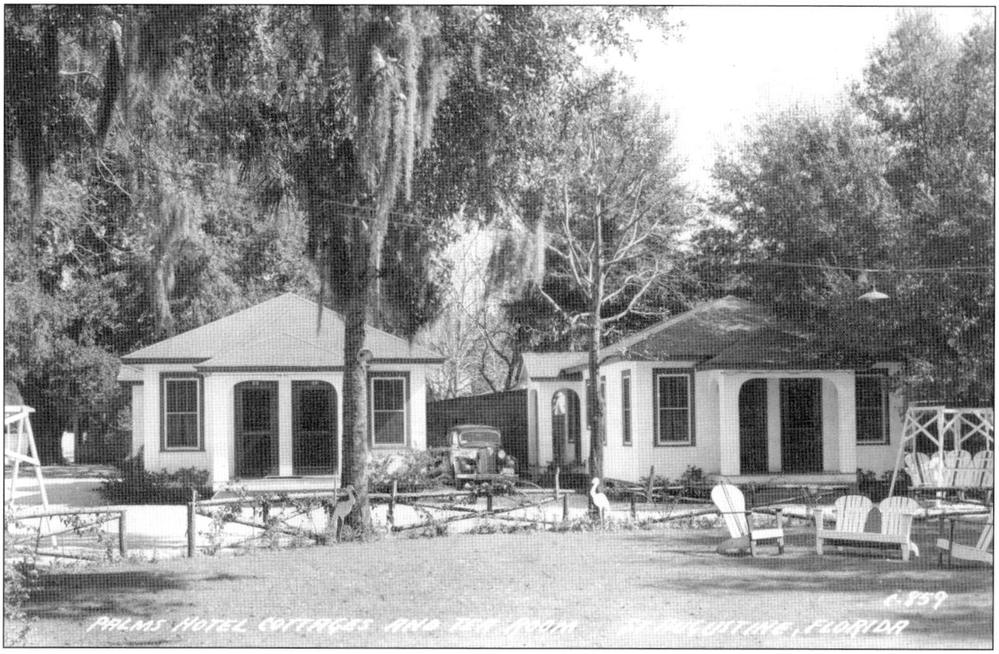

These postcards show the rental cottages at the Palms. The large complex occupied the entire block east from San Marco Avenue to Magnolia Avenue. As more tourists began to travel by car rather than train, it became an important convenience to park right next to one's cottage. On the postcard below a guest has noted the cottage occupied on October 10, 1940. When the tourist court was converted to a modern motel in the late 1950s, the cottages were sold off and moved from the property. Rev. Charles Seymour, of Trinity Episcopal Church, bought two of the cottages and moved them—furniture and all—to property off A1A South, where he joined them to each end of a center room to make his beach house.

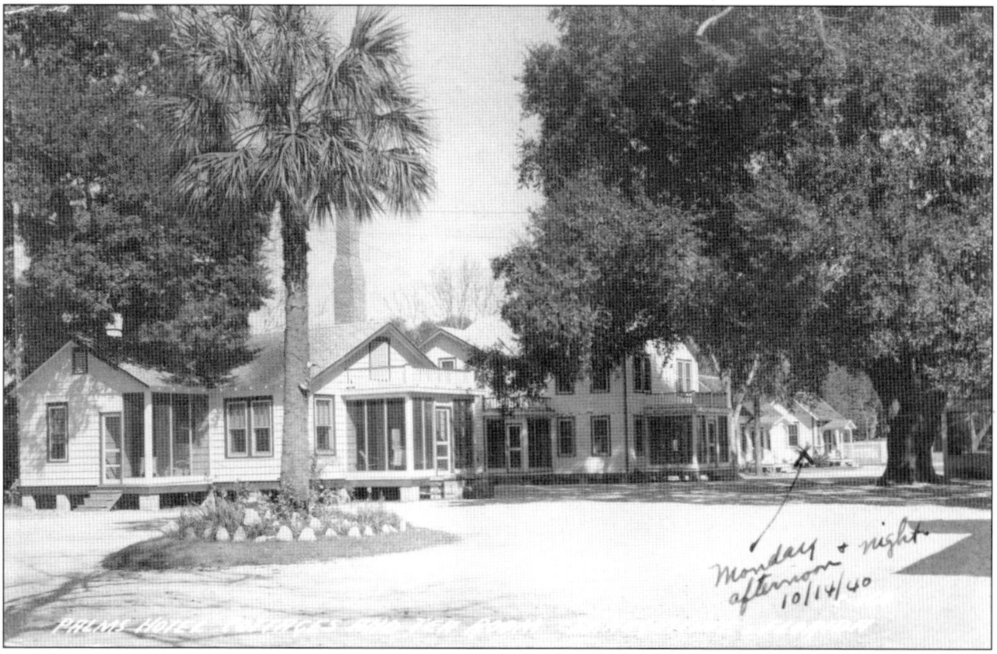

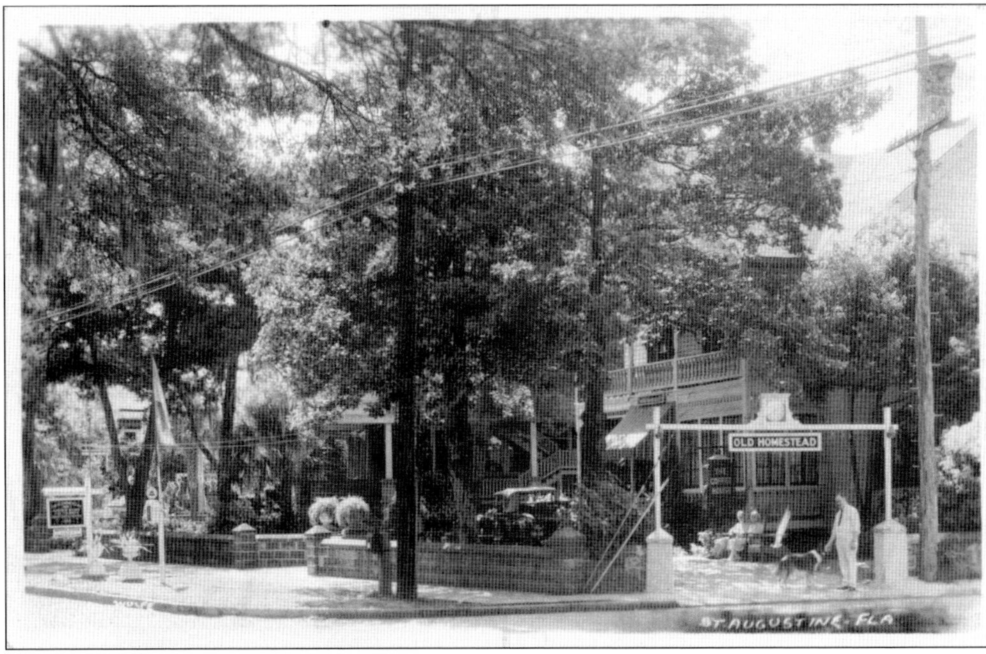

These two views depict the Homestead Guest House at 100 San Marco Avenue, on the corner of Bernard Street. During the 1930s and 1940s, the Homestead was operated by Bernice Masters, who married Halford P. Mills, former manager of the Don Toledo House. In the more recent view below, trees in front of the house have been removed and the front concrete wall lowered. At the far left is Fairlawn, the large guesthouse at 94 San Marco. After Bernice Mills's death in 1970, the house was demolished, and the location became the longtime home of a Dairy Queen restaurant.

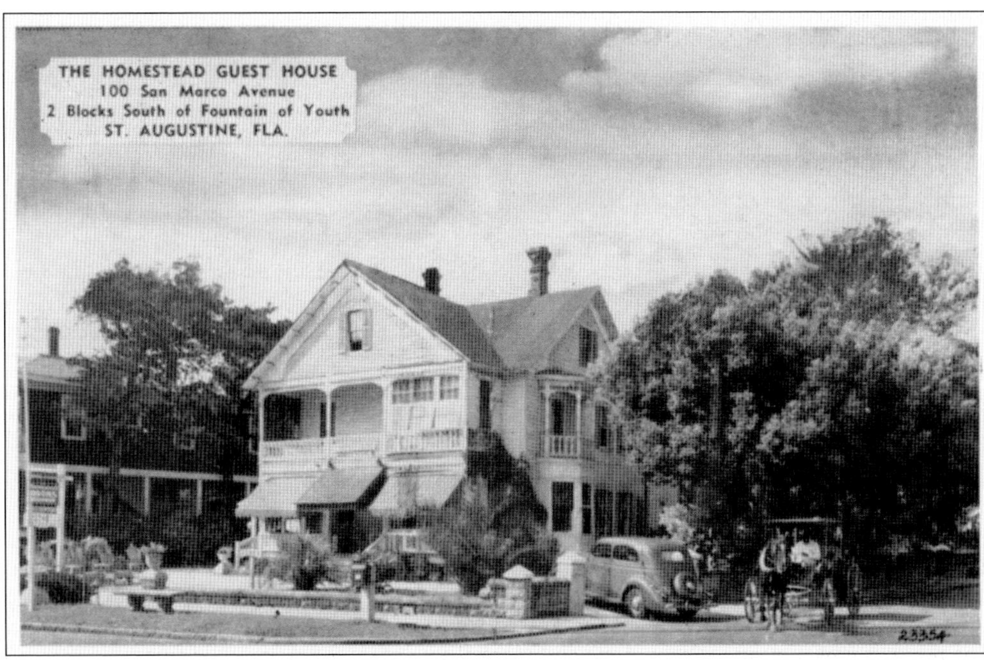

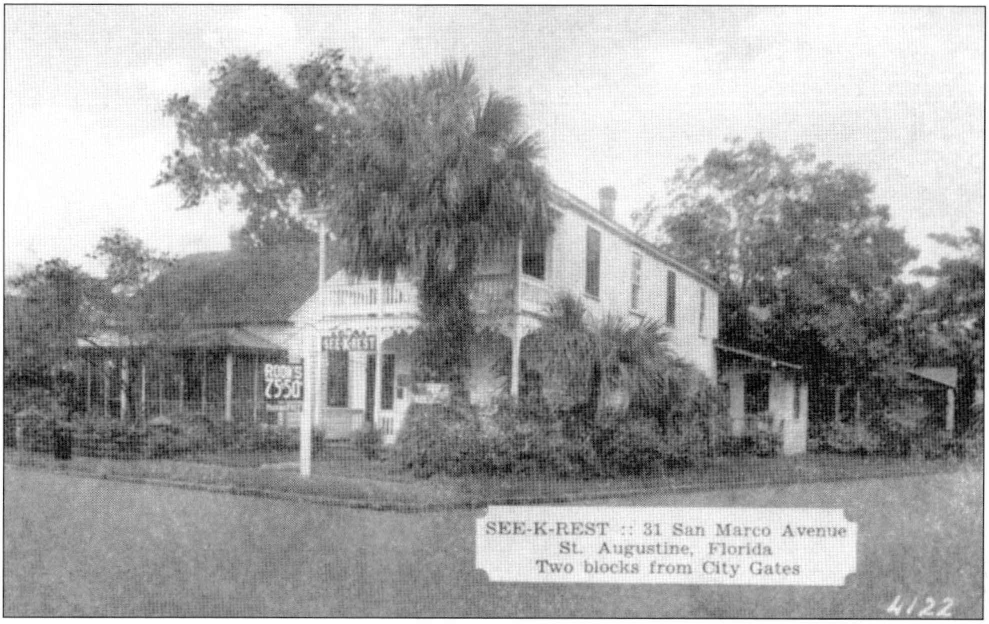

The home at 31 San Marco Avenue, on the corner of Joiner Street, was constructed between 1865 and 1885 and is one of the oldest buildings in the Abbott Tract. In the 1930s, it was See-K-Rest, a guesthouse operated by Helen Ryan, whose sign advertised rooms for 50¢ and 75¢. The home is now converted to commercial use, with enclosed porches, and retains little of its original appearance.

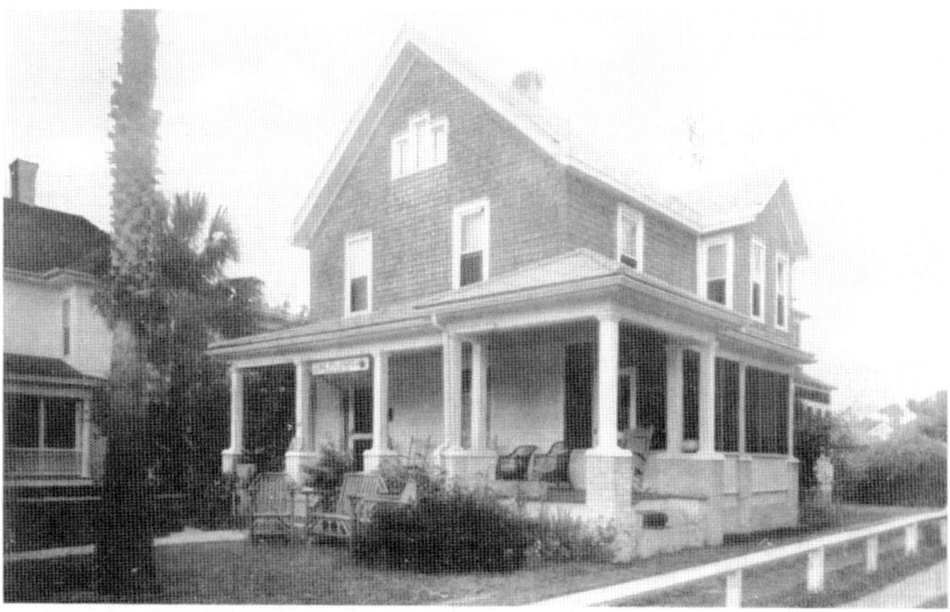

THE FLORIDAN. 73 SAN MARCO AVENUE - U. S. 1 - ST. AUGUSTINE. FLORIDA

Built in 1905, this 2.5-story home at 73 San Marco Avenue was the residence of Vincent D. and Leonora Capo. San Marco Avenue was the main artery into the city from the north, and many of its beautiful residential properties were converted into guesthouses similar to the Capo's Floridan. The house is now a business, part of the commercial area of Uptown St. Augustine.

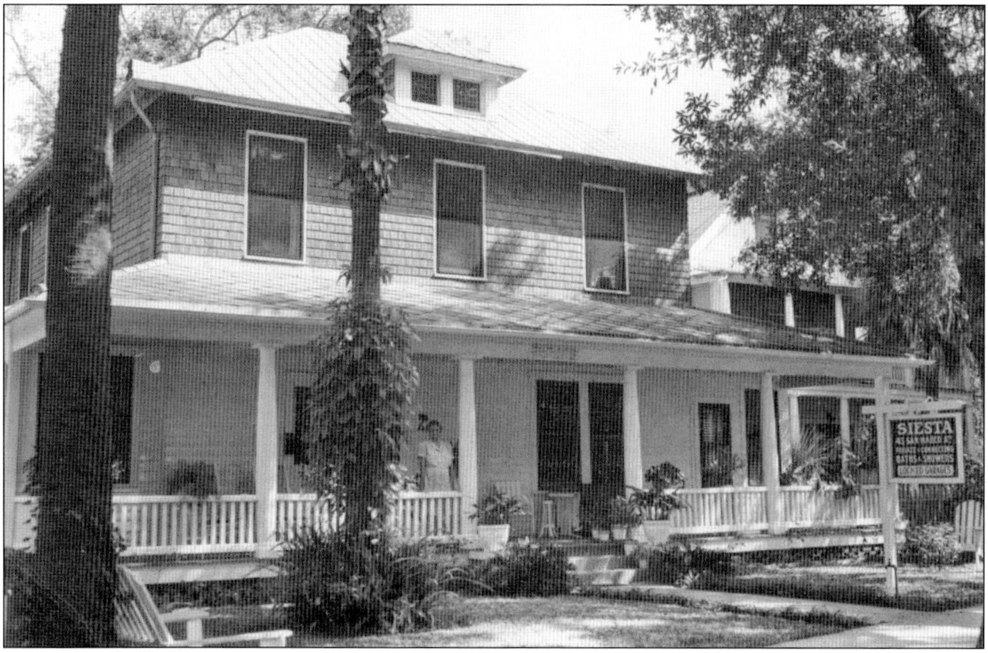

The Colonial Revival house at 45 San Marco Avenue was built between 1904 and 1910. In the late 1930s, it became the longtime home of Bernice Roe, shown here on the porch of her rooming house, the Siesta. The house is now Le Pavilion Restaurant, and the porch has been enclosed and extended closer to San Marco Avenue. Earlier in the 1930s, it was the home of fire chief William B. Parkhill, whose daughters Virginia and Betty are pictured on a goat cart in March 1932. Itinerant photographers with portable darkrooms traveled the country and captured countless images of children posed on these carts or small ponies. The negatives could then be developed directly onto photographic paper with a preprinted postcard backing. Even during the Great Depression, parents would eagerly purchase these charming images of their children. (Above, Desvousges Collection.)

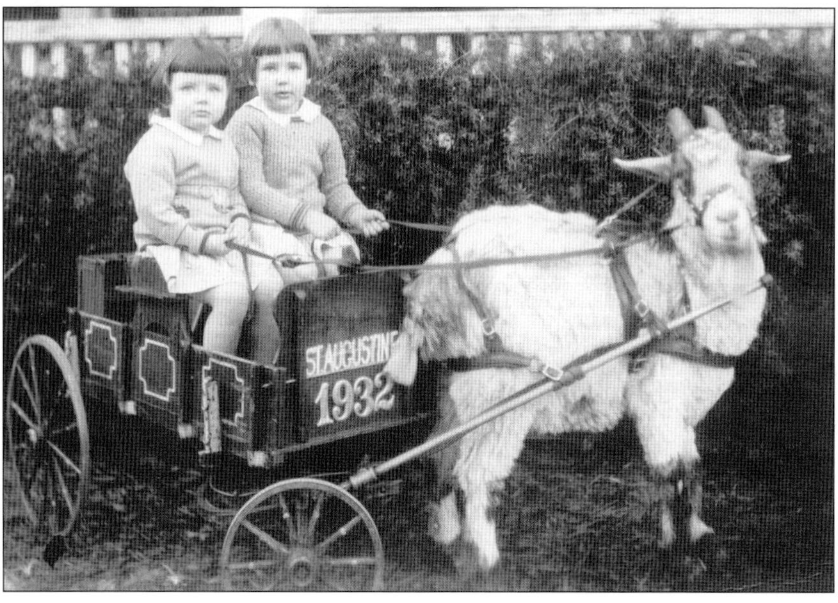

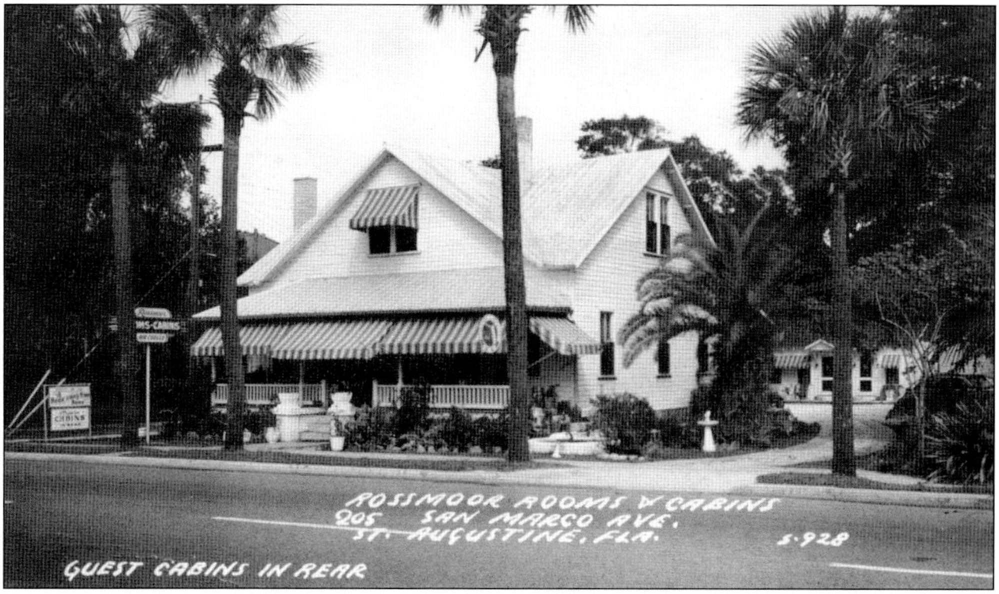

Rossmoor was located at 205 San Marco Avenue at Genopoly Street and featured rooms in the main house with guest cabins in the rear. It was named by Richard Ross, who owned the house around 1940. Later, starting in the mid-1940s, it was operated for many years by Jane Roche. The Rossmoor property was purchased by the Florida School for the Deaf and Blind, and the site is now Ray Charles Hall.

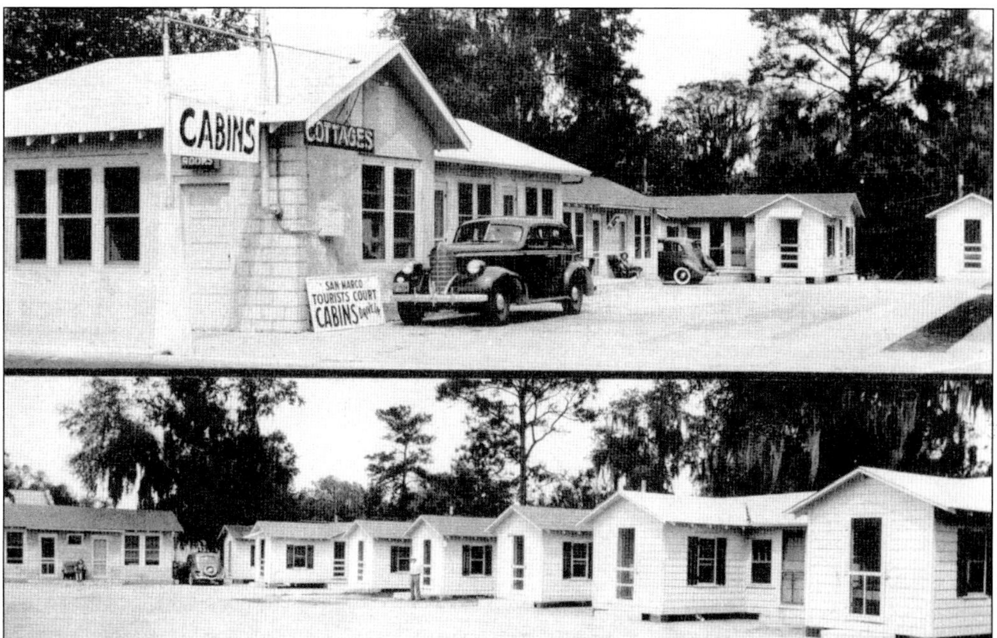

These tourist cabins, operated by A.L. Marsh, were located at 231 San Marco Avenue, between Fullerwood and Bay View Drives. The 1930s saw the rise of cottage courts that were more automobile friendly than the downtown hotels, allowing guests to park right next to their individual cabin. The Marsh cabins were later razed for the San Marco Court, and the site is now the Country Inn and Suites.

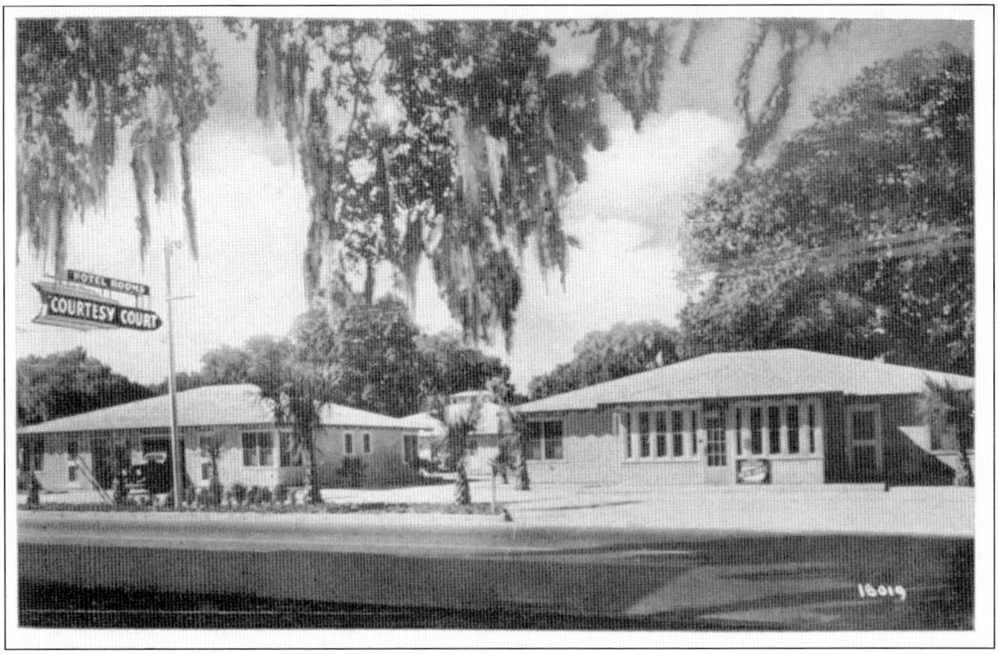

Courtesy Court was located at 264 San Marco Avenue, near the busy intersection of Picolata Road (today's State Road 16). This postcard lists Lloyd G. Thompson as the owner and Ann Schowalter as manager. It featured locked garages, which can be seen at left between two guest rooms.

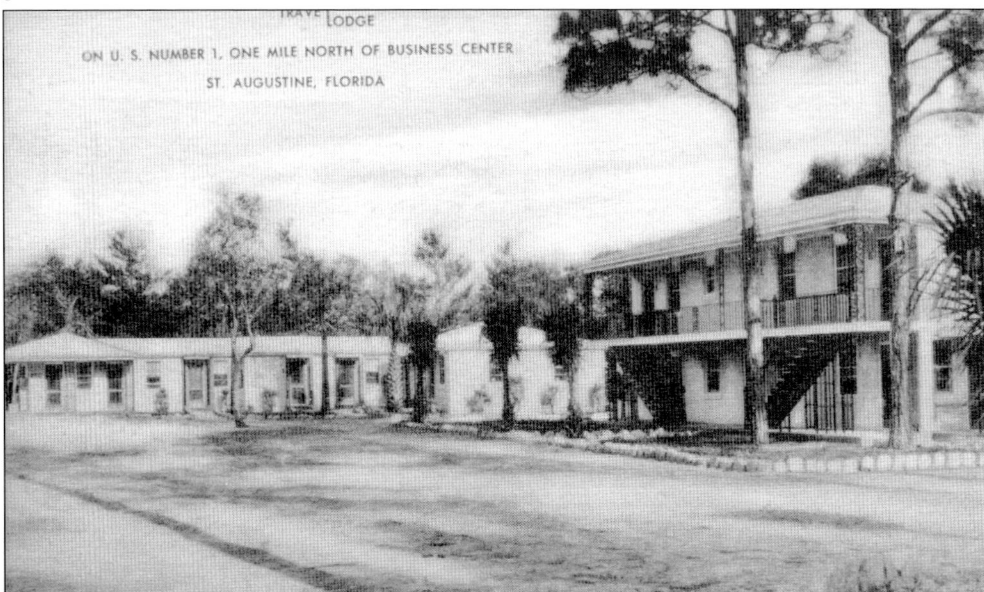

Built in the mid-1940s by Norman L. Hailey, the Travelodge was St. Augustine's first modern motel—a word coined to describe the new "motor hotels." Travelodge was one of the county's first motel chains, opening in California in 1940. Located on US 1 North, the motel was only recently demolished, and the site is now the VyStar Credit Union at 3654 North Ponce de Leon Boulevard.

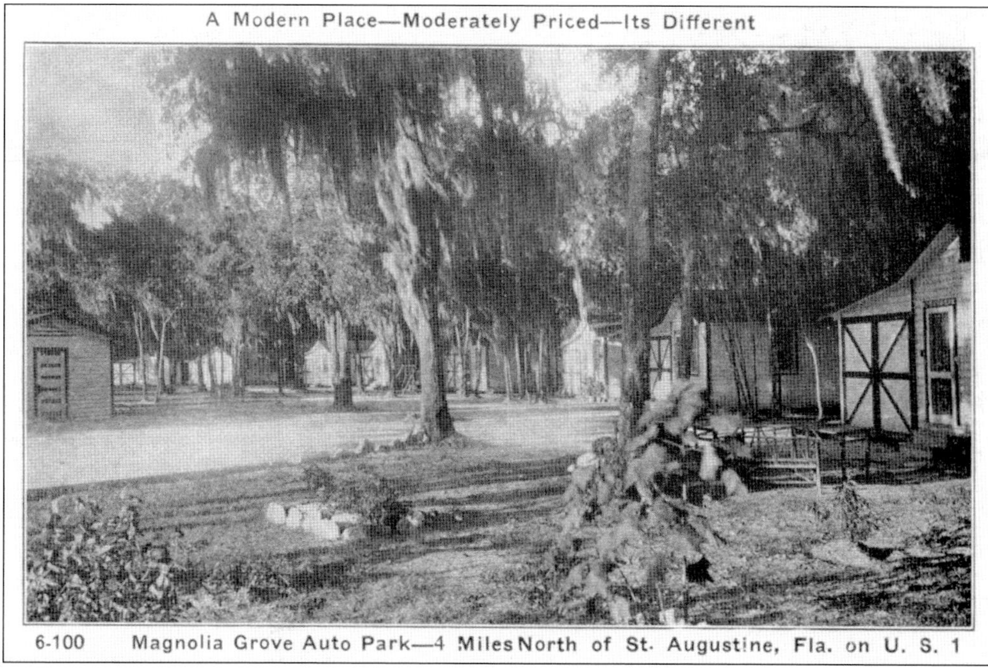

Once a stop on the Florida East Coast Railway, Magnolia Grove was located on Florida Route 4 (US 1) just north of today's St. Augustine Airport. These postcards depict the Magnolia Grove Auto Park, which featured a Sinclair gas station on the highway and rear guest cabins with garages. In 1940, J.W. Copsey and his wife, Joella, were the owners of the auto park. Another resident of Magnolia Grove at that time was James Casper, who is listed as running a small alligator farm. Just after World War II, he opened Casper's Alligator Farm on US 1 North in the Araquay Park area.

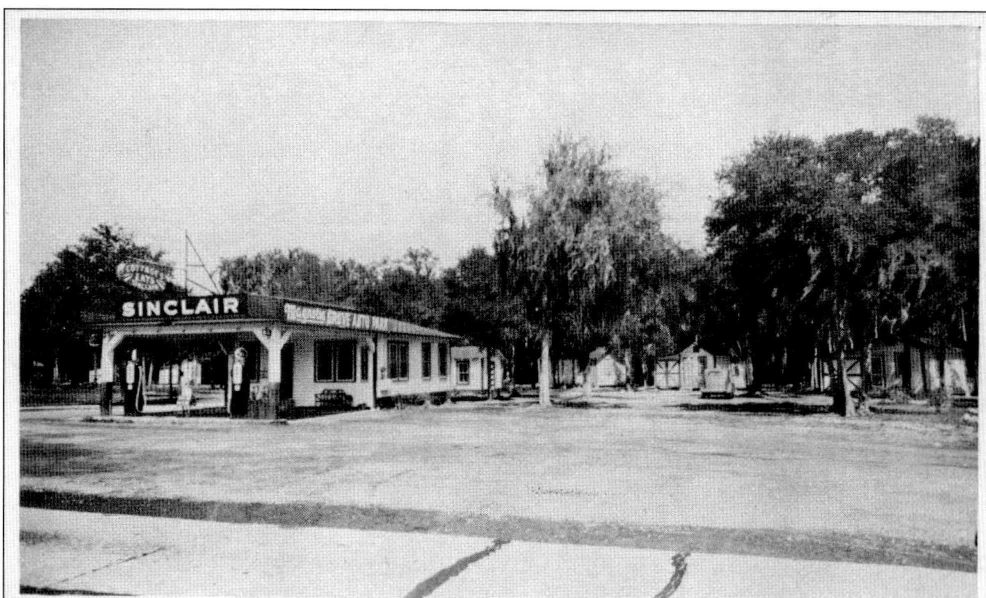

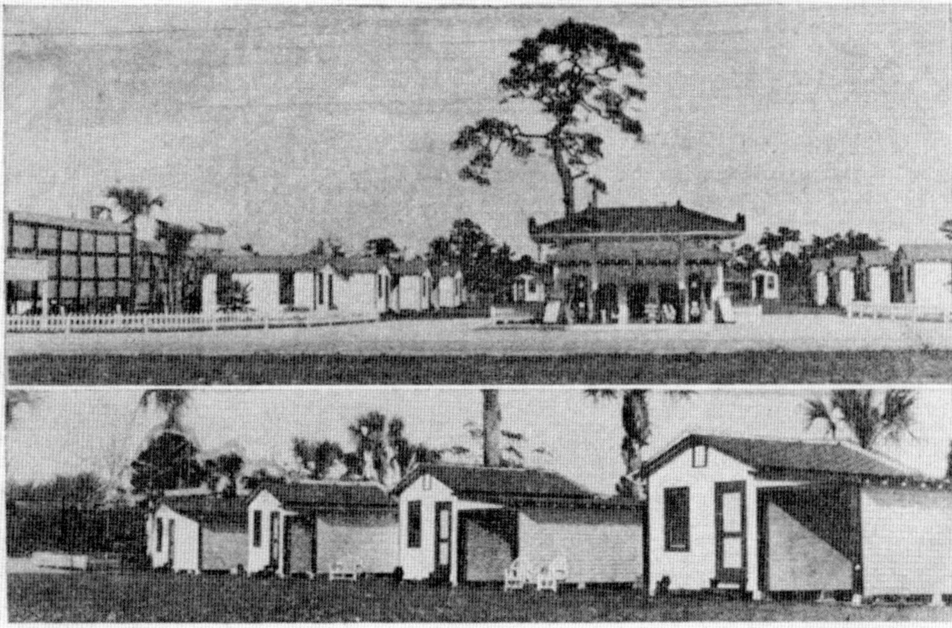

SNUG HARBOR COTTAGES . . . U. S. HY. No. 1 . . . 3 MI. NO. ST. AUGUSTINE, FLA.

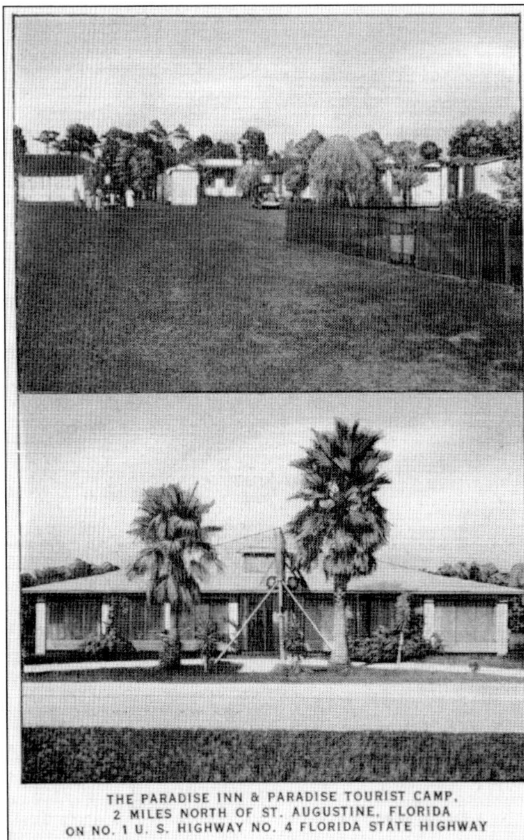

THE PARADISE INN & PARADISE TOURIST CAMP,
2 MILES NORTH OF ST. AUGUSTINE, FLORIDA
ON NO. 1 U. S. HIGHWAY NO. 4 FLORIDA STATE HIGHWAY

Snug Harbor Cottages were among several tourists courts built to lure highway travelers as they approached the city from Jacksonville. The back of this postcard advertises the Snug Harbor Cottages as being the "most modern, with hot and cold showers, innerspring mattresses, gas heated. Three miles north of St. Augustine, US Hwy. No 1. Capt. and Mrs. G. D. Tipton, owners."

The Paradise Inn was located on US 1 North at Magnolia Grove. According to the postcard, the restaurant featured lunches, dinners, and sandwiches, while the camp had Beautyrest coil spring mattresses, baths, and hot and cold running water 24 hours a day. In a 1941 newspaper advertisement, owner Frank Illes advertised the Paradise as a nightclub with a live band.

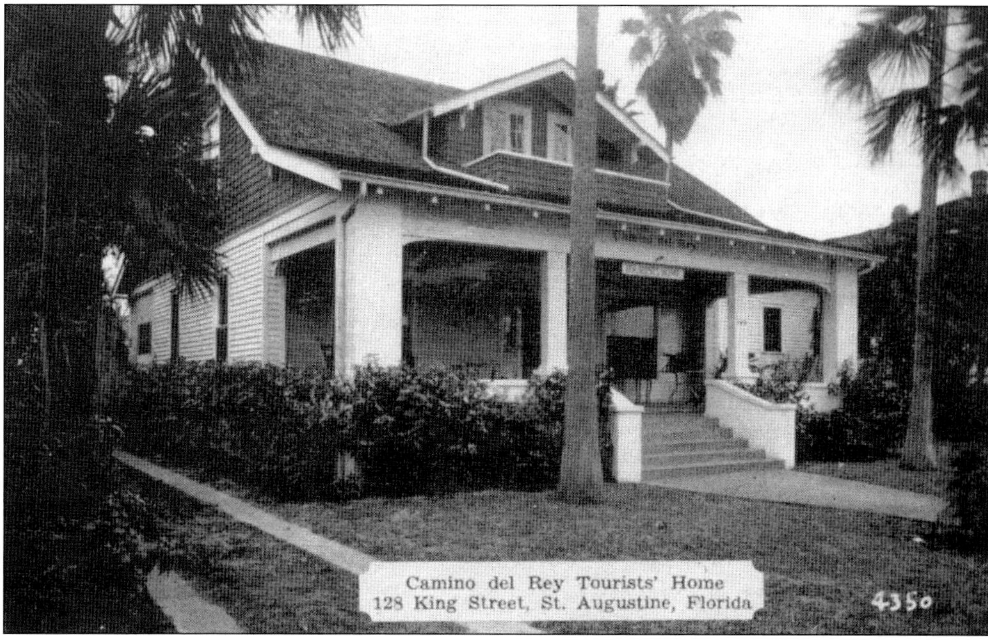

The 1.5-story bungalow at 128 King Street was built between 1910 and 1914. In the 1930s, it became Camino del Rey ("King's Road" in Spanish), one of several guesthouses along King Street, then the route of US 1 through St. Augustine. The house today retains much of its original appearance. (O'Neill Collection.)

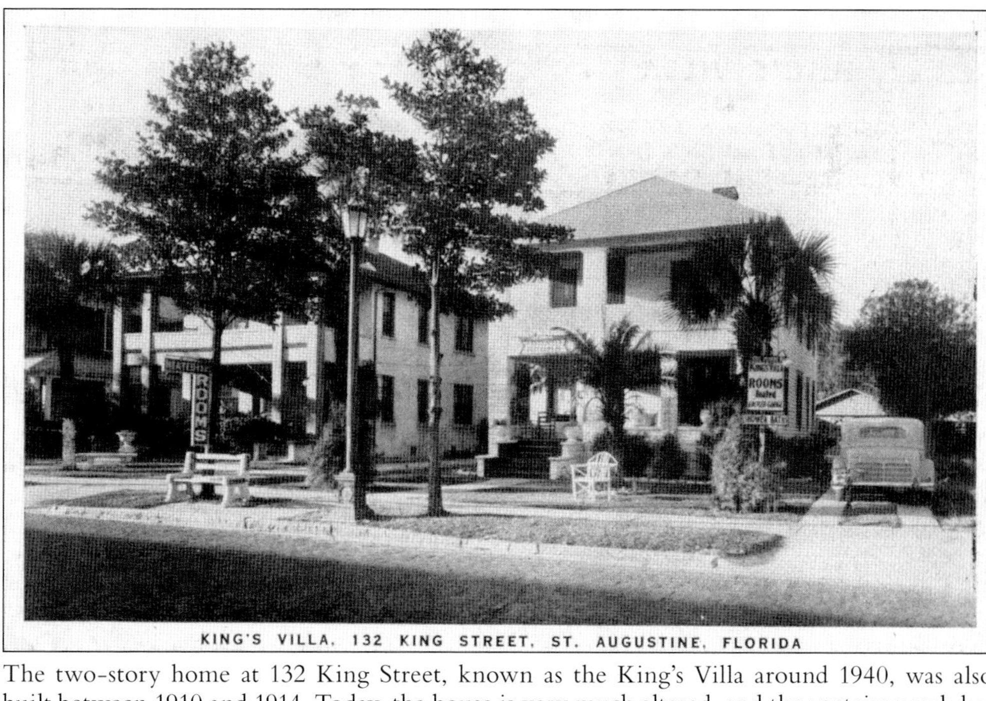

The two-story home at 132 King Street, known as the King's Villa around 1940, was also built between 1910 and 1914. Today, the house is very much altered, and the upstairs porch has been enclosed. The house on the left at 134 King Street was the longtime home of Robert and Mamie Andreu, parents of local attorney and judge Robbie Andreu.

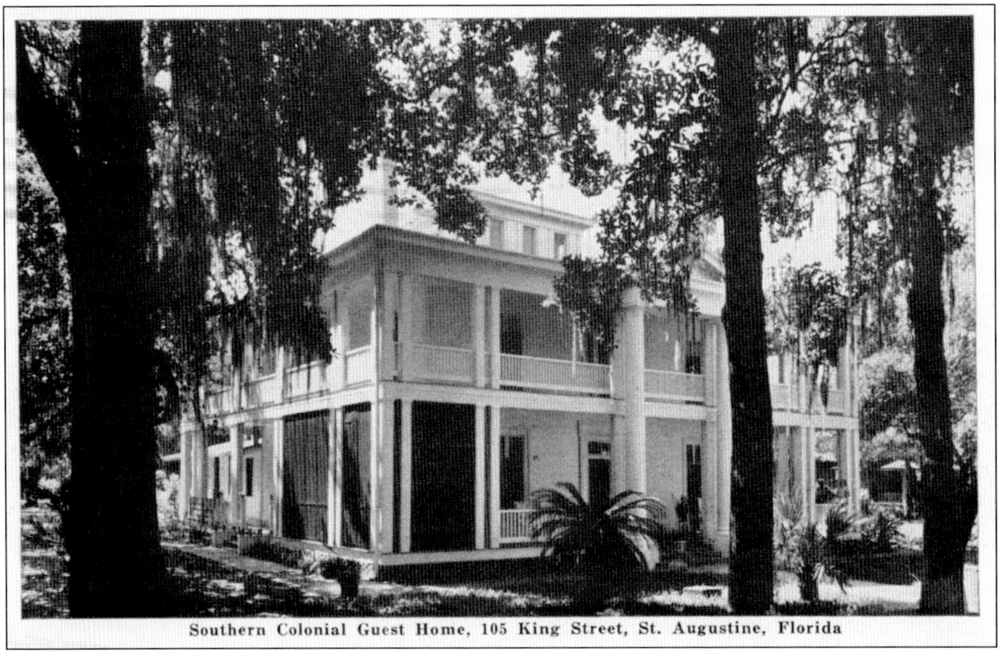

This stately home at 105 King Street was built before the Civil War for sea captain Nathan Cobb. After the war, it was the home of New Yorker Abijah Gilbert, Florida's senator during Reconstruction. It later became the Southern Colonial Guest Home and was demolished in the 1950s to build St. Augustine's first modern supermarket, an A&P grocery.

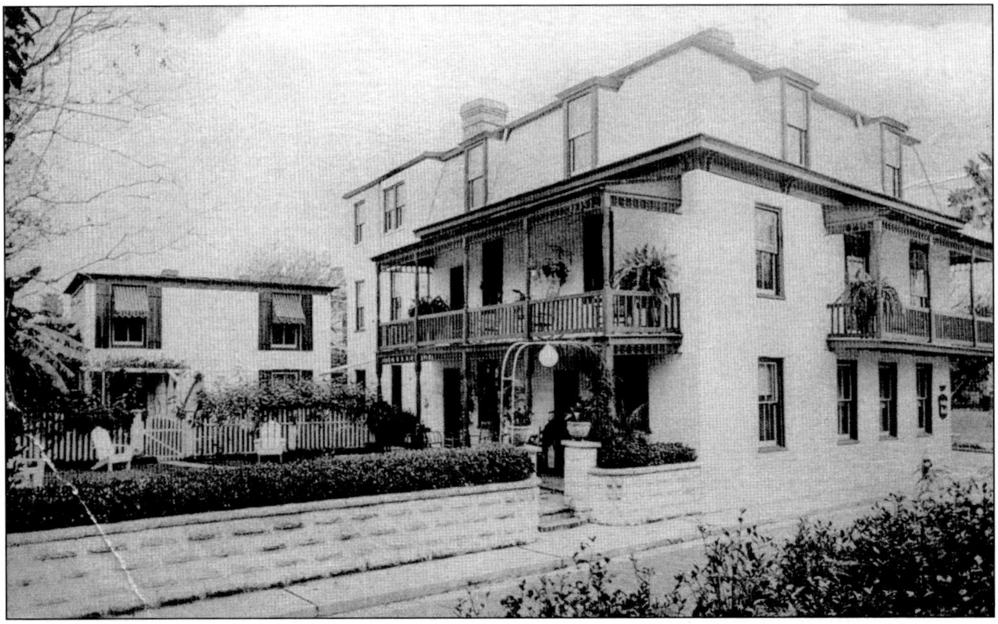

The Graham House at 279 St. George Street dates from 1791. In 1838, it became the property of Col. Thomas Henry Dummett, whose daughter Anna led the drive to erect the Confederate monument now located in the plaza. Thomas W. Graham acquired the house around 1926 and operated a tearoom and inn. In 1948, it became the St. Francis Inn and continues to be one of St. Augustine's most popular B&Bs.

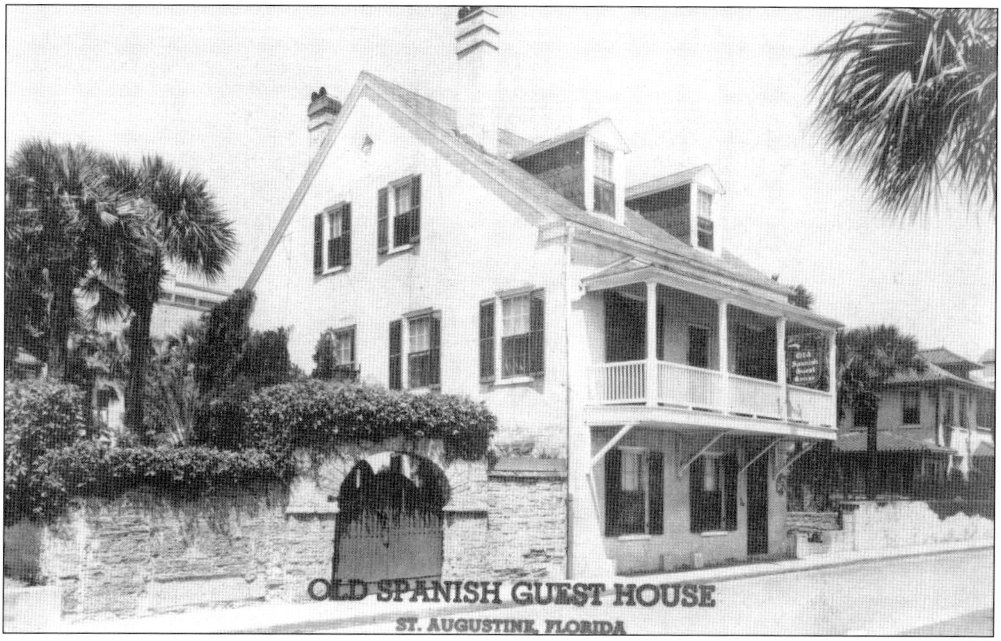

The home at 46 Bay Street (today's Avenida Menendez) was once the home of Burroughs Carr, merchant and owner of the Magnolia Hotel on St. George Street. The house burned in the 1887 fire and was reconstructed exactly the same, except that poured concrete used instead of the original coquina. But the front coquina wall and gate were retained from the previous era. The house was occupied for many years by Bartolo Genovar, who often rented it out to winter visitors. In the late 1930s, it was the residence of tax assessor Ray Hellier. After his death in 1942, his widow, Aline, operated the Old Spanish Guest House in the home. Since the 1970s, it has housed a restaurant, and its front coquina wall and gate have become a familiar landmark of St. Augustine.

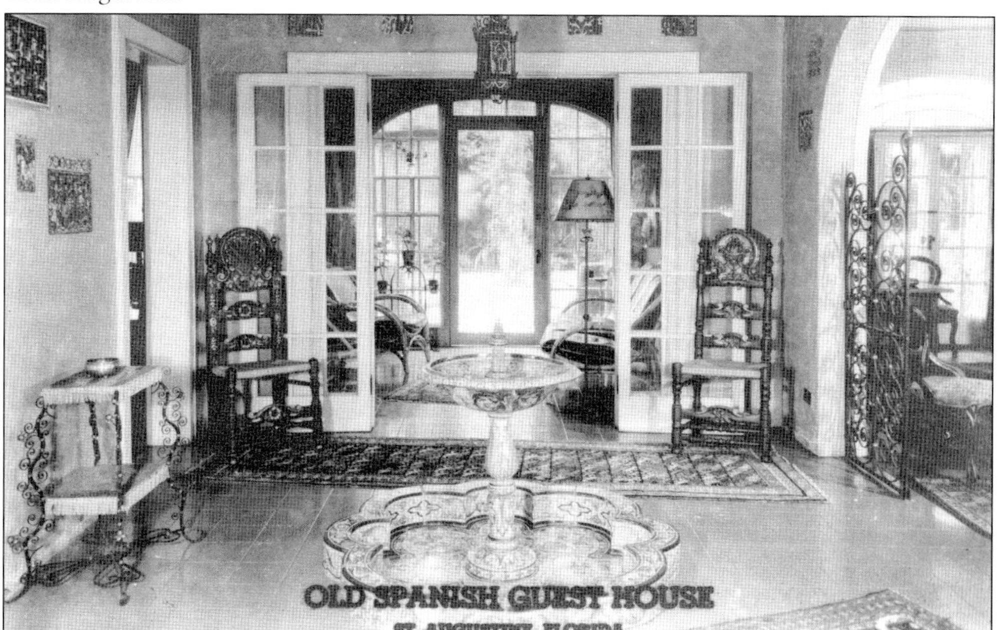

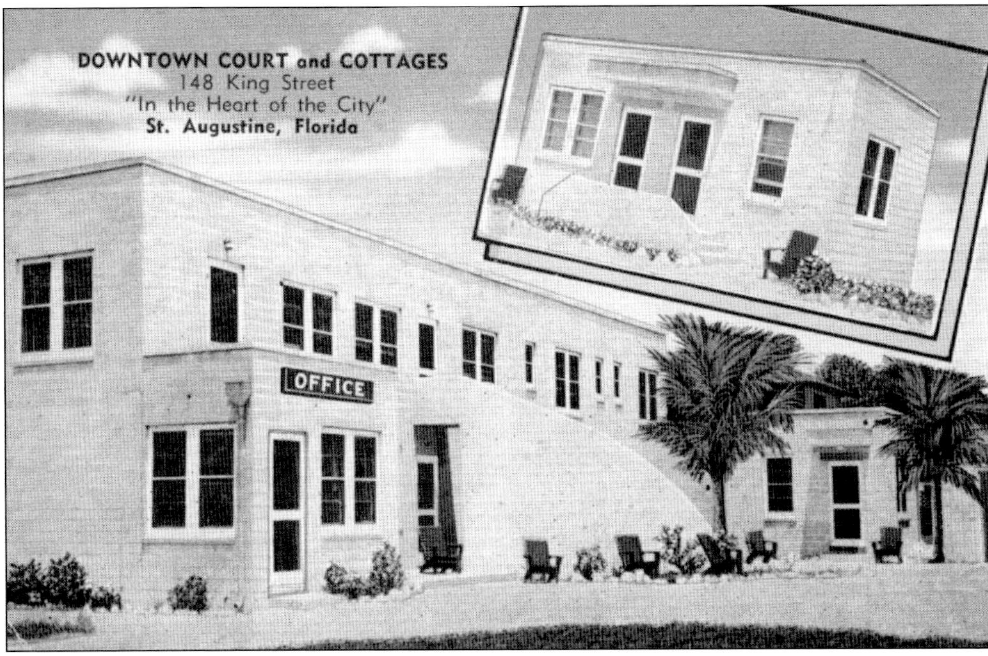

The Downtown Court and Cottages were built in the late 1940s at 148 King Street, next to Ben Adams's filling station at the corner of King and Malaga Streets. Owners Larry and Mollie Wolff advertised modern fireproof buildings, with steam heat and private tiled baths. The site is now the location of Carmelo's Marketplace and Pizzeria.

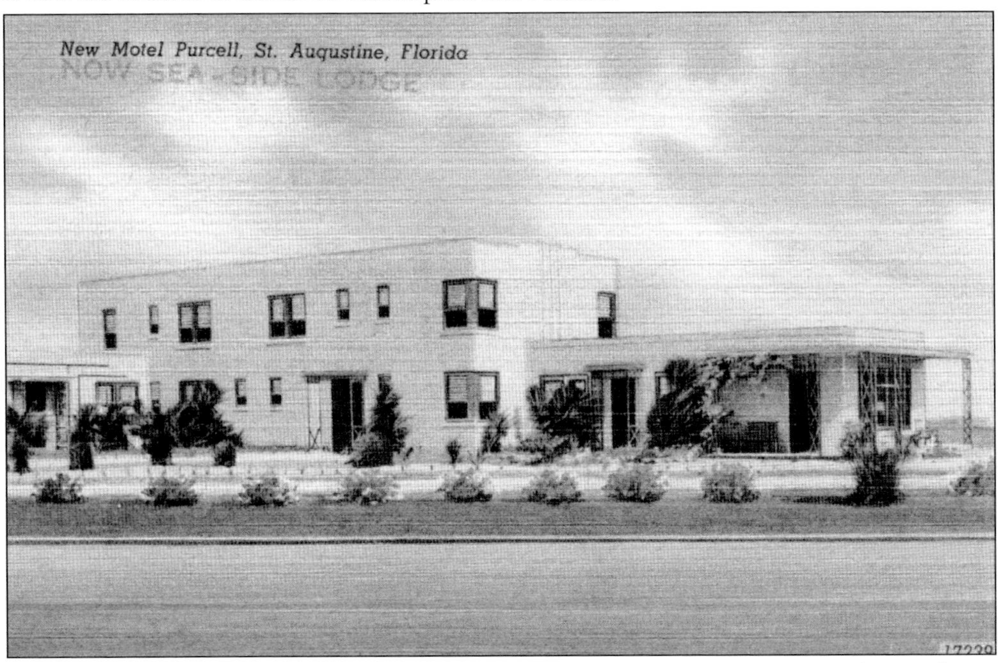

Built in the 1940s by W. Walt and Harry L. Brown, the Art Deco–style Motel Purcell was located at 512 Anastasia Boulevard, at the corner of Comares Avenue. The name was soon changed to the Sea Side Lodge, under the ownership of J.H. Roemer, and later taken over by Stanley V. Colee. It was recently renovated in a 1950s style and is now the Island Shores Inn.

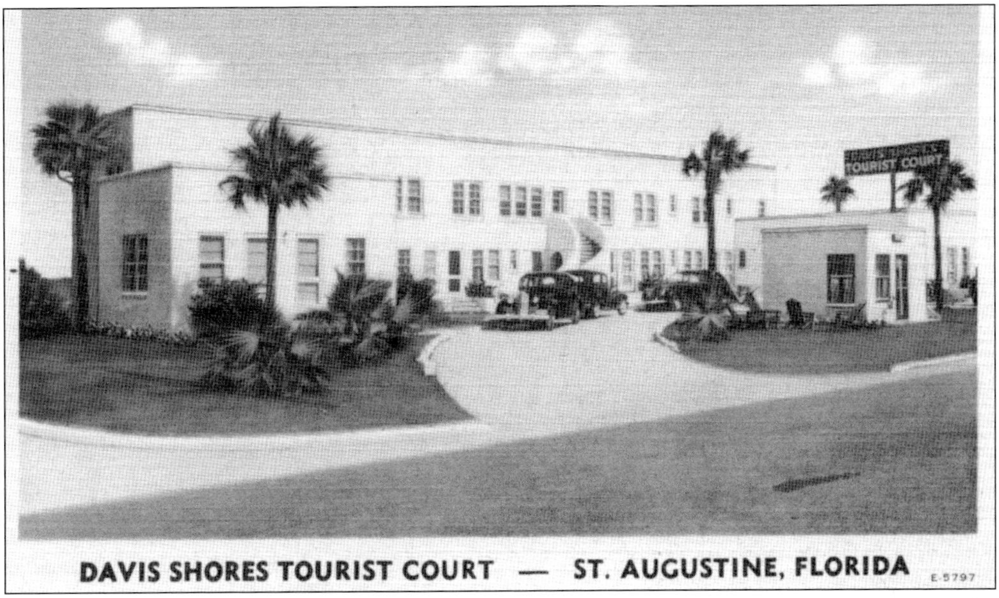

The Davis Shores Tourist Court was built in the late 1930s at 400 Anastasia Boulevard on the corner of Matanzas Boulevard. Owners were Arthur and Florine "Flo" McQuaig, who was elected St. Augustine's first female city commissioner in 1949. The court was later owned by L.H. Baas and is now converted into rental apartments with an added second-floor porch and the front office demolished. (SAHS.)

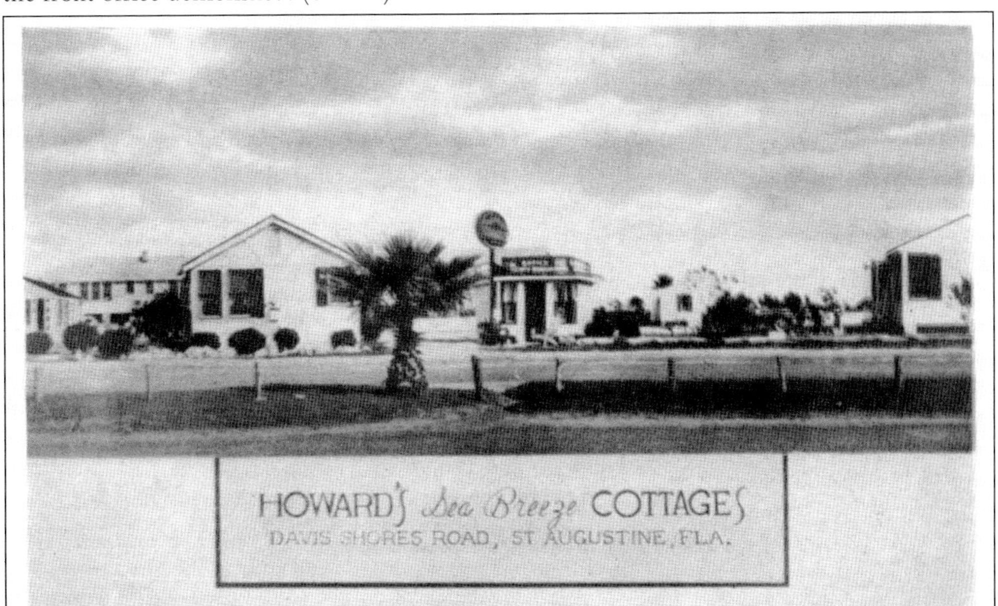

Howard's Sea Breeze Cottages at 208 Anastasia Boulevard were built in the late 1930s by owners Howard B. McClain and Everett B. Meade. This postcard touts them as having "innerspring mattresses, Frigidaires, electric ranges, private baths, radios, and continuous hot water." The cottages were gradually converted into a more modern accommodations, and today, they are the Seabreeze Motel.

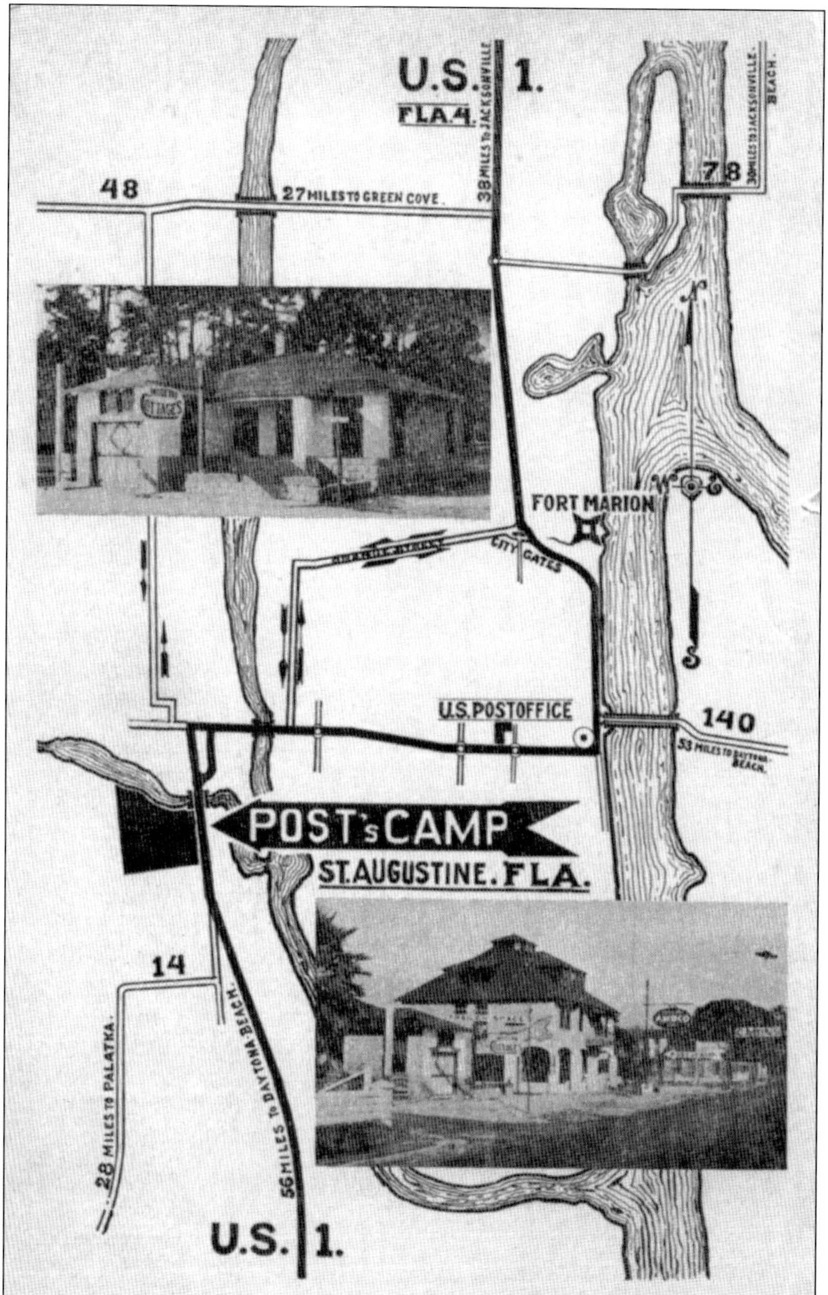

Onno and Susan Post offered rental cottages, a gas station, and a campground at their location on South Dixie Highway, just south of Oyster Creek. This postcard shows the route of US 1 through the city—San Marco Avenue to Bay Street, then west on King Street and turning south in West Augustine on Leonardi Street to South Dixie Highway. The card also pictures an alternate route using the Mill Creek, or Picolata, Road (today's State Route 16) to Masters Drive, and another optional route of Orange Street west to Malaga Street and onto King Street. In the days before Ponce de Leon Boulevard was constructed and became US 1, traffic on the downtown streets was often very congested.

Three

Restaurants and Bars

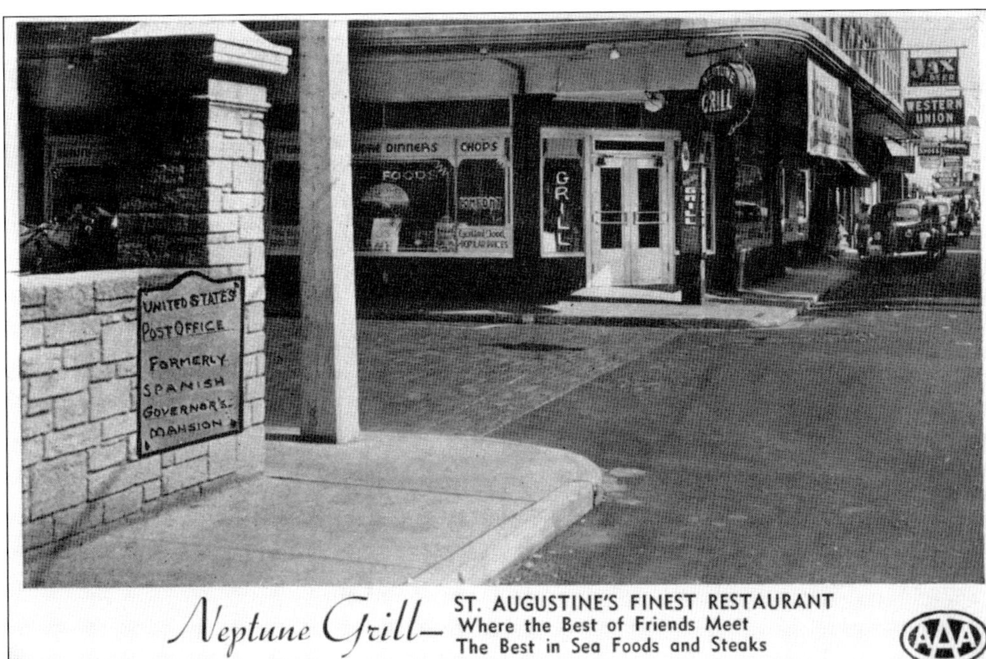

The Neptune Grill was located on the busy northwest corner of St. George Street and Cathedral Place. It was established in the mid-1930s by Spero Zepatos, one of many Greek restaurant owners in downtown St. Augustine at that time. The restaurant was located in the Bishop's Building and was closed in 1960 when the structure was demolished.

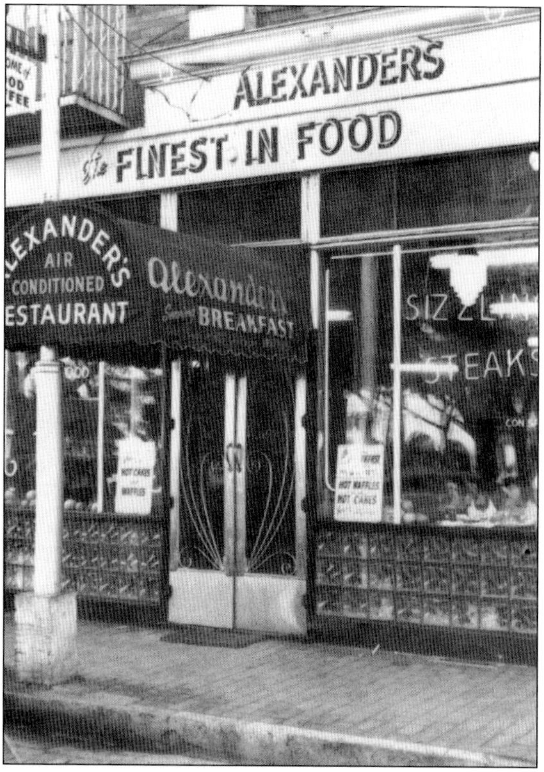

Peter and Virginia Alexander opened a fruit stand at 25 King Street around 1920. By the early 1930s, it became a restaurant serving traditional foods as well as Greek dishes. After World War II, their son James R. (Jimmy) and his wife, Emily, gradually took over the business. In 1955, the building housing their location was demolished, and the Alexanders opened the Ranch House Restaurant on Anastasia Boulevard. (Alexander collection.)

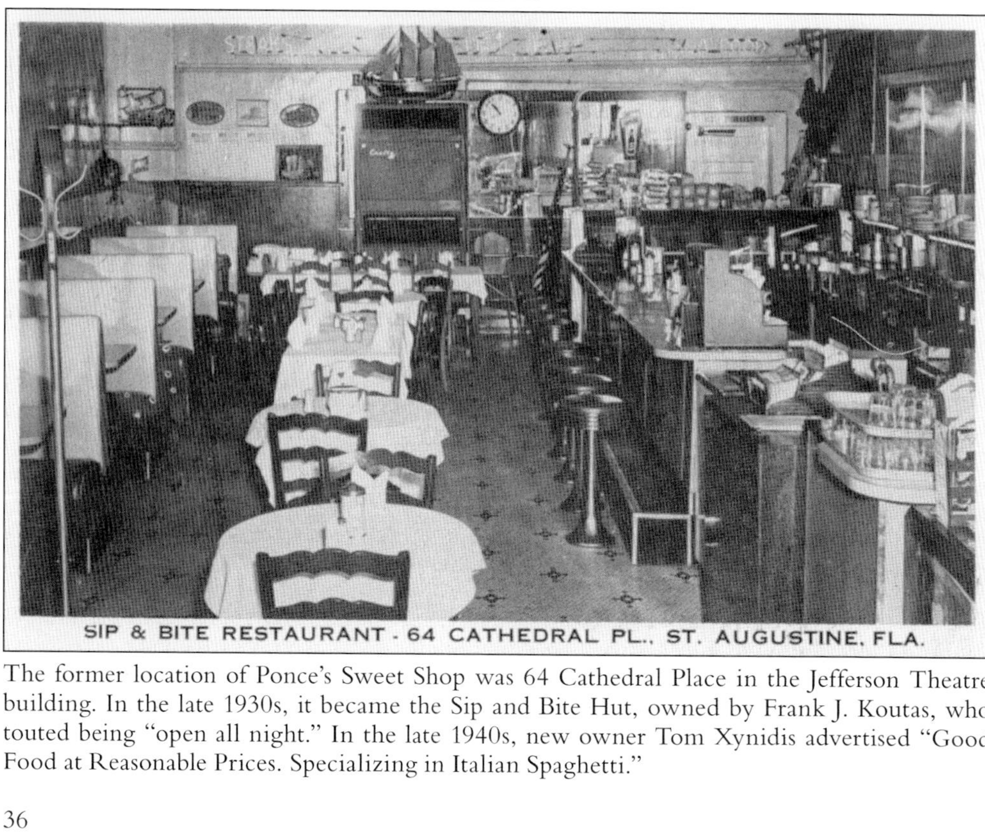

The former location of Ponce's Sweet Shop was 64 Cathedral Place in the Jefferson Theatre building. In the late 1930s, it became the Sip and Bite Hut, owned by Frank J. Koutas, who touted being "open all night." In the late 1940s, new owner Tom Xynidis advertised "Good Food at Reasonable Prices. Specializing in Italian Spaghetti."

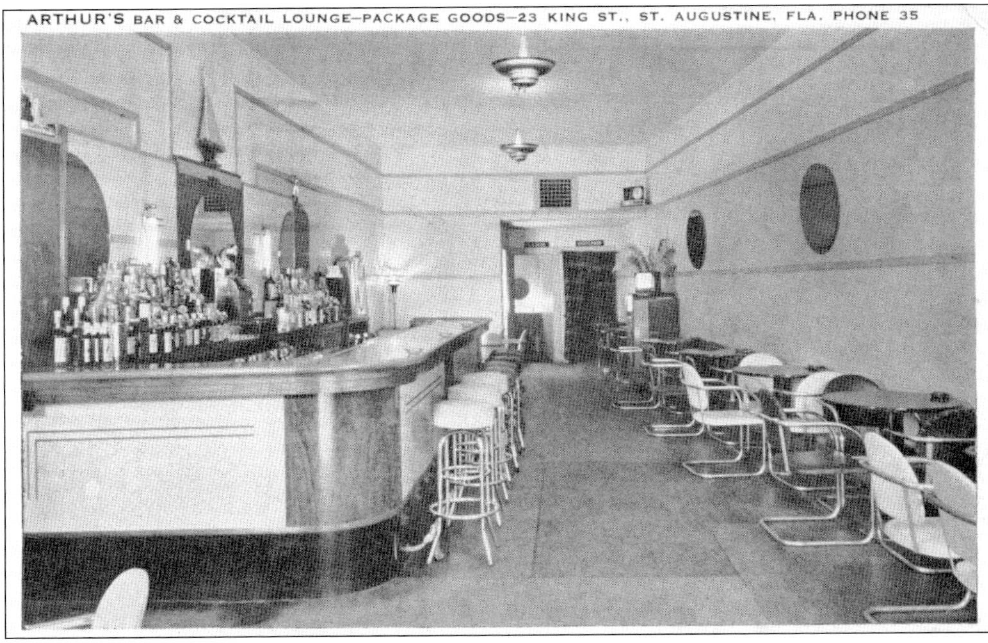

Arthur's Bar at 23 King Street boasted this beautiful Art Deco interior. Originally opened in the mid-1930s as Driz and Charlie's (for owners W. Irving Drysdale and F. Charles Usina, also owners of the St. Augustine Alligator Farm), by 1940 it was renamed for current owner Arthur C. Wendel. With repeal of the 18th Amendment and end of Prohibition in December 1933, many bars and package stores opened in the city.

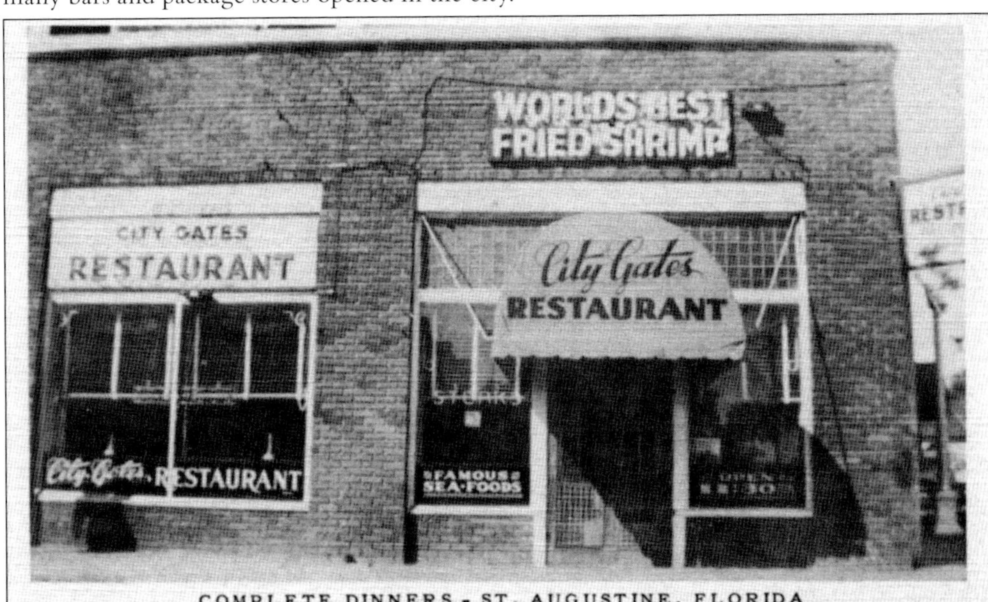

Twin brothers Granville and Leonard Grissom opened the City Gates Restaurant at 2 St. George Street in the mid-1940s. The sign over the front door advertised the "World's Best Fried Shrimp." Both brothers would remain in the restaurant business, with Granville opening the Blue Heron on Anastasia Boulevard in 1947 and Leonard later running the South Seas Restaurant at 841 Anastasia Boulevard.

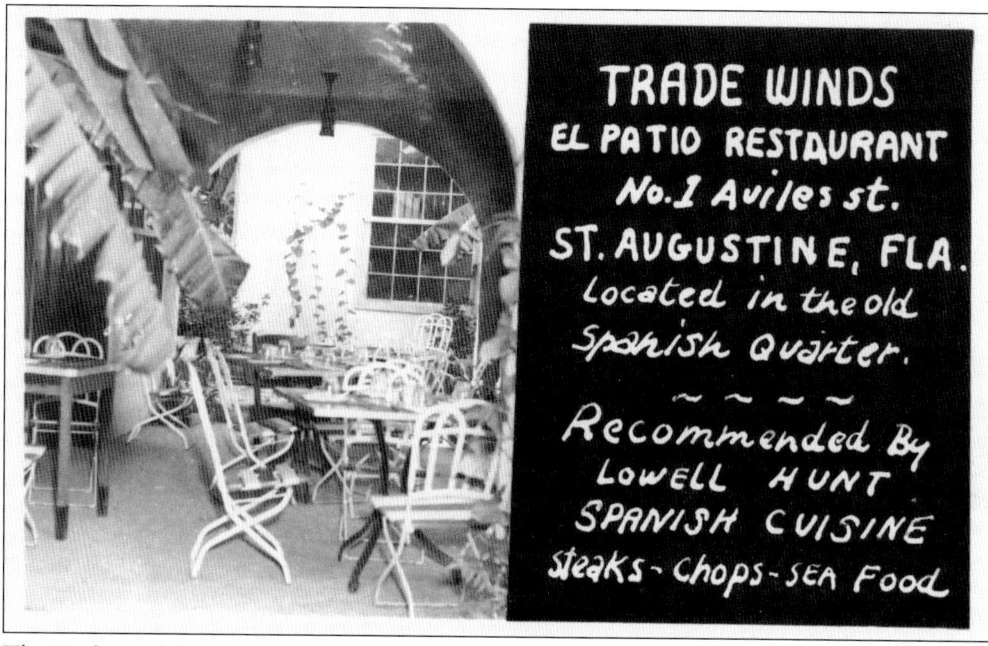

The Tradewinds began as an Aviles Street restaurant run by Clara Mier, a descendant of families who came to St. Augustine in the late 1700s from the Mediterranean island of Menorca. Kenneth Dow purchased the building where the restaurant was located, and he and John Meigs opened the lounge in February 1945. The bar became famous for its indoor tropical storm and musical entertainment. In 1964, the Tradewinds relocated to its current address at 124 Charlotte Street and continues to be one of St. Augustine's most enduring and popular nightspots. Kenneth Dow sold the Tradewinds building in 1949 and began buying the properties that now comprise the Collector Luxury Inn and Gardens.

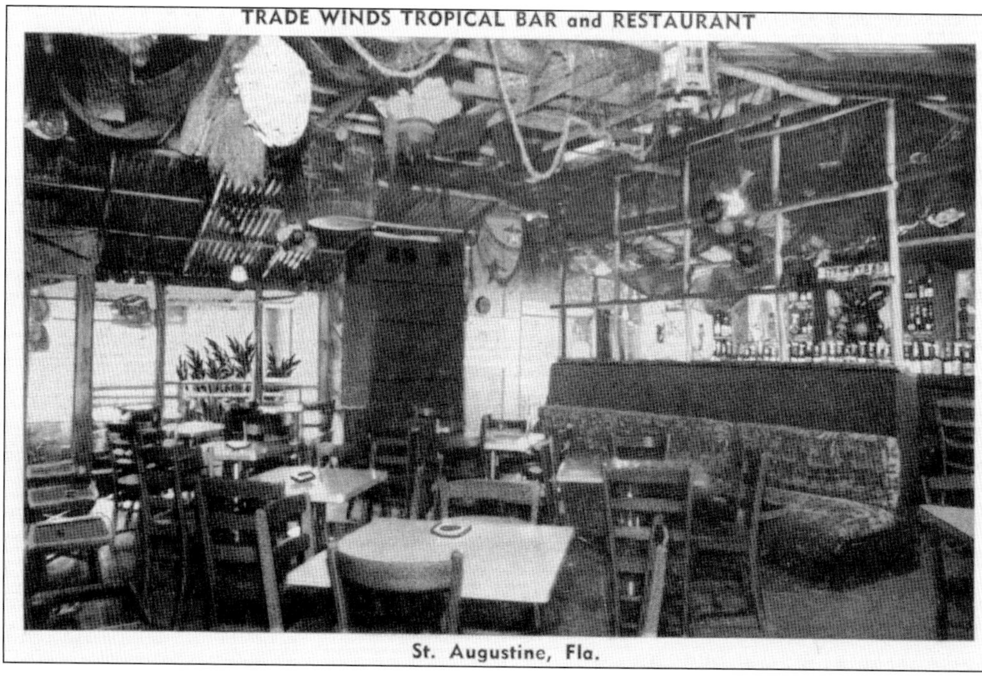

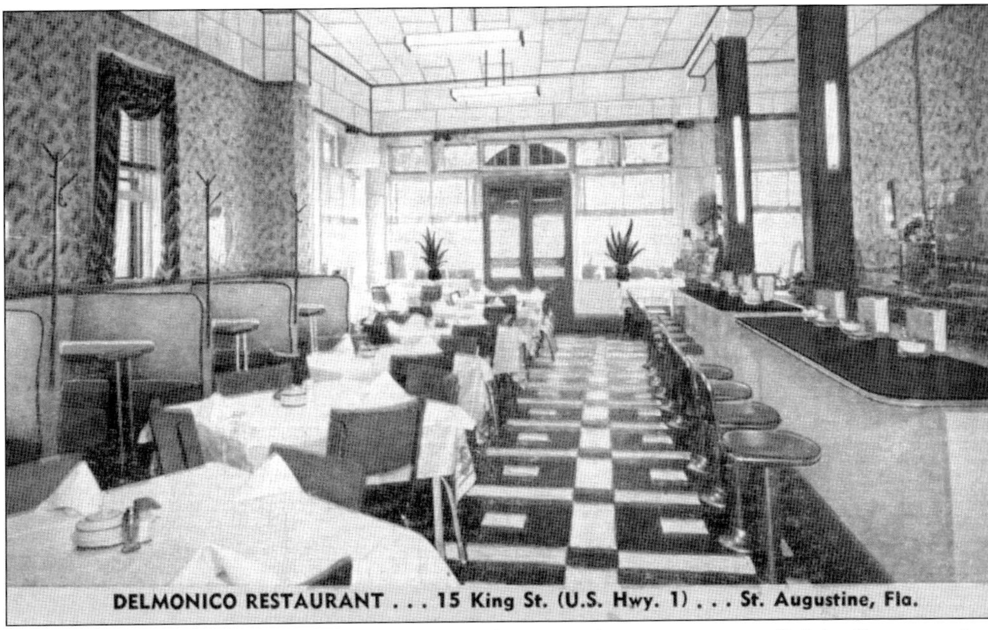

The site of 15 King Street was a restaurant location for many years. Originally opened as the Twentieth Century Café around 1930, by the mid-1940s it became the Park View Café, operated by Mike and Mina Manitopoulos. By the late 1940s, it was Nick Petroglou's Delmonico Restaurant, shown in this postcard.

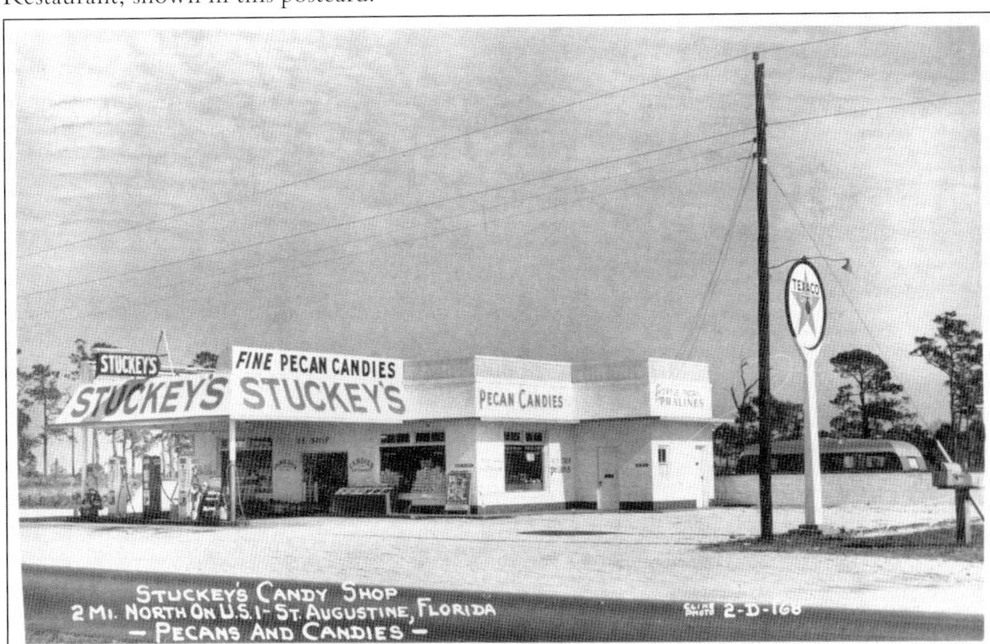

Opened in 1946 on US 1 North, Stuckey's originated in Eastman, Georgia, in the early 1930s when W.S. Stuckey Sr. began selling pecans from a roadside stand along a major route to Florida. After World War II, he franchised locations that featured Texaco gas, a restaurant, and clean restrooms. The St. Augustine Stuckey's later became Linda's, a roadside feature in the Araquay Park area for many years.

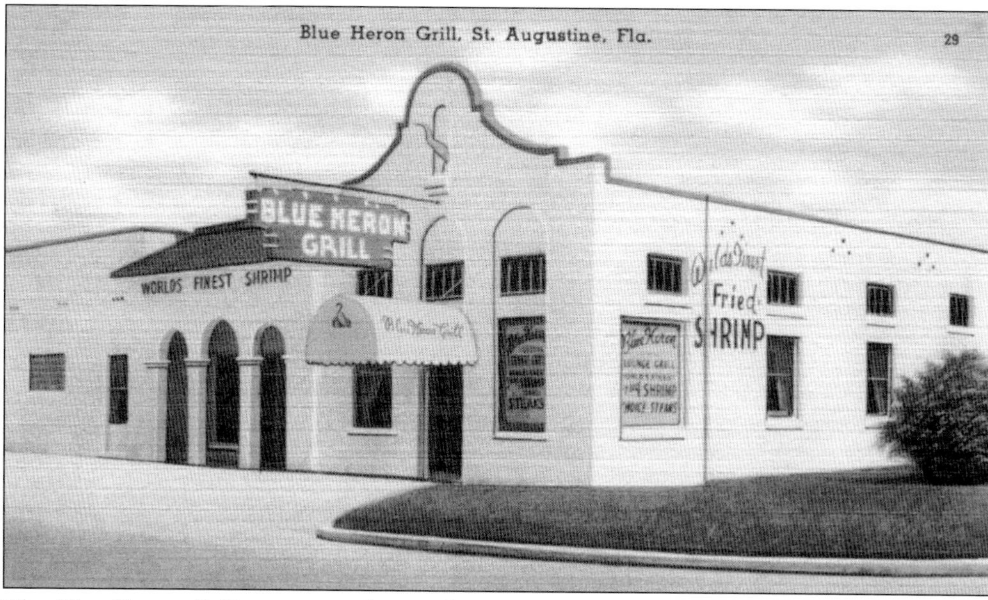

The Blue Heron Grill was one of many businesses that opened along a booming Anastasia Boulevard in the years immediately following World War II. Located at 218 Anastasia Boulevard at the corner of Arredondo Avenue, owners Granville Grissom and Sterling Andrew boasted the "World's Finest Fried Shrimp," and the restaurant soon became one of the town's most popular eateries. The location is now a modern motel, the Anastasia Inn.

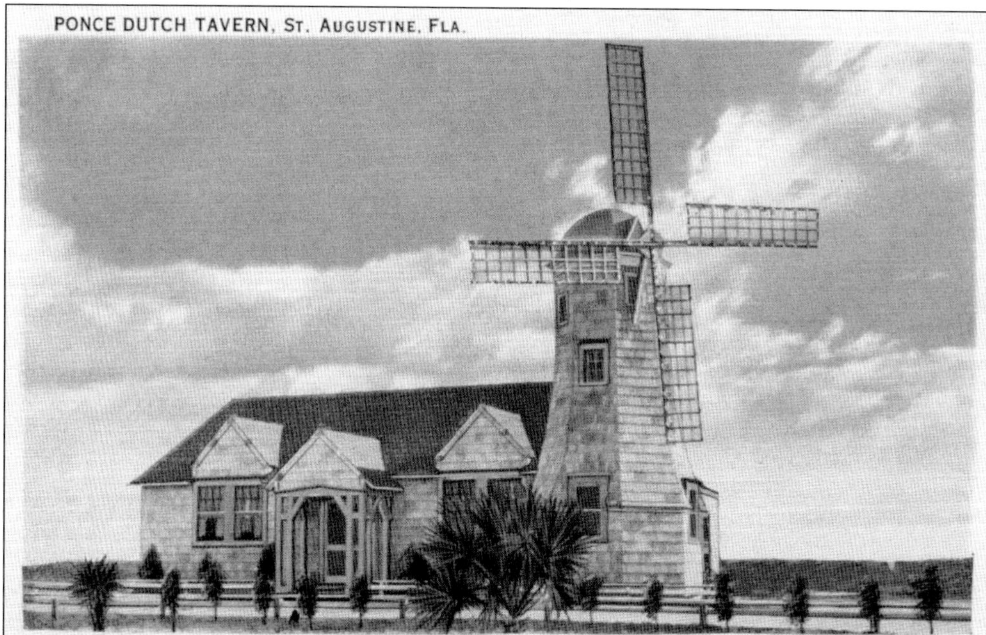

This unique restaurant at 101 Anastasia Boulevard was opened in the mid-1930s by Joseph X. Ponce, whose previous business was Ponce's Sweet Shop in the Jefferson Theater building on Cathedral Place. Ponce's son James A. Ponce founded By The Sea Court on Comares Avenue, which later became the Conch House Marina. In the 1960s, the restaurant became Norman's Windmill Restaurant, owned by Norman P. and Barry W. Myers. (O'Neill Collection.)

Four

PUBLIC LANDS AND BUILDINGS

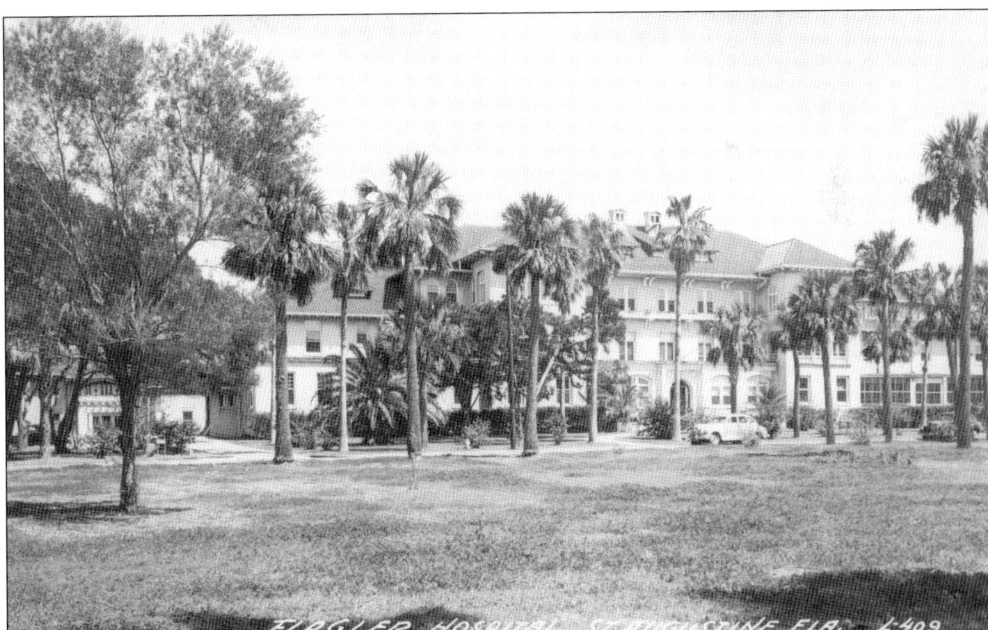

This second Flagler Hospital opened on January 5, 1921, replacing the original wooden hospital that burned in 1916. Designed by architect Fred A. Henderich, construction was funded by a bequest from Henry Flagler's third wife, Mary Lily Kenan, and funds raised by the hospital's ladies auxiliary. In 1989, the hospital moved from its south Marine Street location to a larger facility on US 1 South.

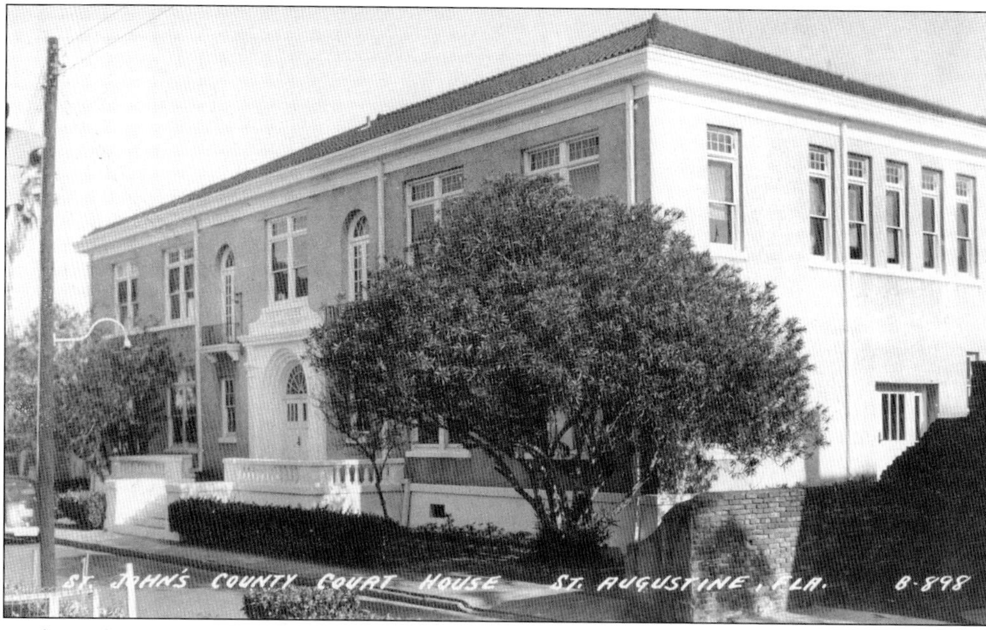

Dedicated in March 1918, the St. Johns County Courthouse was located on the southwest corner of Charlotte and Treasury Streets. Designed by architect Fred A. Henderich, it replaced an earlier courthouse that was destroyed in the 1914 fire. It remained in use until 1968, when county government moved into the former Cordova Hotel. The building was demolished in 1971 for a bank parking lot.

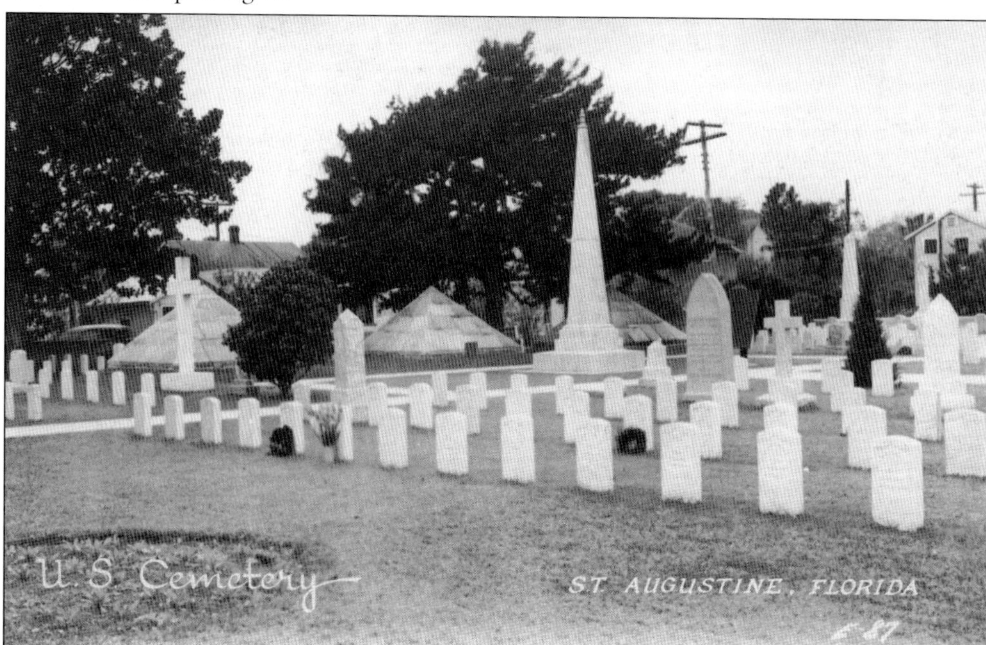

The St. Augustine National Cemetery is located at 104 Marine Street, just south of the headquarters of the Florida National Guard. Three coquina pyramids mark the mass graves of soldiers killed during the Seminole Wars. The white marble obelisk was dedicated in 1881 to Maj. Francis Dade and the victims of the 1835 massacre near Bushnell, Florida.

St. Augustine's plaza was first laid out in 1573 and is the nation's oldest public space. Near the center is the Constitution Monument, erected in 1813 to commemorate the Spanish constitution of 1812. The monarchy was restored in 1814, and King Ferdinand VII ordered all constitution monuments destroyed. But St. Augustine's obelisk remains and may be the only surviving monument to Spain's first constitutional government. At the east end of the plaza is the public market, built in 1824. Postcards from the early 1900s onward by William J. Harris and other photographers touted the structure as a slave market, but debate continues as to whether that was ever its primary purpose. Tables and benches in the market made it a popular spot for a relaxing game of checkers.

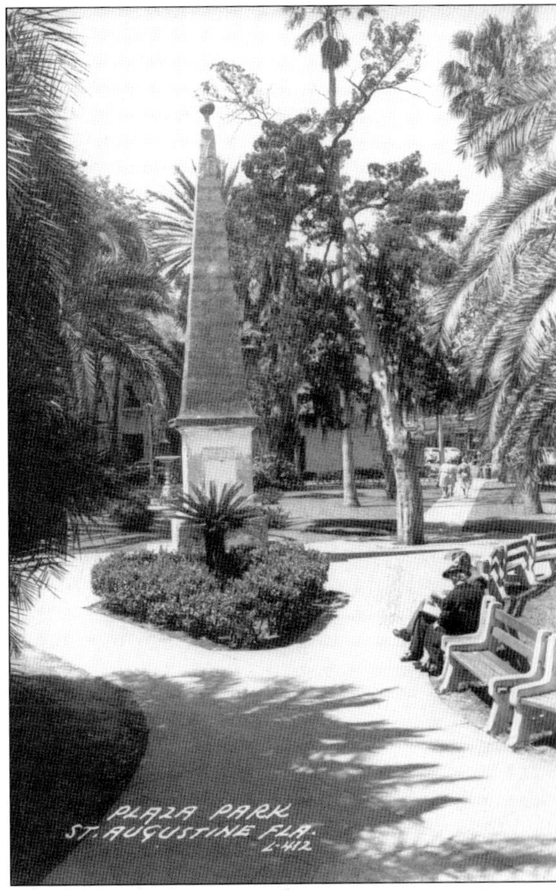

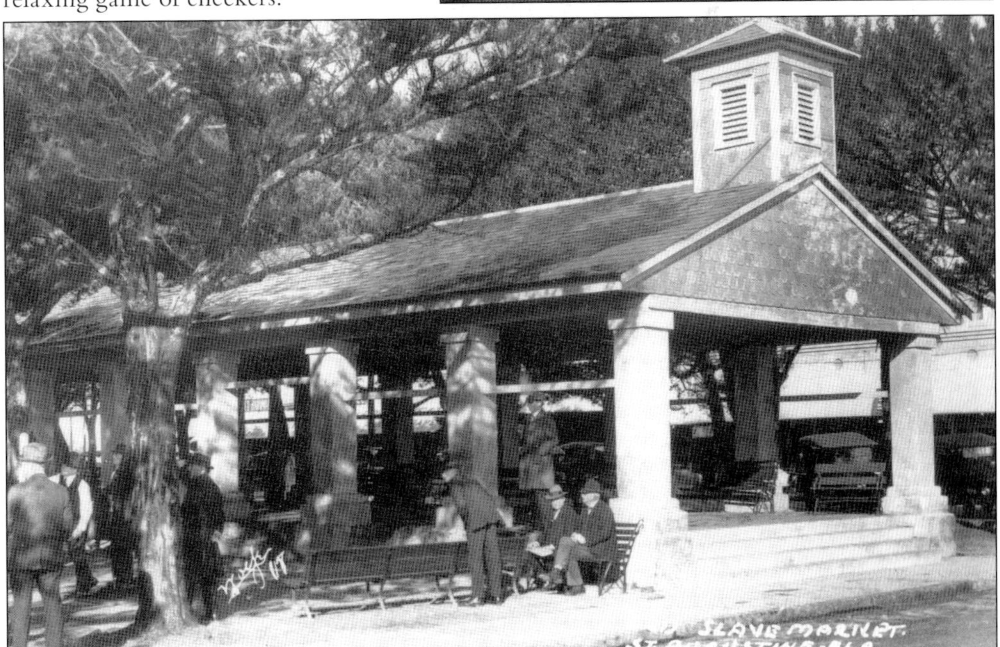

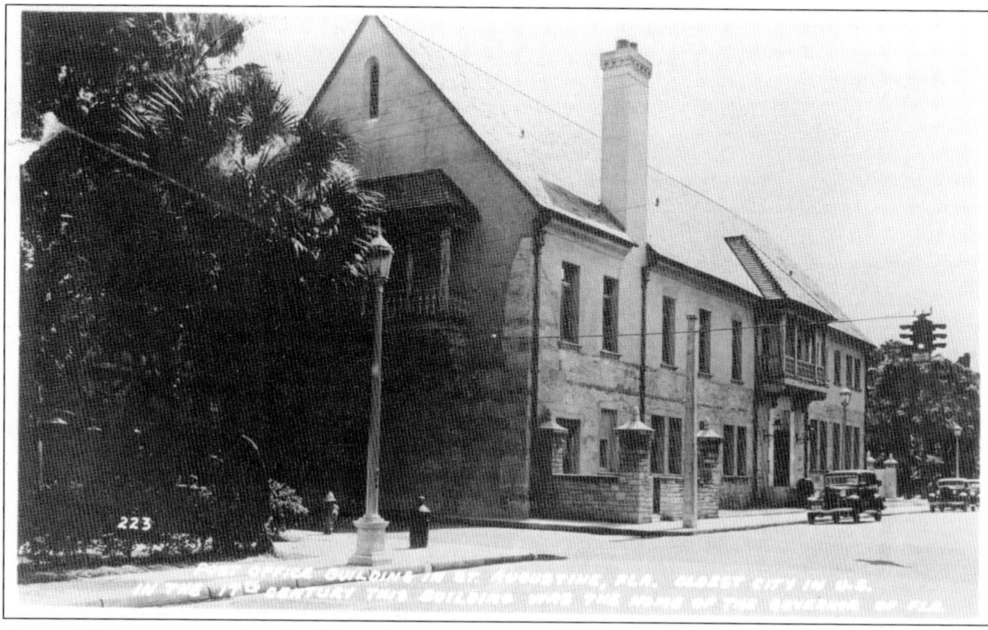

Since 1598, a government building has stood on this site, housing administrative offices and the residence of colonial governors. By the time Florida became a US territory in 1821, the structure was in ruins and rebuilt for use as a post office, courtroom, and customs house. During the Civil War, Federal troops were housed in the building. In 1873, another remodeling was undertaken. Between 1936 and 1937, the building was completely rebuilt as a Works Progress Administration project. It continued to serve as a post office until 1965, when a new facility was built on King Street. Ownership of the building was transferred to the State of Florida in 1966 and today is the Government House Cultural Center and Museum managed by the University of Florida Historic St. Augustine, Inc.

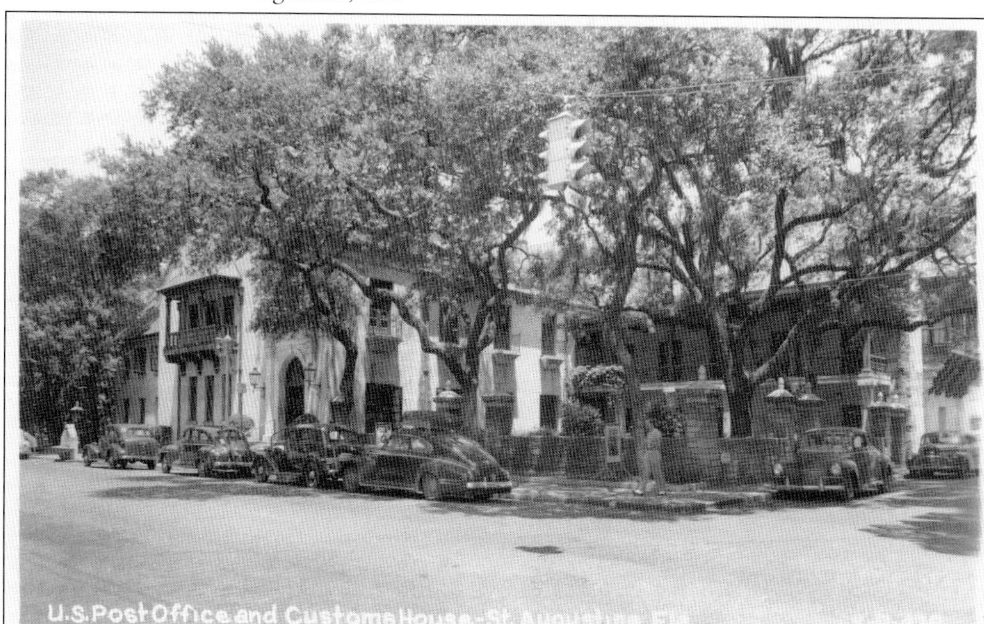

The Florida Council for the Blind ran a newsstand in the lobby of the post office. The operator shown here is Emmanuel "Manny" Ross, a lifelong resident of St. Augustine and graduate of the Florida School for the Deaf and Blind. He worked at the post office for many years and is remembered for knowing everyone by name and never missing a day of work.

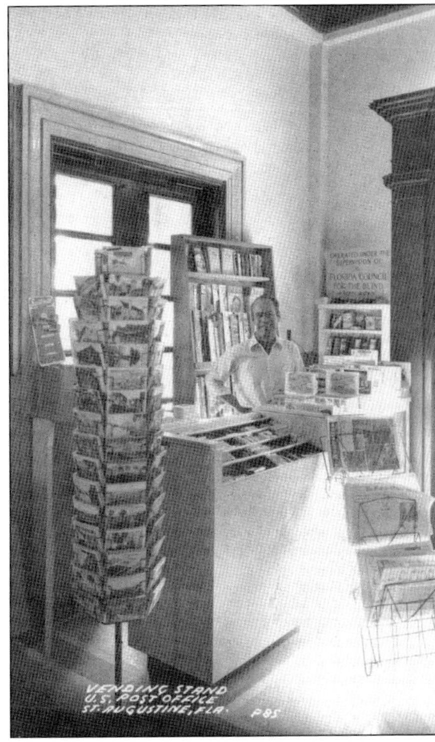

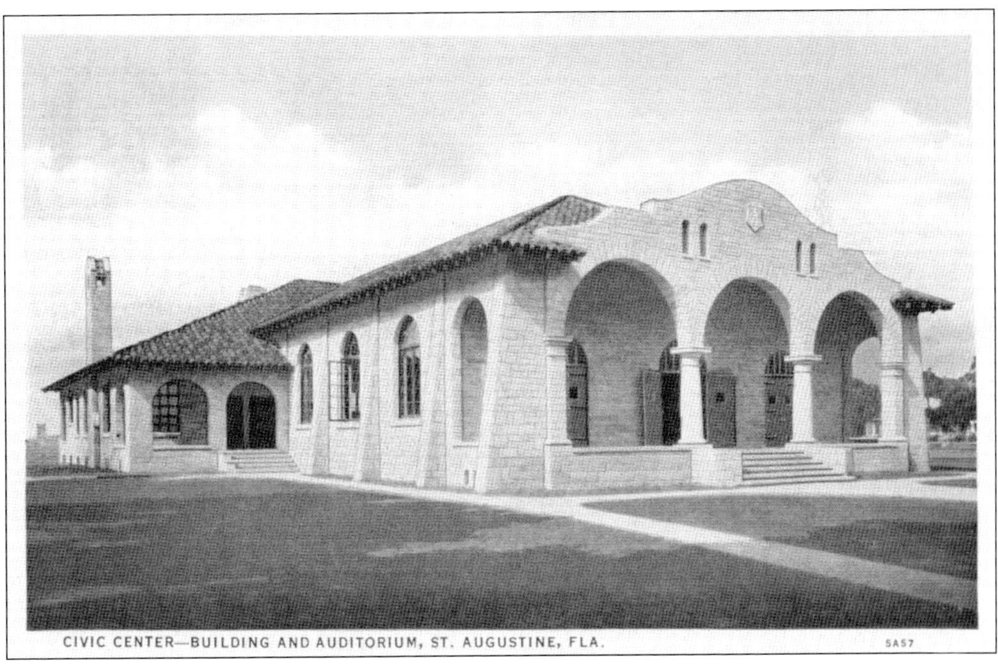

The Civic Center—today's Visitor Information Center—was one of the public works projects undertaken to provide employment during the Depression. Opened in February 1935, it was built of coquina stone and financed by the Federal Emergency Relief Administration. Designed by architect Frederick A. Henderich, the Civic Center featured a large main hall with a stage and side rooms for meetings and offices.

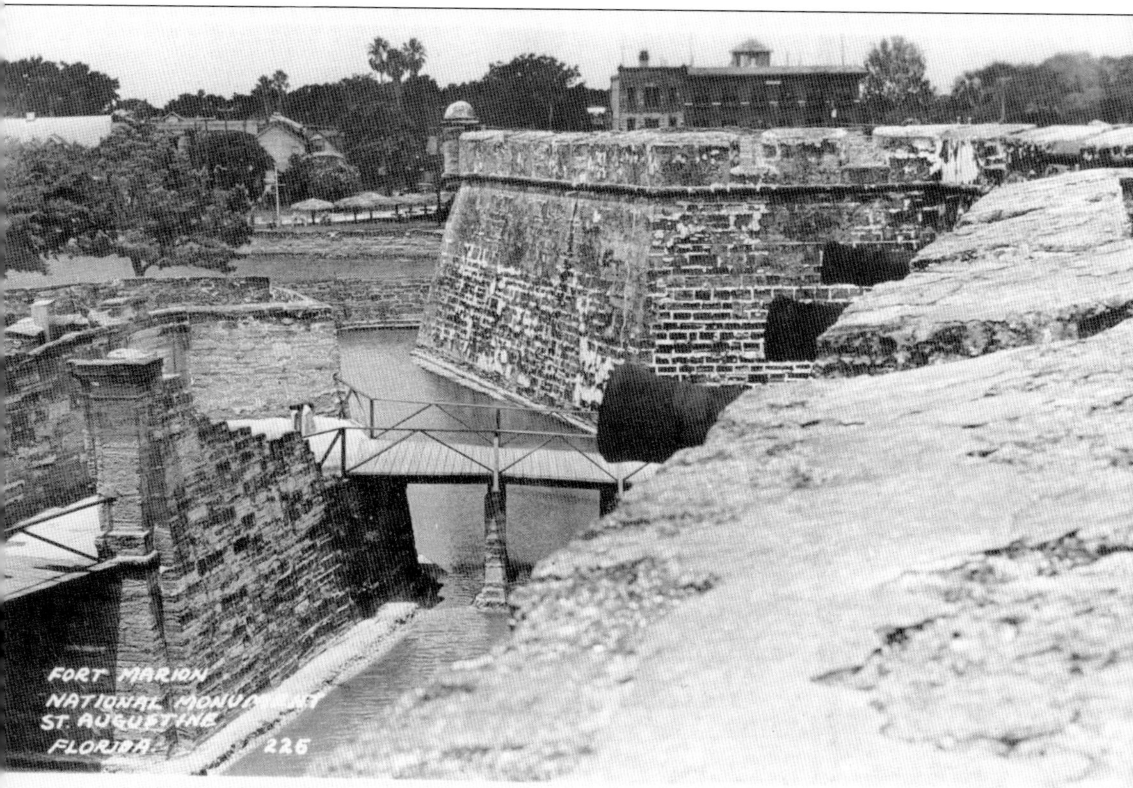

The Castillo de San Marcos, built by the Spanish between 1672 and 1696 using coquina stone quarried on Anastasia Island, is the oldest masonry fort in the continental United States. When the Americans arrived in 1821, they changed the name to Fort Marion, in honor of the "Swamp Fox," Gen. Francis Marion, of Revolutionary War fame. This view looking to the west was taken sometime after the fort was declared a national monument in 1924 but prior to the name change back to Castillo de San Marcos in 1942. In the distance on St. George Street is the Byrne Building and former City Gates Hotel, now converted into the Byrne Apartments.

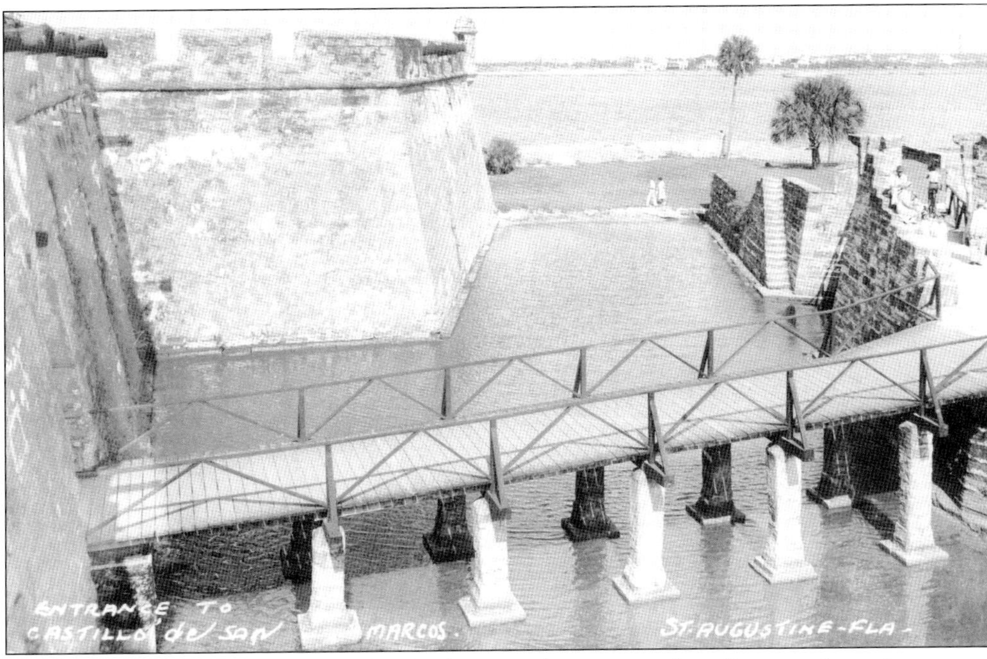

A wooden bridge, once a drawbridge, leads across the moat to the sally port, the only entrance into the fort. At right, an outer defense, the barbican, guards the fort's entrance. Between 1936 and 1996, the moat was filled with water but drained when it was determined that the water was causing the coquina to weaken. In the distance is the Matanzas River and Davis Shores.

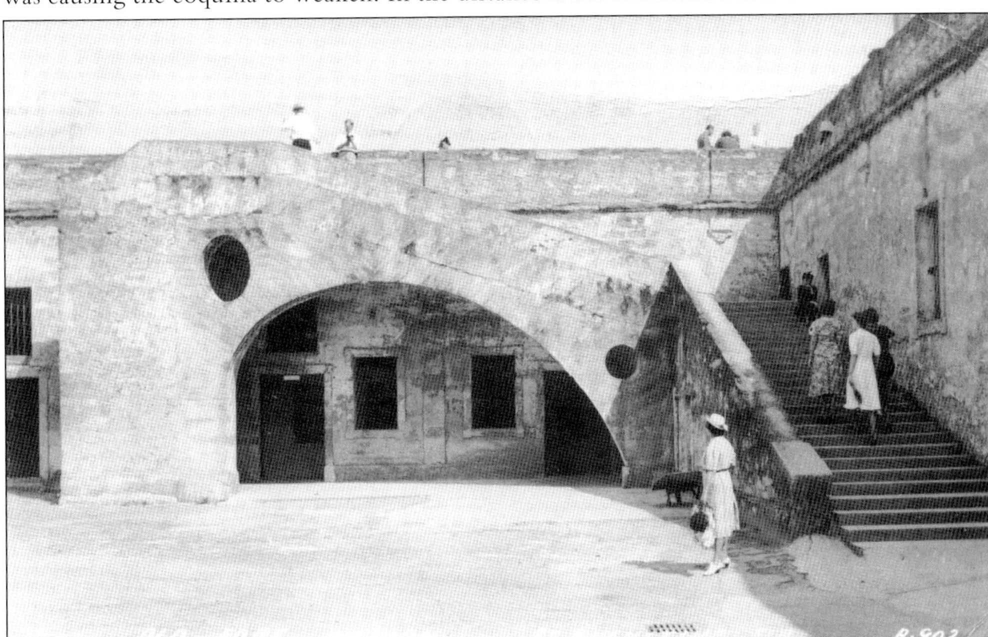

The steps at the fort were once a ramp leading to the gun deck. Deactivated as a military post in 1900, the St. Augustine Historical Society became the custodian of the fort from 1914 to 1935 and provided tours and souvenirs to tourists. In 1933, Fort Marion was transferred from the War Department to the National Park Service.

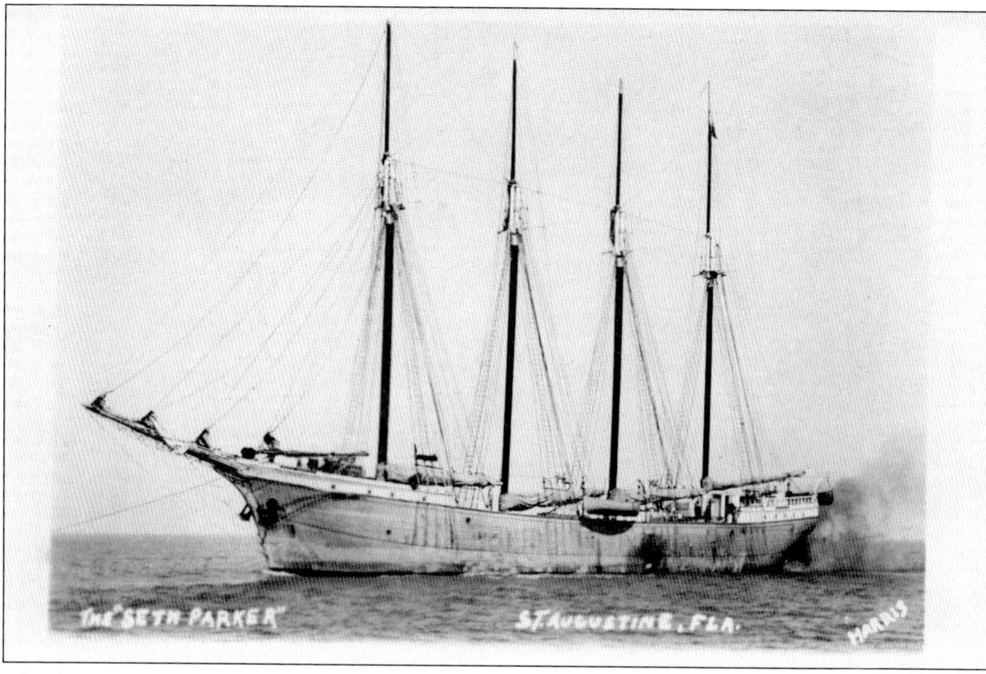

The four-masted schooner *Seth Parker* docked in St. Augustine on March 13, 1934. Owned by radio personality Phillips Lord, the ship traveled the world doing live broadcasts for his show, *Sunday Evenings with Seth Parker.* That evening, the program was broadcast live on NBC Radio from a room at Fort Marion. Shown are, from left to right, Victorino Capo, John Osceola (great-great grandson of Osceola, who was imprisoned at the fort in 1837), Phillips Lord (portraying Seth Parker), and Harry Hernandez (grandson of John Masters, who was present at the capture of Osceola under a white flag of truce in the Moultrie area). (Below, SAHS.)

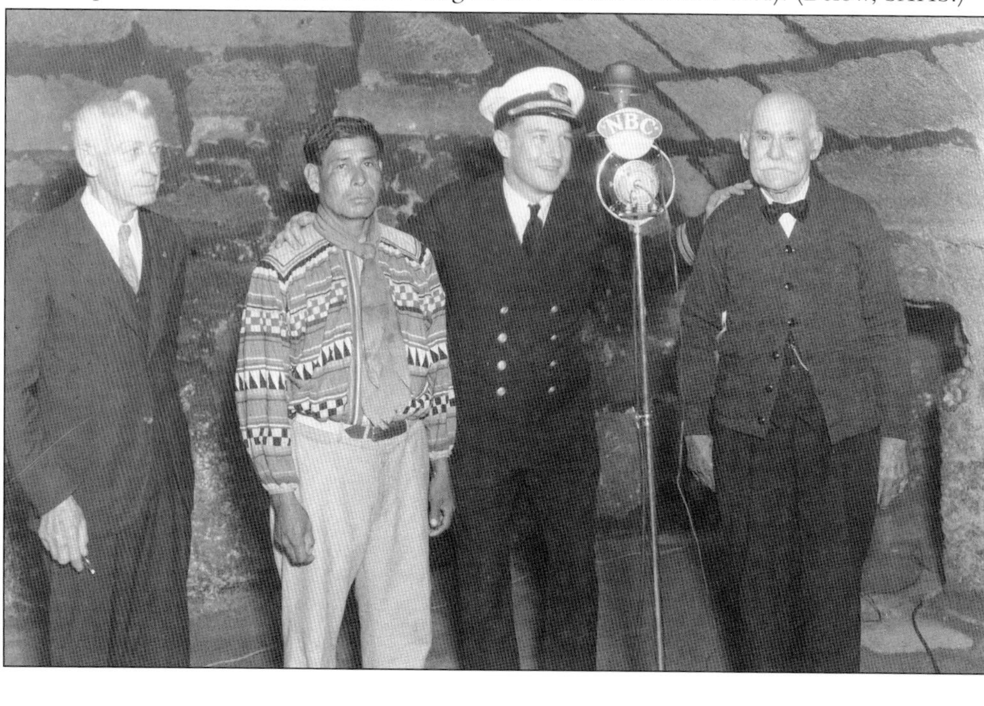

This is the courtyard of the Segui-Kirby Smith House at 12 Aviles Street. Constructed in the late 1700s by Bernardo Segui, it was the birthplace of Confederate general Edmund Kirby Smith in 1824. In 1896, it opened as a public library, at the bequest of John and Frances Wilson. The library moved to a larger facility in 1987, and the building is now the Research Library of the St. Augustine Historical Society. (SAHS.)

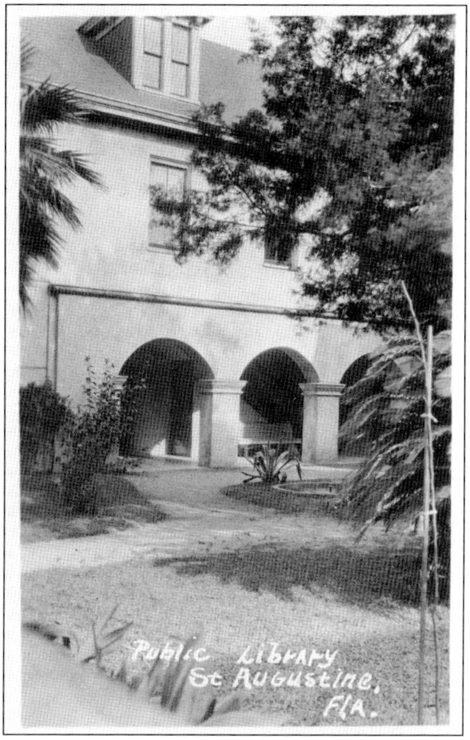

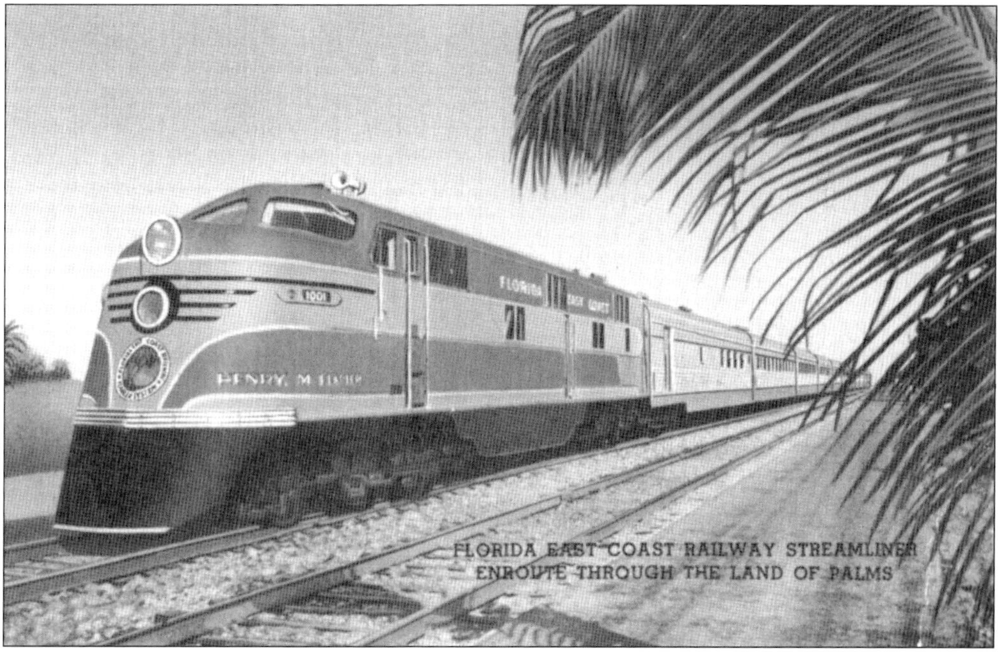

The Florida East Coast Railway's first streamliner, the *Henry M. Flagler,* began operation in December 1939. The single diesel engine and seven cars made the trip from Jacksonville to Miami in 5 hours and 59 minutes. The FEC depot on Malaga Street was one of 18 stops on the line, but it was the only one where the train had to back out of the station to rejoin the main track. (SAHS.)

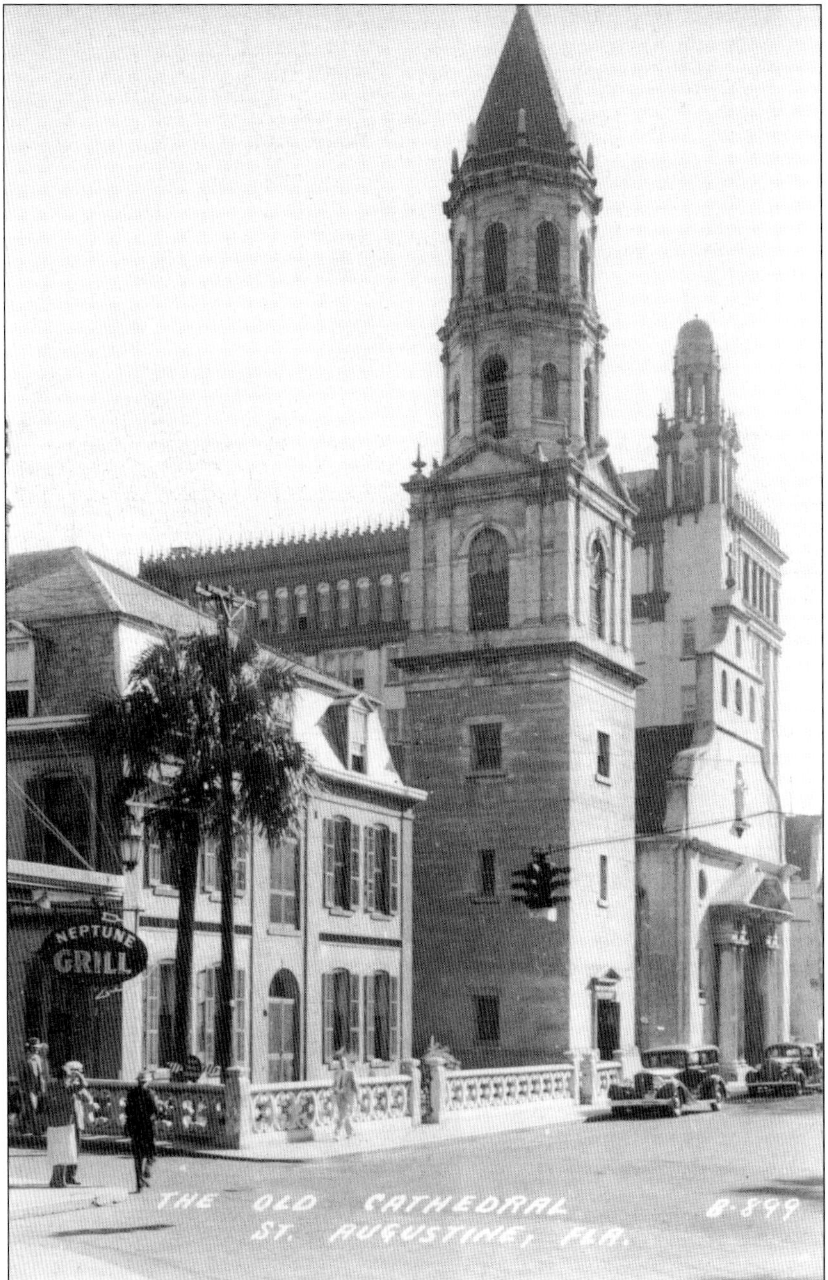

The Spanish Mission–style cathedral was constructed between 1793 and 1797 using local coquina. In 1887, the cathedral was gutted by a fire that destroyed the wooden St. Augustine Hotel and other structures around the plaza. The cathedral was rebuilt with the help of architect James Renwick, who happened to be staying in St. Augustine at the time of the fire. The architect of St. Patrick's Cathedral in New York City, Renwick also designed a new bell tower. Henry Flagler contributed $5,000 to the cathedral's restoration. The bishop's house and rectory, shown to the left of the bell tower, was built in the 1870s. It was demolished in 1965 when a new rectory was built behind the cathedral on Treasury Street.

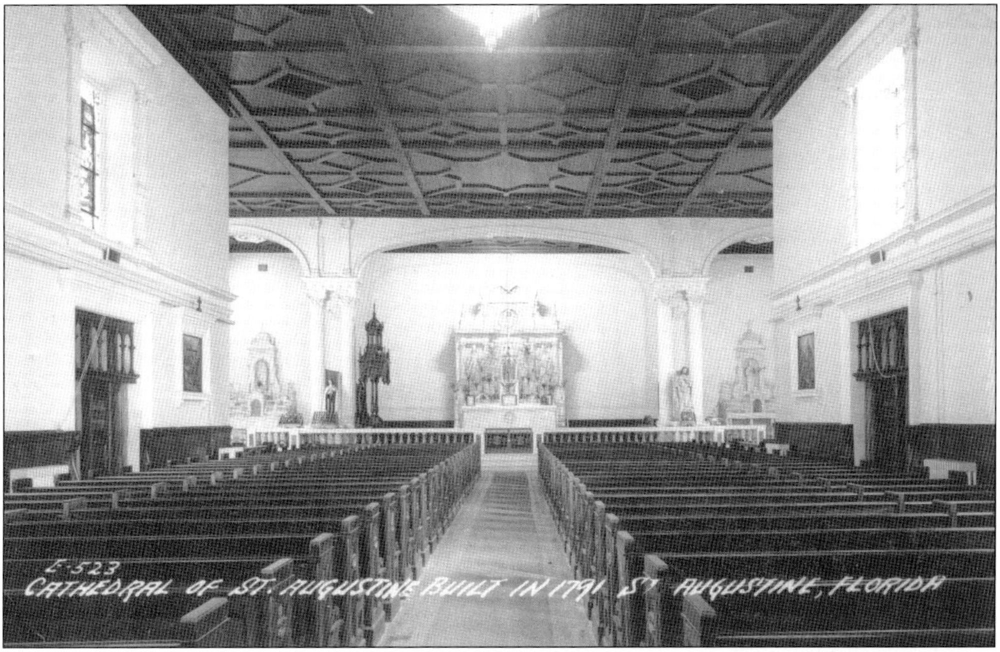

The interior of the cathedral, shown here around 1940, looks essentially the same since its reconstruction after the 1887 fire and would remain so until the extensive renovation that was undertaken for St. Augustine's 400th anniversary in 1965. During the 1930s and 1940s, the Diocese of St. Augustine covered the entire state, as the southern part of Florida did not become a separate entity until 1958. Joseph Patrick Barry served as bishop from 1922 until his death in 1940. His sister, Mother Gerald Barry, was a Dominican prioress general and founded Barry College in Miami Springs in 1940. Archbishop Joseph P. Hurley headed the diocese from 1940 until 1967.

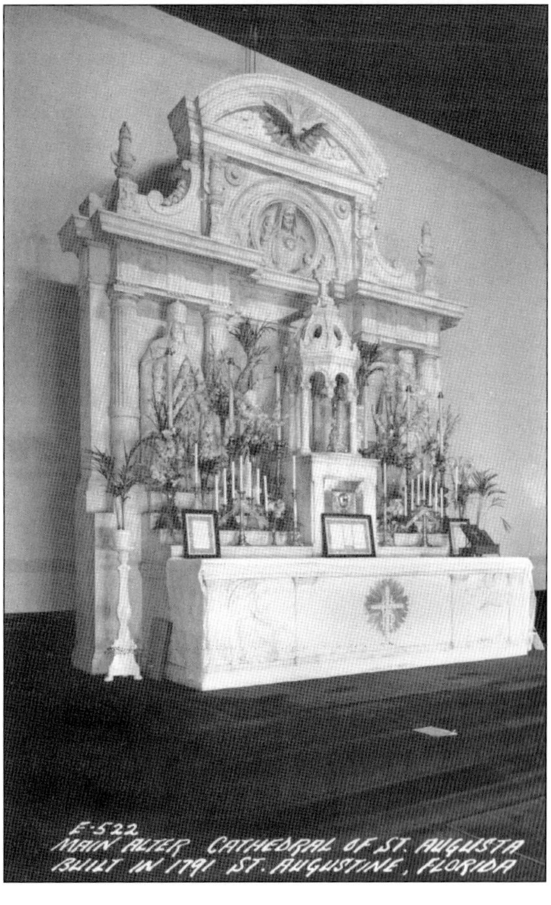

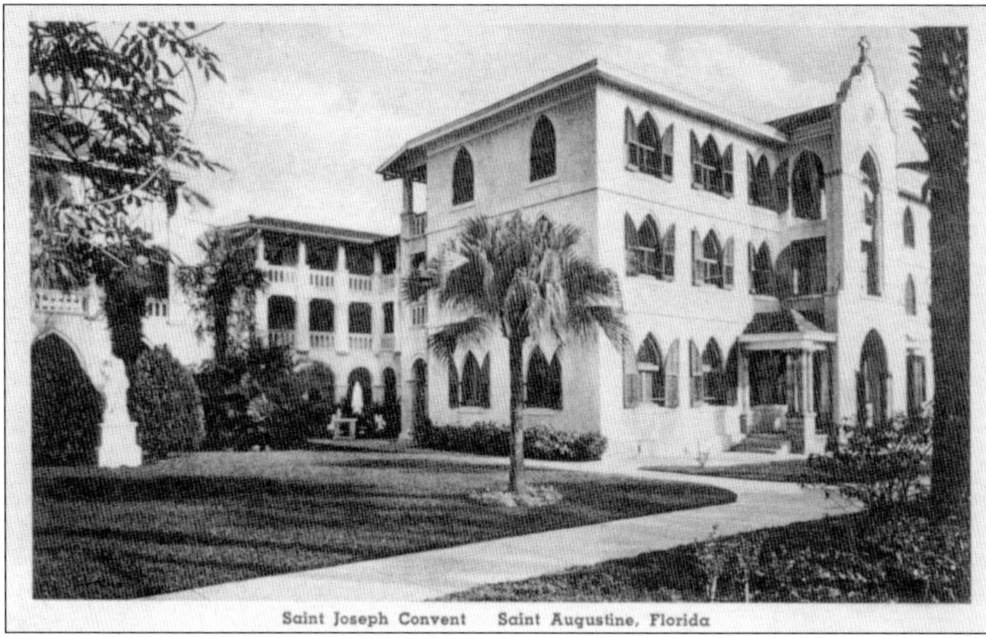

The Sisters of St. Joseph came to St. Augustine in 1866 from LePuy, France, to educate the black children of the city. Built between 1874 and 1876, their convent at 241 St. George Street sits on land donated by Fr. Miguel O'Reilly, whose house is located behind the convent at 32 Aviles Street. The convent was one of the last major structures in St. Augustine constructed of coquina quarried on Anastasia Island.

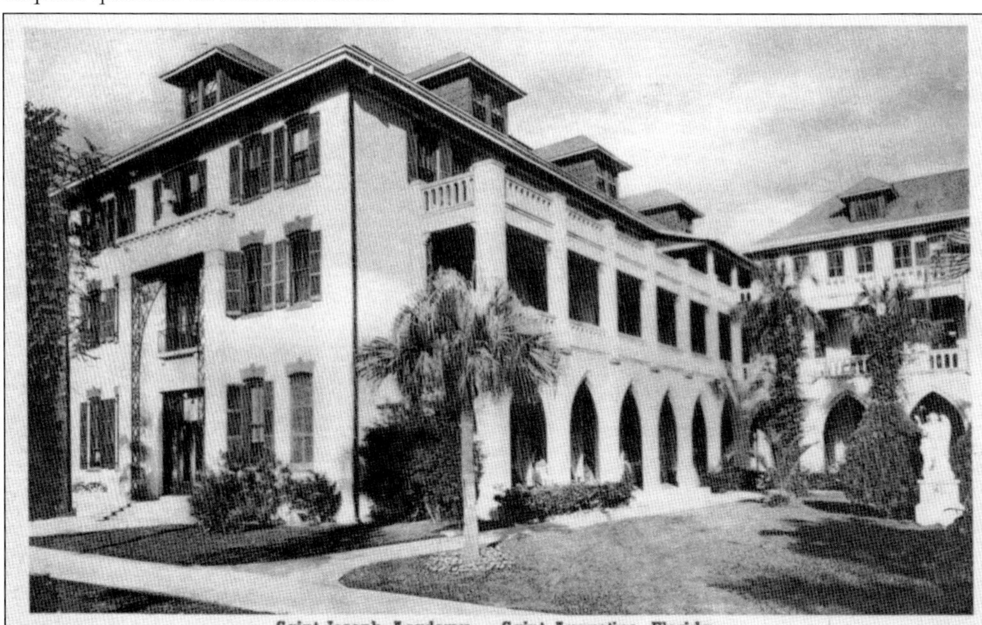

St. Joseph's Academy was built adjacent to the convent and opened in the fall of 1908. Around 1940, its original wooden porches were replaced with the concrete cloisters shown in this postcard. A new St. Joseph's Academy opened west of the city in 1980, and the old academy buildings were demolished in 1982, but its coquina gate remains at 235 St. George Street.

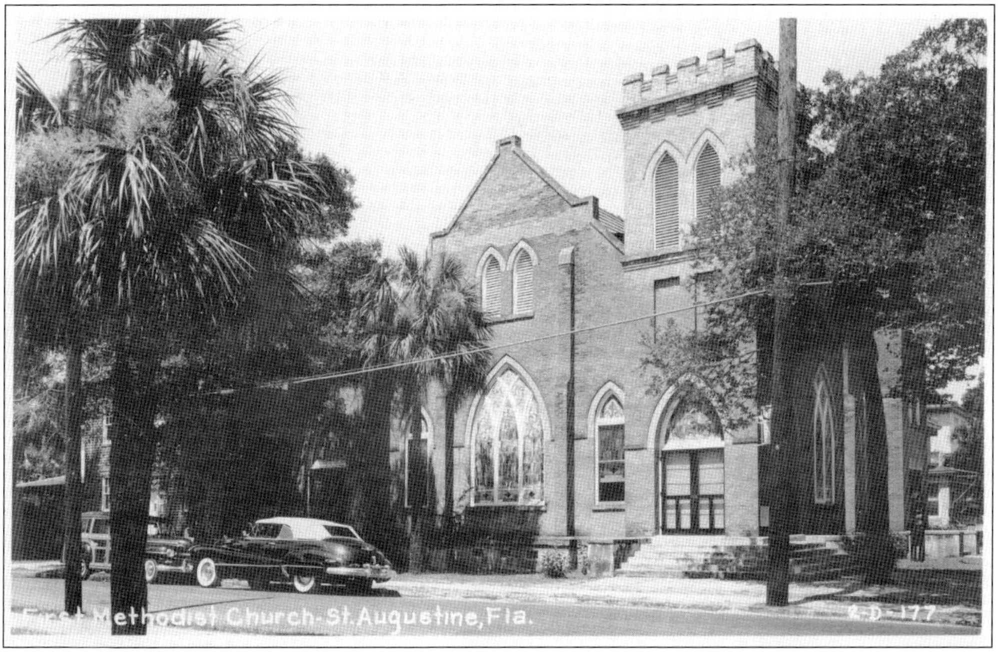

First Methodist Church was built in 1910 as the First Methodist Episcopal Church South. Constructed in a Gothic Revival style, the church's architect was Wilbur B. Talley, of Jacksonville. The entrance originally faced the corner of King and Riberia Streets, as shown in this postcard, but the church was enlarged and reconfigured in 1954 and now has its main entrance on King Street. (SAHS.)

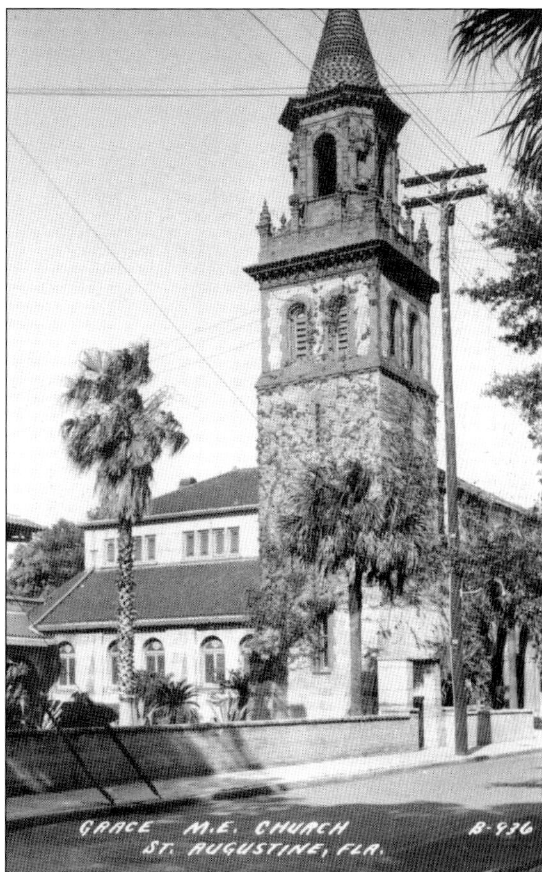

Grace Methodist Episcopal Church, located on the northwest corner of Cordova and Carrera Streets, was dedicated in January 1888. It was built by Henry Flagler at a cost of $85,000 and designed by architects Carrere and Hastings. Flagler needed the land of the Olivet Methodist Episcopal Church on King Street to build his Ponce de Leon Hotel, so he offered to build the congregation a new church if they would move.

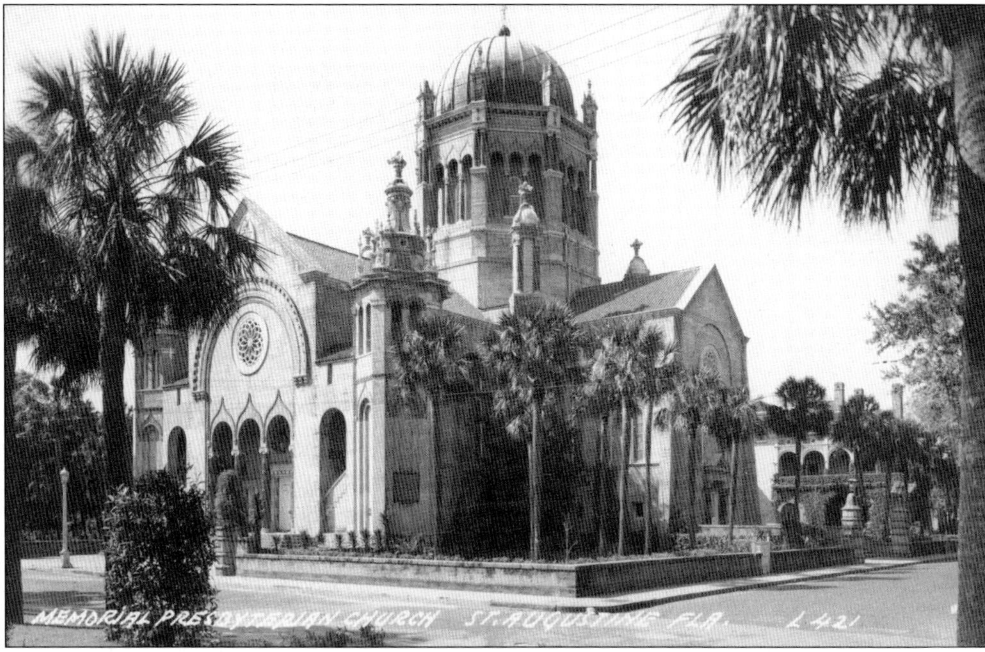

Henry Flagler built the Memorial Presbyterian Church in memory of his daughter Jennie Louise Benedict, who died in 1889 soon after giving birth. He used the same architects, Carrere and Hastings, who had designed his recently opened Ponce de Leon and Alcazar Hotels. The building was completed in less than one year using the same poured concrete construction employed in those hotels.

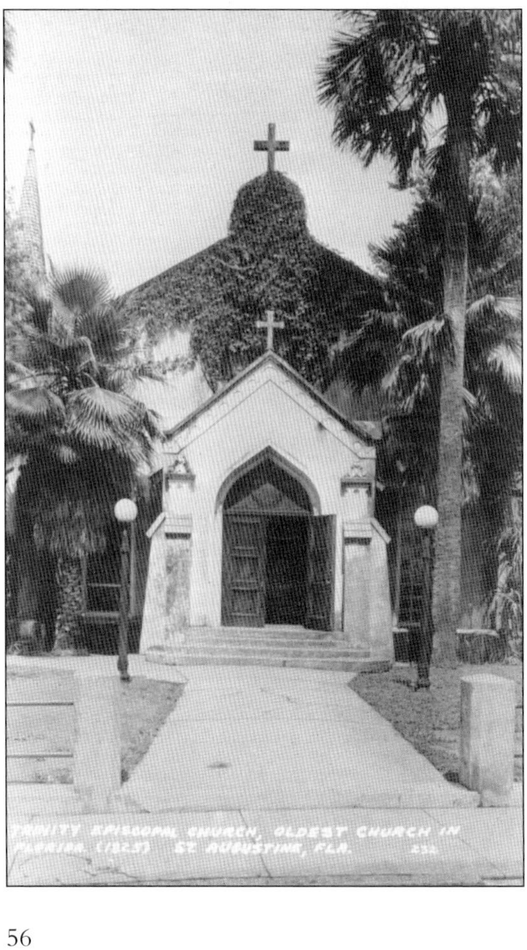

Established in 1821, Trinity Parish Episcopal Church is the oldest Protestant church in Florida. The original building was constructed in 1830–1831 in a north-south direction, with its entrance on King Street. The church was enlarged in 1902–1903 with a new east-west transept and entrance facing St. George Street, shown here. At left is the church's steeple, which rises above the King Street entrance.

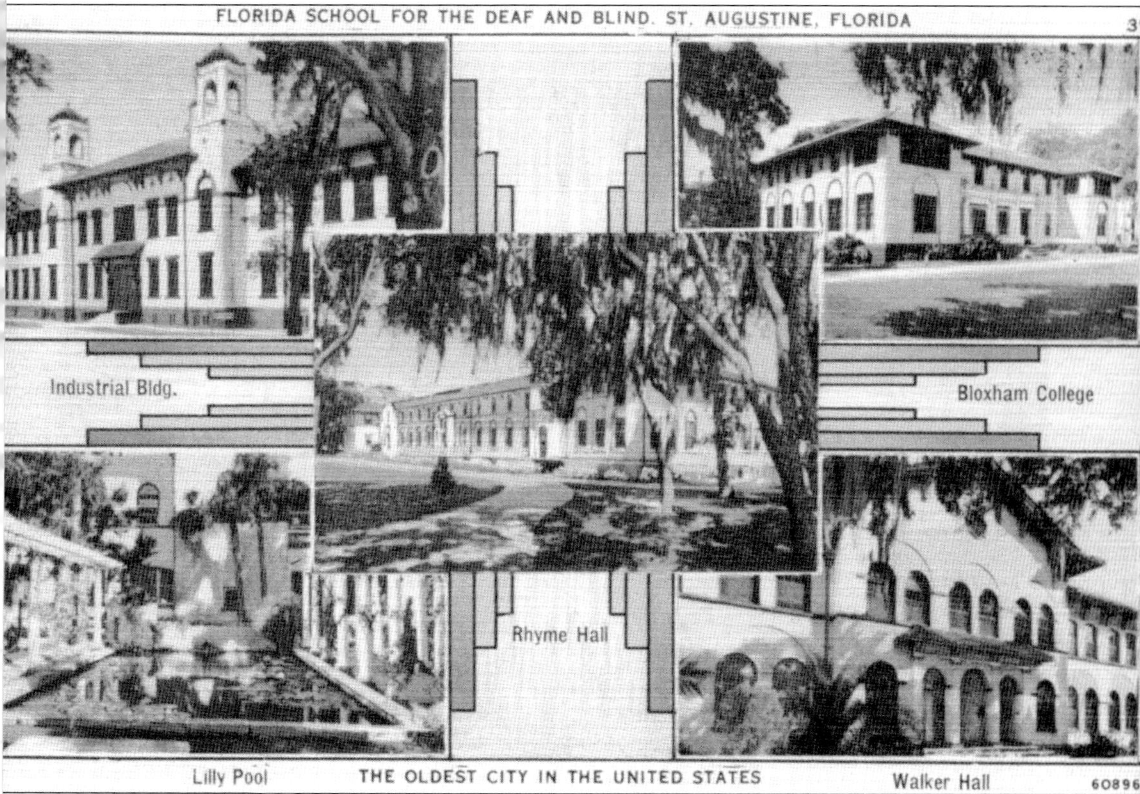

The Florida School for the Deaf and Blind opened in 1885 on San Marco Avenue on five acres of land donated by Capt. Edward E. Vaill, owner of the St. Augustine Hotel. This postcard from the mid-1930s depicts some of the major buildings on campus. Built in 1924, Bloxham College was named for William D. Bloxham, Florida governor from 1881 to 1885, who was instrumental in establishing the school. Walker Hall, opened as the Administration Building in 1910, was renamed in 1927 to honor Albert H. Walker, president of school from 1906 to 1927. Rhyne Hall, built in 1927, is named for Mary Knox Rhyne, a deaf sewing teacher and houseparent. Constructed in 1915, the Industrial Building was renamed the Pope Vocational Building in 1963 to honor Artemas Winfred Pope, the first male deaf graduate and father of state senator Verle A. Pope.

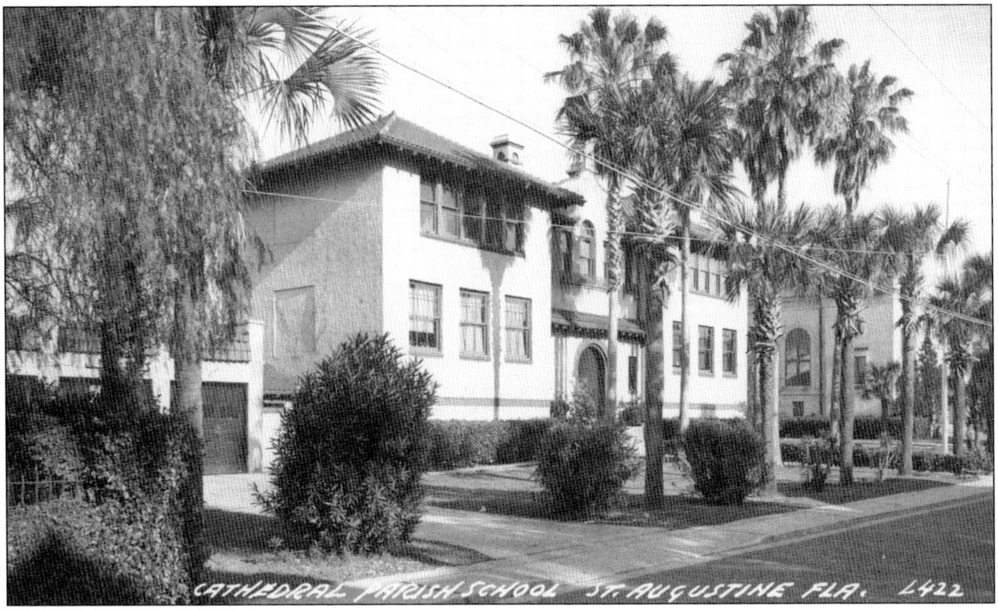

Located at 259 St. George Street, Cathedral Parish School opened in 1916 and was staffed by the Sisters of St. Joseph. To the right of the school is the Cathedral Parish Lyceum, built in 1926, which featured an auditorium and gymnasium. The original Cathedral Parish School was demolished in 1960 and replaced with a modern facility, and the Lyceum was rebuilt to become the Bishop Baker Center.

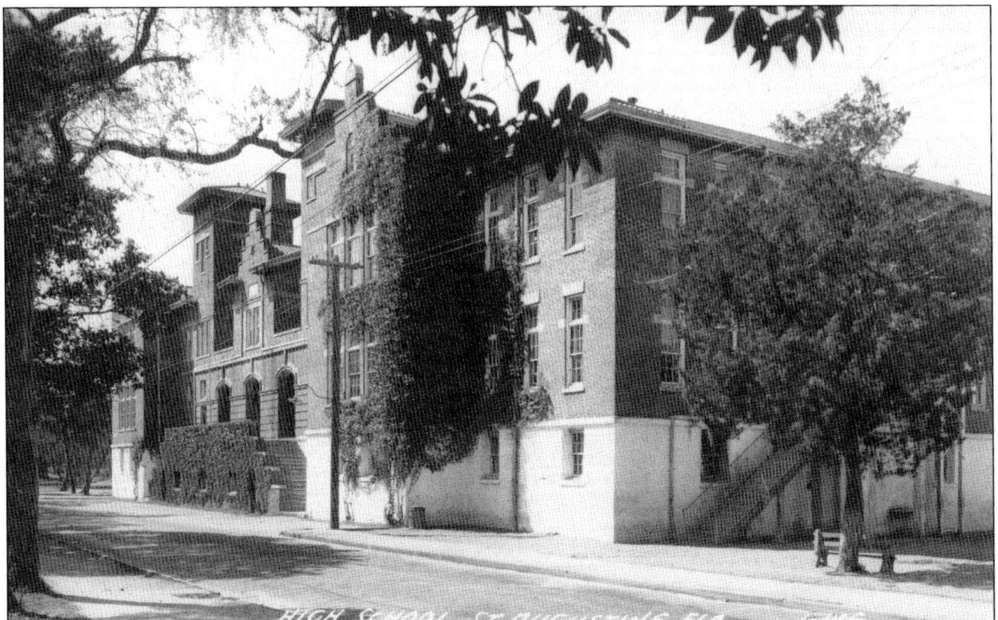

Built in 1910 for students in grades one through 12, Orange Street School was the inspiration of W.S.M. Pinkham, St. Augustine mayor and superintendent of public instruction for St. Johns County. However, the caption on this 1940s postcard is not accurate, as Orange Street School was only for students in grades one through eight after Ketterlinus High School opened one block west on Orange Street in 1925.

Six

Attractions

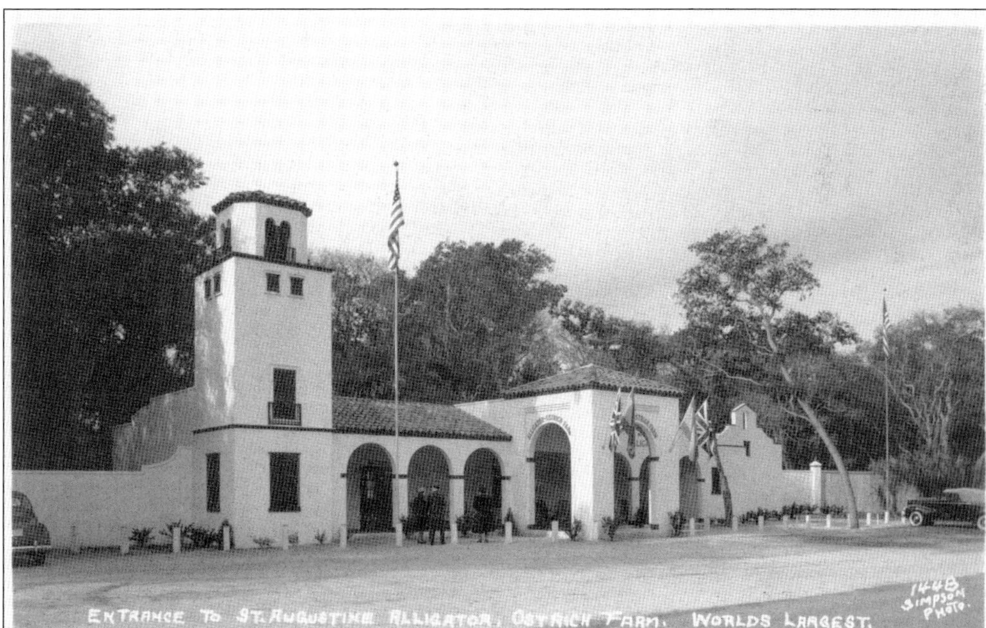

The St. Augustine Alligator Farm was founded in 1893 at South Beach, near the east end of today's Pope Road. Beach erosion forced the relocation of the attraction in the early 1920s to its present location on A1A. The original wooden entrance building on Young Avenue (today's Old Quarry Road) was destroyed by fire in 1936 and replaced by this attractive Mission Revival building on Anastasia Boulevard.

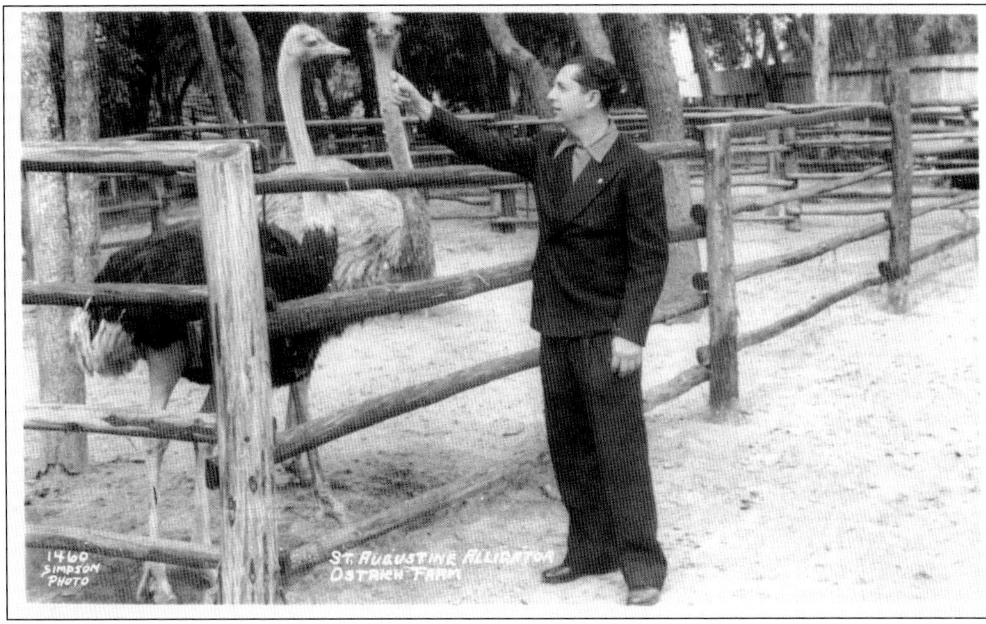

In 1937, local businessmen W.I. Drysdale and F. Charles Usina purchased the alligator farm from the original owner, George Reddington. They improved the exhibits and added more animals, including crocodiles, tortoises, monkeys, and birds. Usina, who served as a longtime state representative for St. Johns County beginning in 1943, is seen in the above postcard with two of the ostriches that were added to the exhibits. The name changed to St. Augustine Alligator and Ostrich Farm. Visitors toured the alligator pens on raised walkways, and the small sign at upper right in the postcard below warns them: "No trespassing on this island."

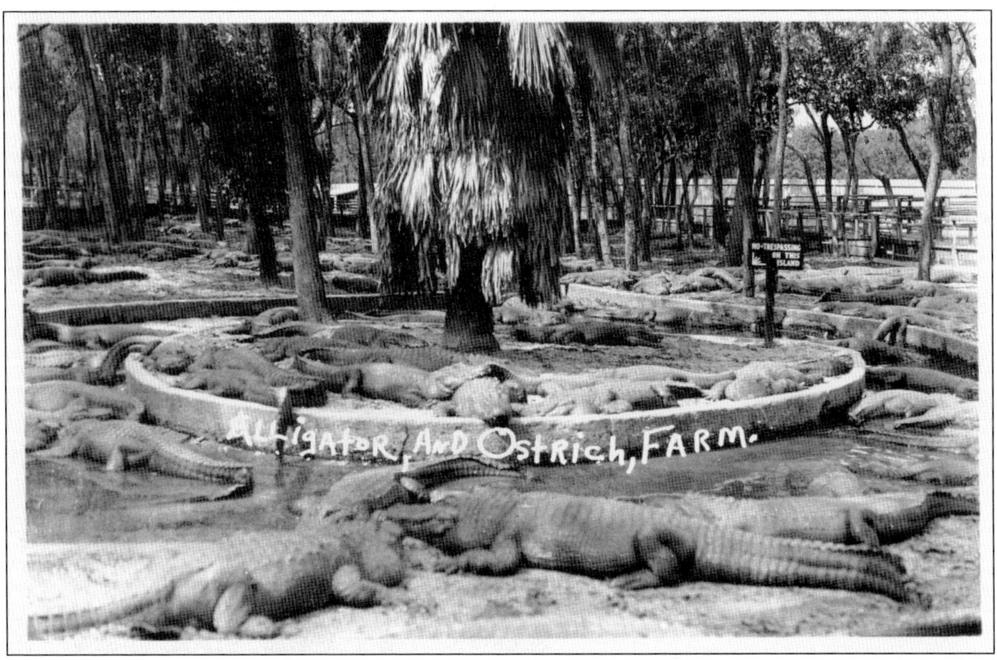

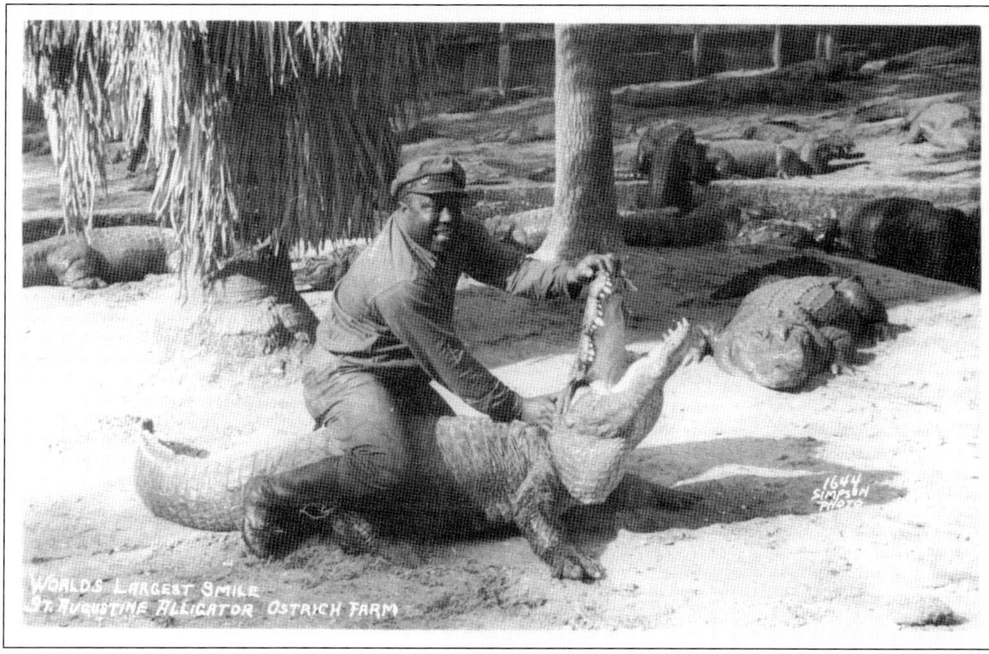

The alligator farm offered scheduled shows where the guides interacted with the animals. Longtime employee George Morgan, pictured in hundreds of postcards, holds a gator's mouth open for visitors' photographs. A popular feature was this sliding board where an alligator would "Shoot the Chutes." Thousands of servicemen visited the alligator farm during World War II, and it continued to gain popularity in the postwar years as a family vacation stop. Today, the attraction continues to evolve as a zoological park and features an exhibit with all known species of the world's crocodilians and a wild bird rookery popular with nature photographers. (Above, O'Neill Collection.)

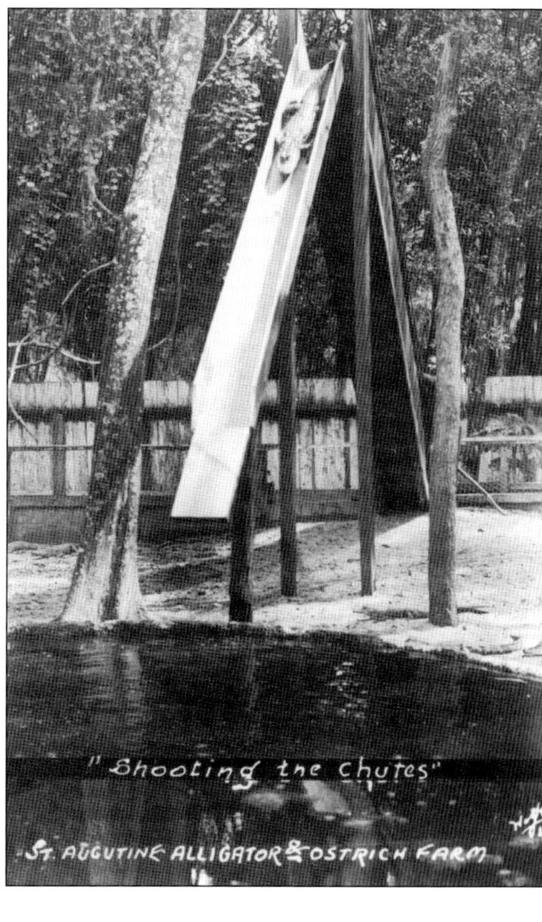

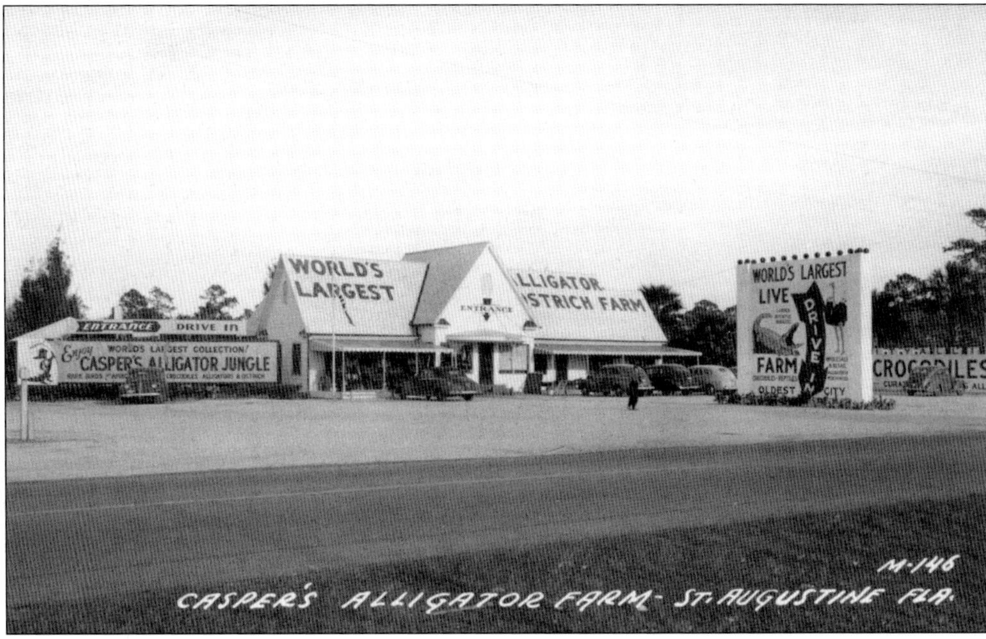

In 1946, James Casper opened a competing alligator and ostrich farm on US 1, north of St. Augustine. It featured a 1/8 mile track where ostriches, trained by veteran ostrich handler F.W. Anderson, competed in races pulling lightweight sulkies. Casper billed himself as the world's largest dealer in alligator hides, supplying the postwar craze for alligator purses, shoes, and belts. In the late 1940s, Casper also operated a retail outlet for alligator goods at 9 King Street. In later years, the attraction changed hands several times and was known as Gatorland when it closed in 1982.

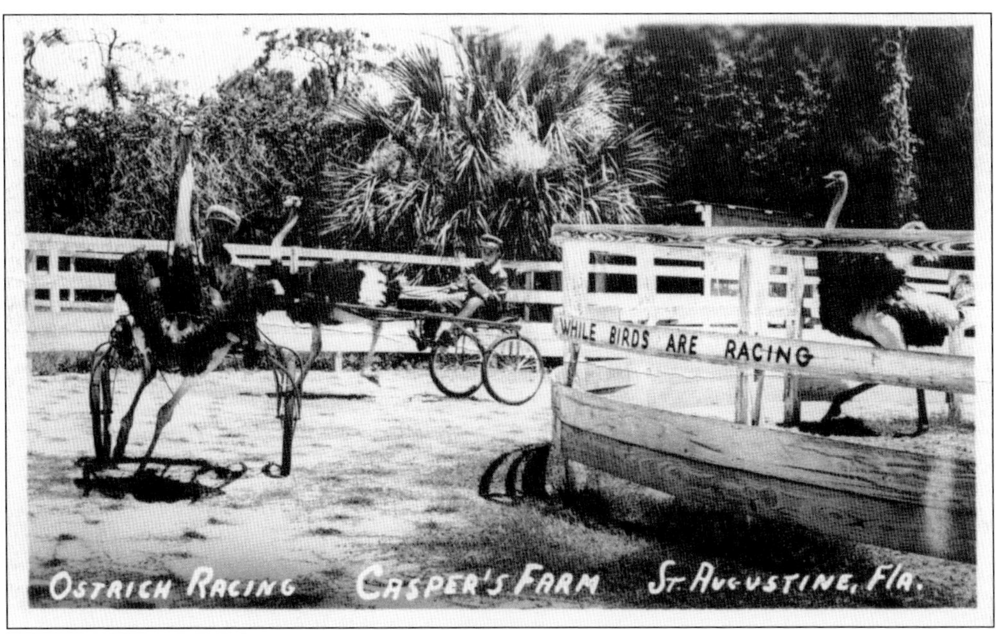

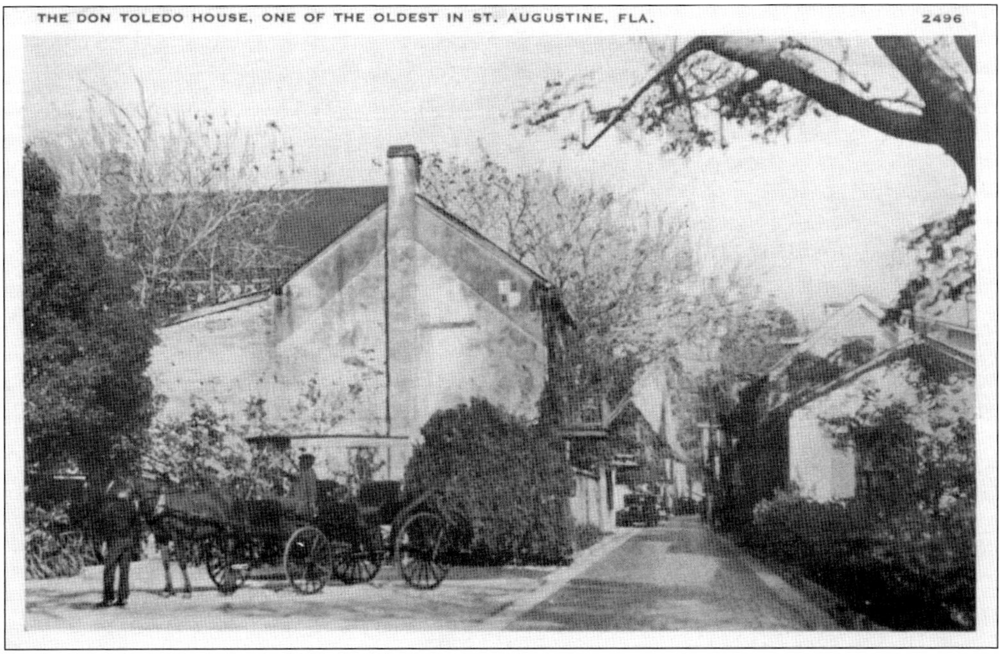

The coquina house at 36 Aviles Street was built between 1803 and 1817 by Gaspar Papy, a Greek who emigrated with the Menorcan colonists, and is one of St. Augustine's oldest houses. In 1903, Everett Whitney, great-grandson of cotton gin inventor Eli Whitney, leased the house and promoted it as "Whitney's Oldest House." The Sisters of St. Joseph purchased the house in 1928 and leased it to various operators, including Clara Mier, until the early 1940s. Promoted as the Don Toledo House, visitors could see antique furnishings, a Spanish bank hidden inside a wall, and this rear patio with a well. The Sisters ended the leases and remodeled the house in 1944, and it retains little of its original appearance today.

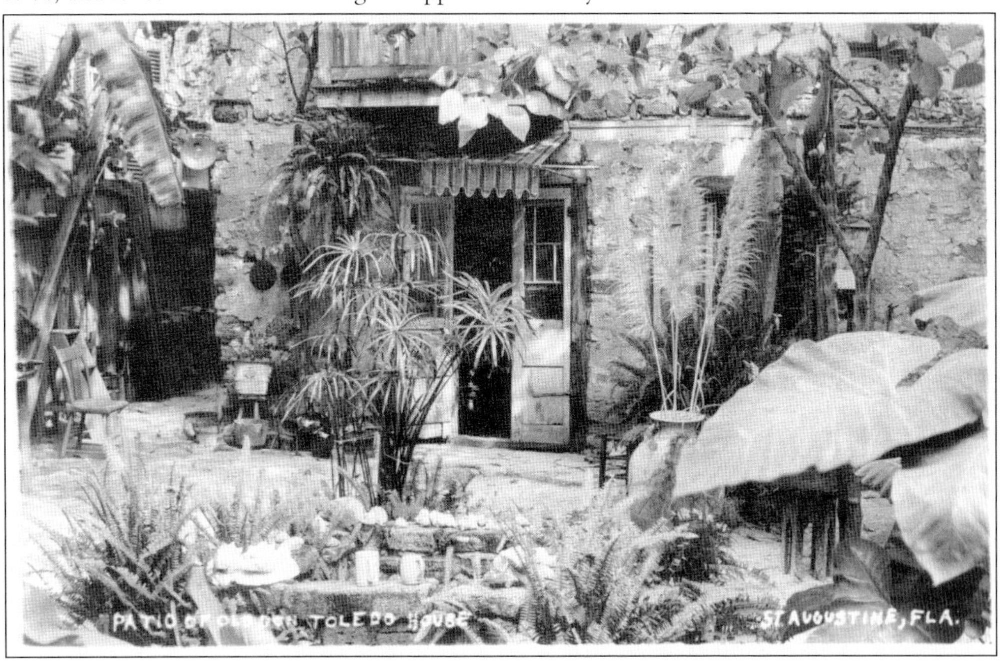

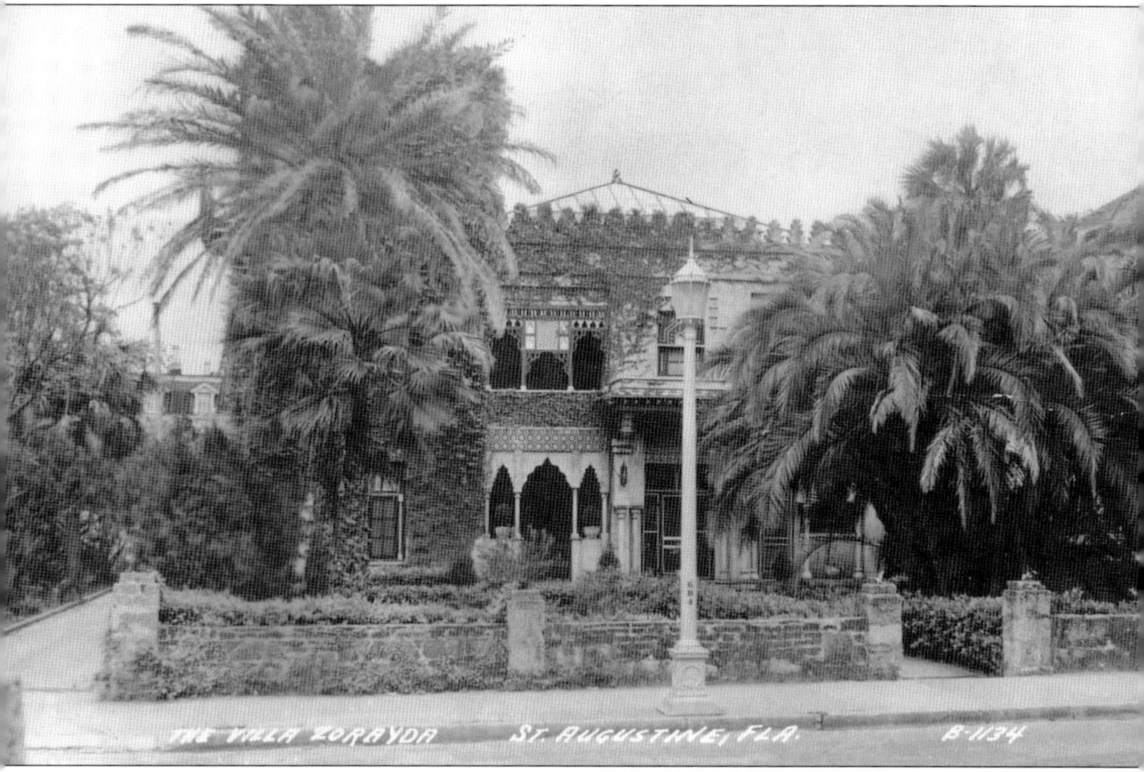

Located at 83 King Street, the Villa Zorayda was built in 1883 as the winter residence of Franklin W. Smith (1826–1911). From a wealthy Boston family, Smith was instrumental in founding the Young Men's Christian Association and was president of its first chapter in that city. To build the Villa Zorayda, Smith developed a new construction method using poured concrete mixed with coquina shell, a technique that Henry Flagler would later employ in his Ponce de Leon and Alcazar Hotels. The villa's Moorish Revival style would soon be copied in many of the city's new structures and homes, including the Lyon Building and the Vaill Block, commercial buildings constructed on Cathedral Place after an 1887 fire destroyed Capt. Edward Vaill's St. Augustine Hotel. (SAHS.)

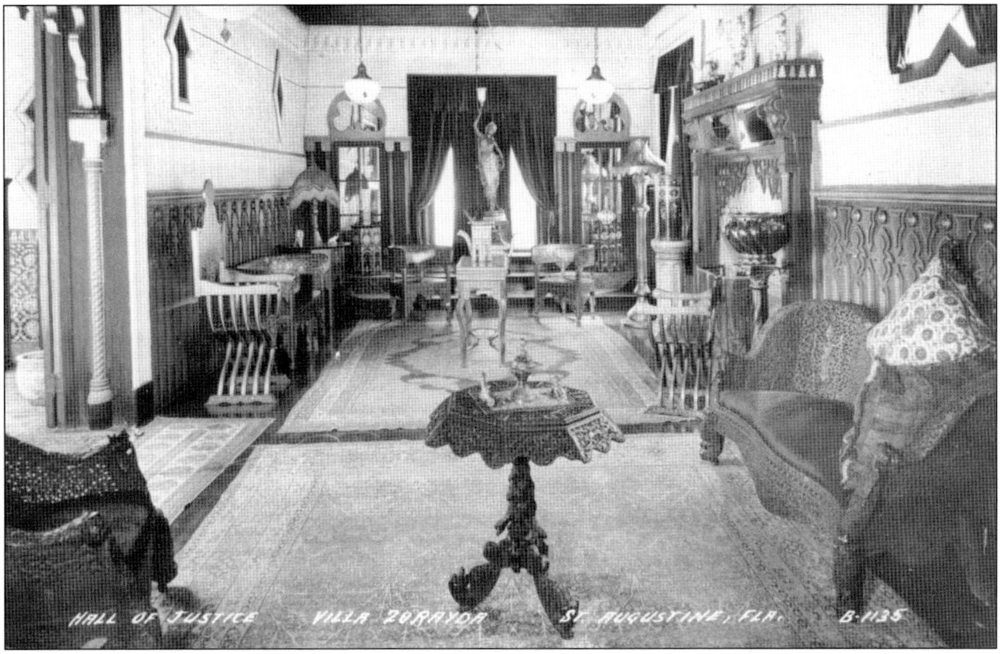

In 1913, the Villa Zorayda and part of Franklin Smith's antiquity collection were purchased by Abraham S. Mussallem, an authority on Oriental rugs, fine arts, and Egyptian artifacts. Mussallem had also purchased the adjacent Hotel Granada and renamed it the Hotel Alhambra, as the Villa Zorayda was modeled after the famous Alhambra Palace in Granada, Spain. During the 1920s, it was the Zorayda Club, a fashionable gambling casino and café. In the mid-1930s, the Villa Zorayda opened as a museum, featuring the antique collections of Smith and Mussallem, pictured in these postcards. The Mussallem family continues to operate this popular attraction today. (Right, SAHS.)

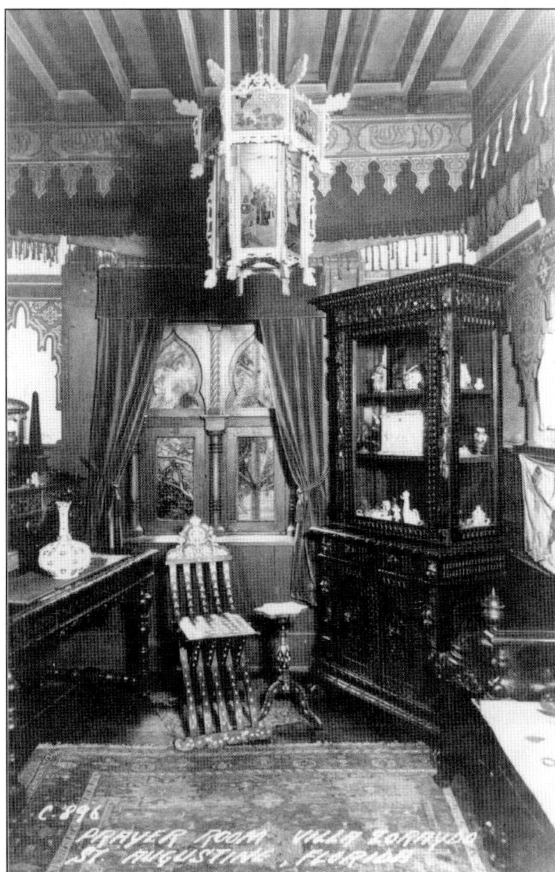

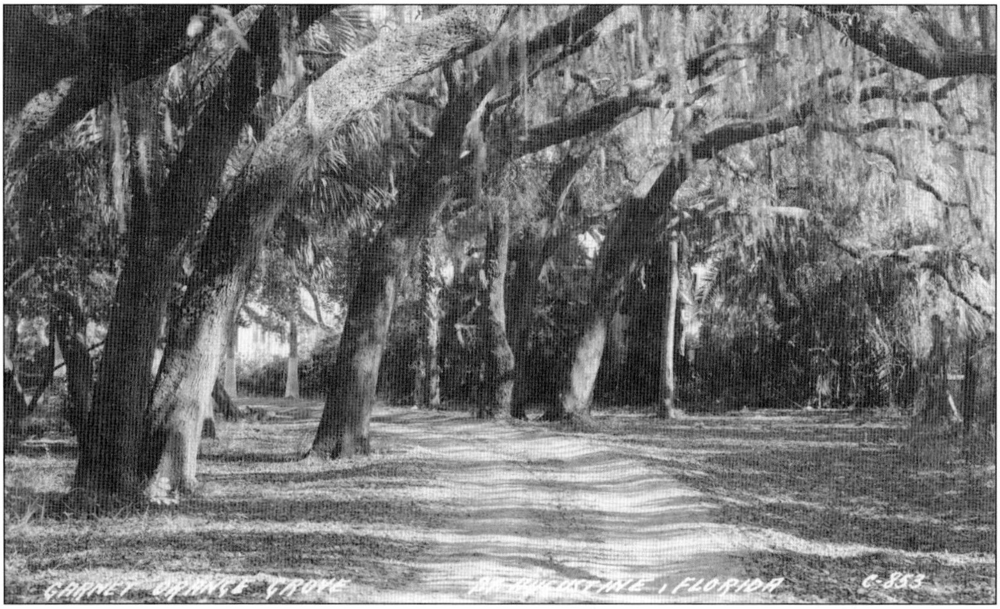

Garnett's Orange Grove was located on San Marco Avenue between St. Louis (today's Old Mission Avenue) and Sebastian Avenues and extended west to the San Sebastian River. In 1883, Dr. Reuben Garnett purchased 20 acres along the Shell Road (today's San Marco Avenue) and planted an orange grove. The grove and the oak-lined paths on the property soon became a tourist destination in the early 1900s. (SAHS.)

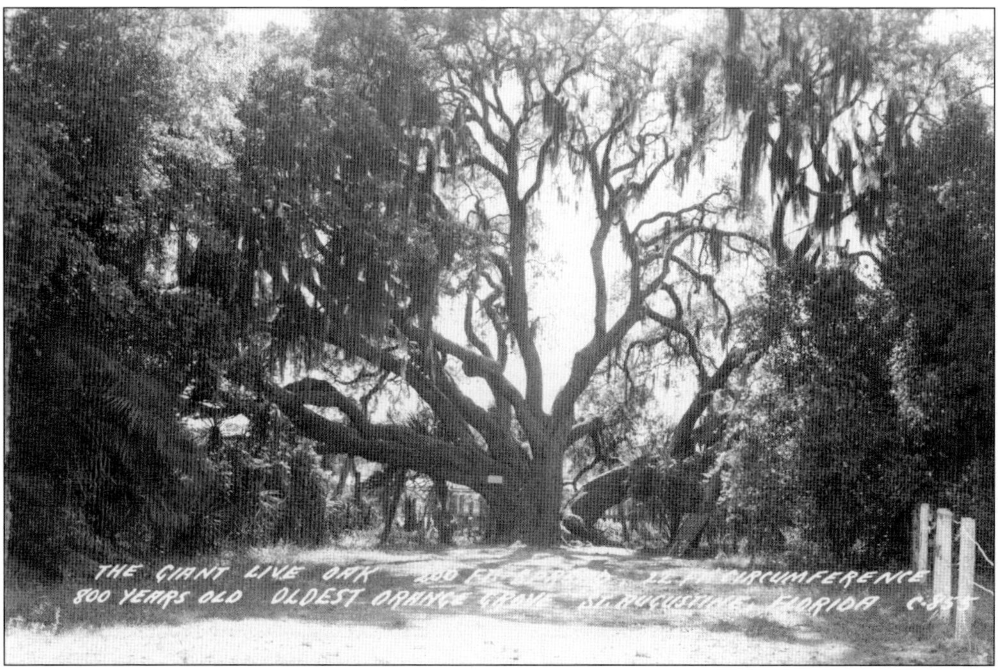

This giant live oak was at the west end of the Garnett Grove on the San Sebastian River. After Dr. Garnett's death in 1922, his daughter Katherine Murphy continued to operate the grove and opened a riding stable. Her daughters June and Mary Katherine (M.K.) were avid horsewomen, and M.K. led St. Augustine's Easter Parade for over 50 years.

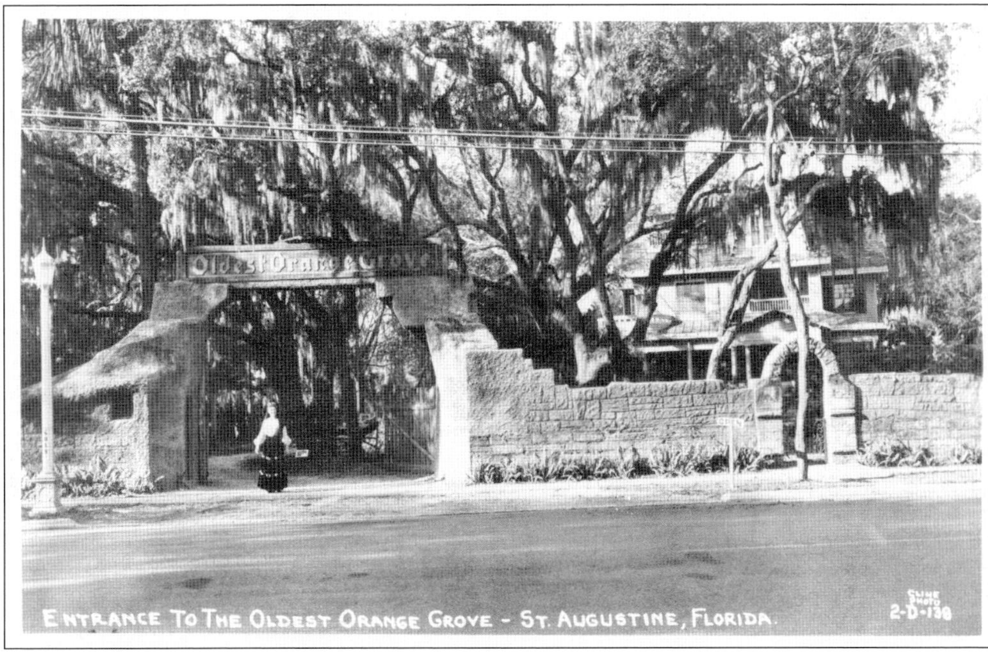

In 1943, the Murphys sold Garnett Grove and moved to a home on Picolata Road (today's State Route 16). Walter B. Fraser, owner of the nearby Fountain of Youth, acquired the property and began operating it as a tourist attraction, the Oldest Orange Grove. Dr. Garnett's house, built around 1890 and demolished in 1954, can be seen to the right of the entrance gate.

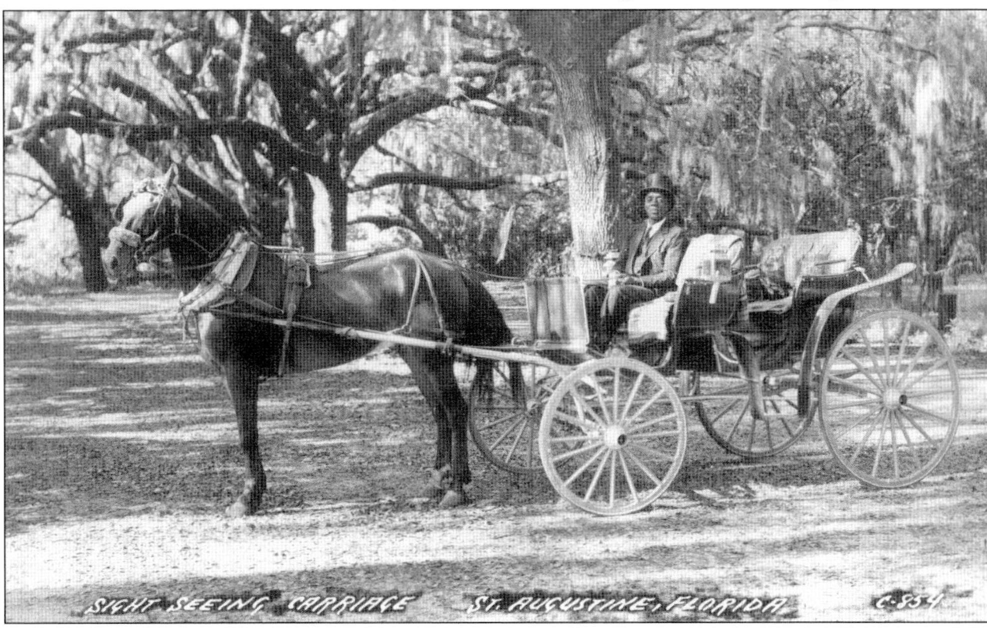

The paths among the grove's moss-draped live oaks were a popular spot for carriage rides. This postcard shows Major Argrett Jr. (1888–1984), a carriage driver for 73 years. He began working for Colee's Stables at age 14 and drove many notables, including Franklin and Eleanor Roosevelt and Katharine Hepburn. The carriage drivers of St. Augustine dedicated a plaque to Argrett's memory on April 11, 1986.

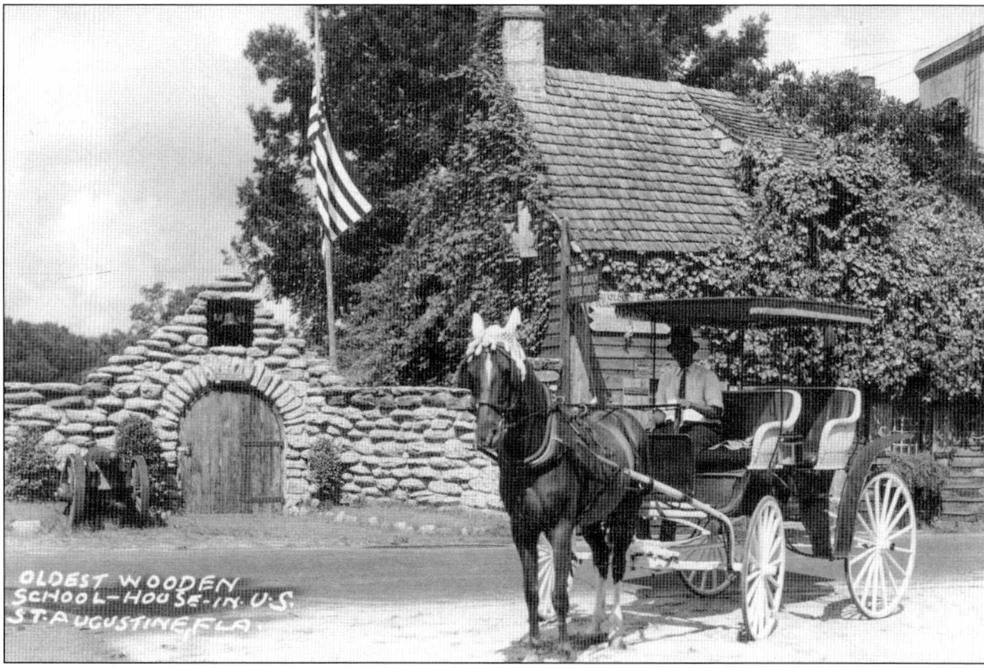

The wooden house at 14 St. George Street was built between 1800 and 1810 by Juan Genopoly, a Greek carpenter who came to St. Augustine with the Menorcan colonists. Genopoly, and later two of his children, operated a small school in the house. The rear yard featured a detached kitchen with a coquina chimney and a well, shown just to the left of the walkway. For many years, the building housed a succession small businesses and souvenir shops. In 1931, it was purchased by photographer W.J. Harris, who began promoting it as the Oldest School House. Walter B. Fraser purchased the house in 1937, and his family still operates the attraction, now known as the Oldest Wooden School House.

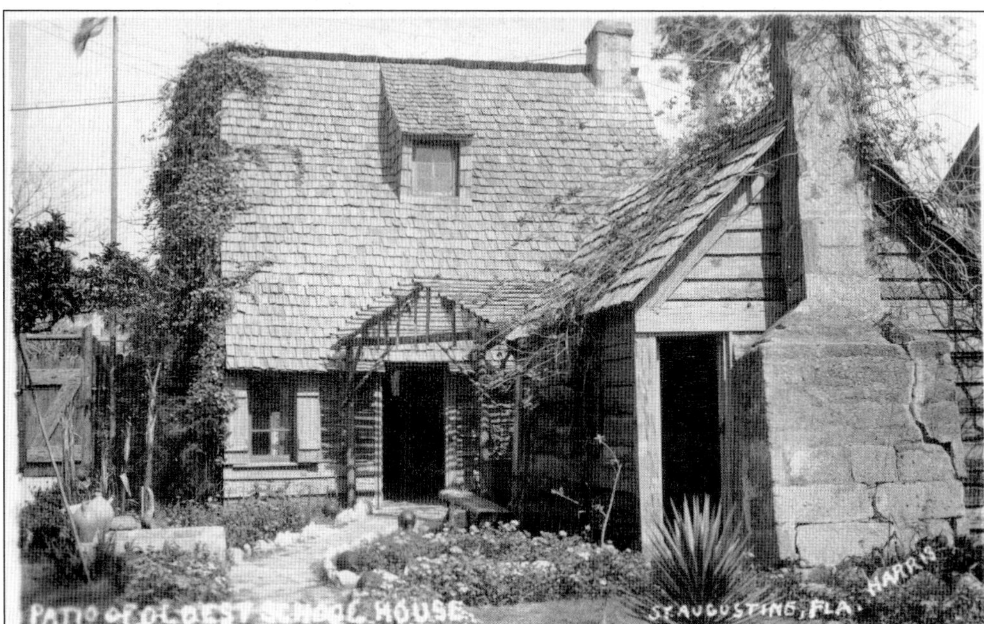

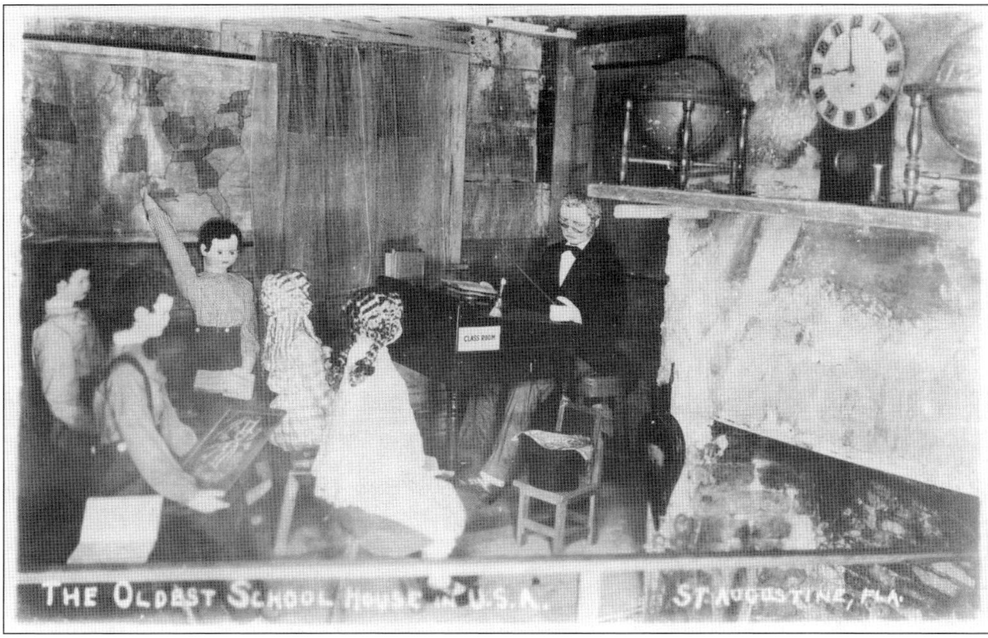

In November 1931, nine former students gathered for a reunion at the Oldest School House. They helped arrange the downstairs room as they remembered it during their days attending the Genopolys' school. Owner W.J. Harris then had mannequins made to represent the teacher and his students, seen in the postcard of the re-created classroom. (SAHS.)

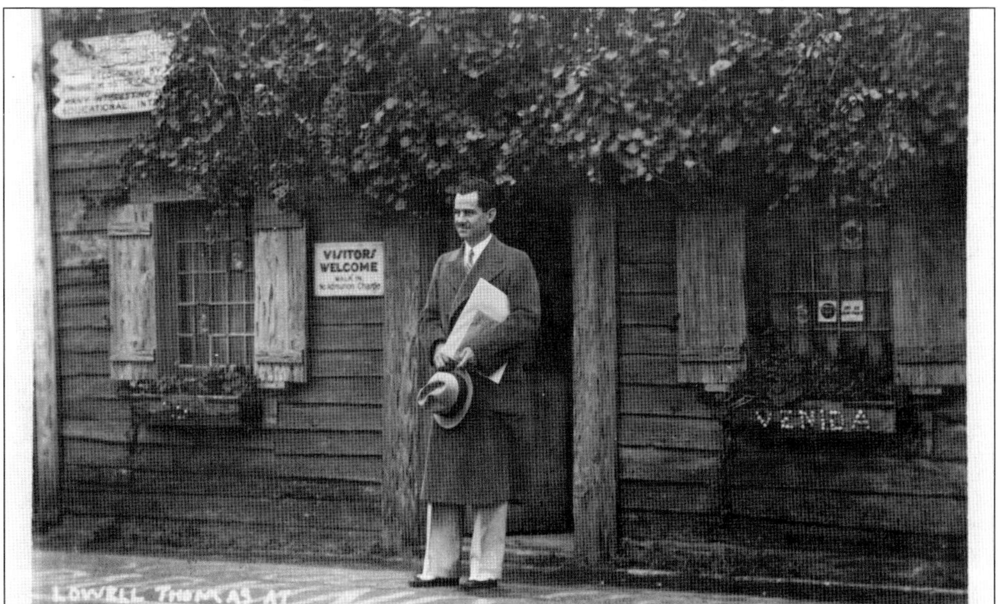

Radio broadcaster Lowell Thomas is pictured in front of the Oldest School House in the mid-1930s. A relentless self-promoter, Thomas first gained fame during World War I when he covered T.E. Lawrence's campaign in Arabia. In 1930, Thomas became a broadcaster with CBS Radio in a career that lasted until his retirement in 1976, a record surpassed only by Paul Harvey. (SAHS.)

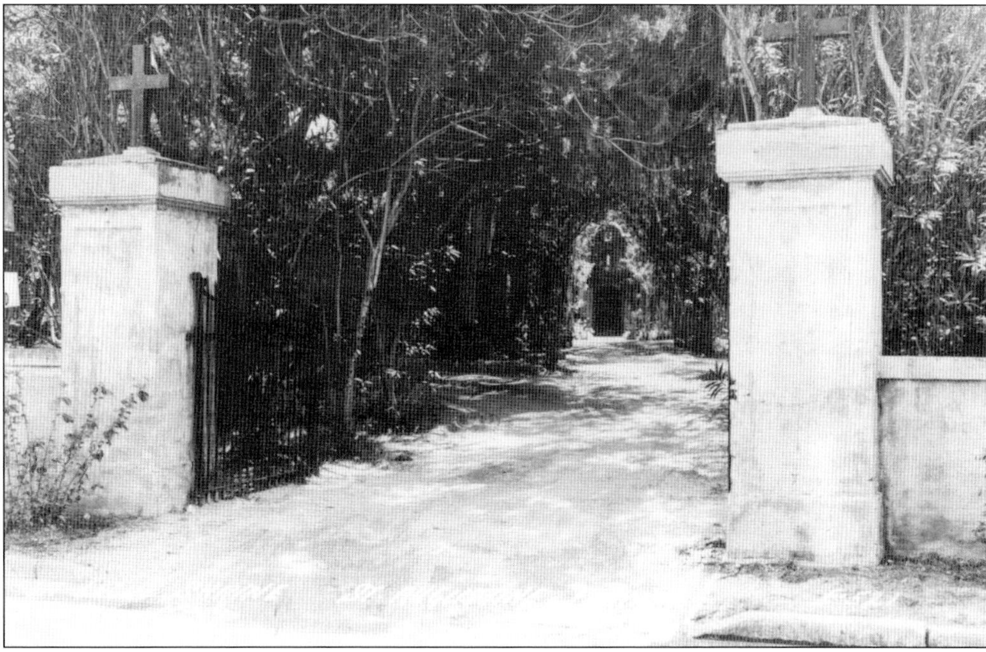

The Franciscan Mission of Nombre de Dios was established in 1587 on the site of a Timucuan Indian village. In the 1930s and 1940s, entrance to the mission site was through these gates at the east end of Ocean Avenue, and its shaded trails were a popular spot for sightseeing carriages.

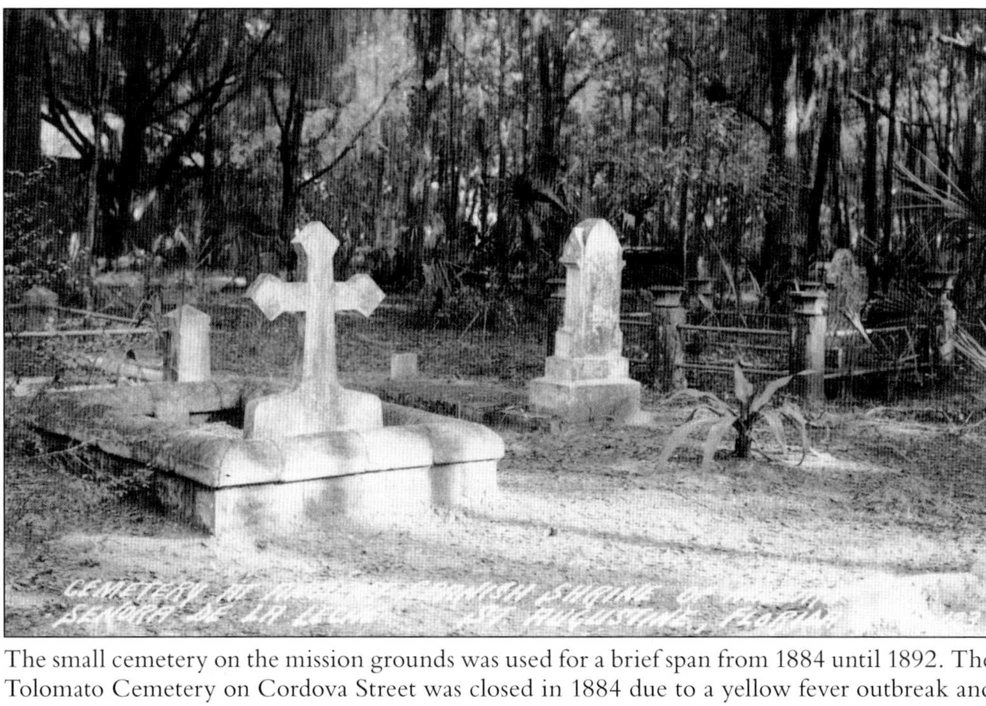

The small cemetery on the mission grounds was used for a brief span from 1884 until 1892. The Tolomato Cemetery on Cordova Street was closed in 1884 due to a yellow fever outbreak and fear of disease from the corpses. San Lorenzo, a new Catholic cemetery located on South Dixie Highway, did not open until 1892.

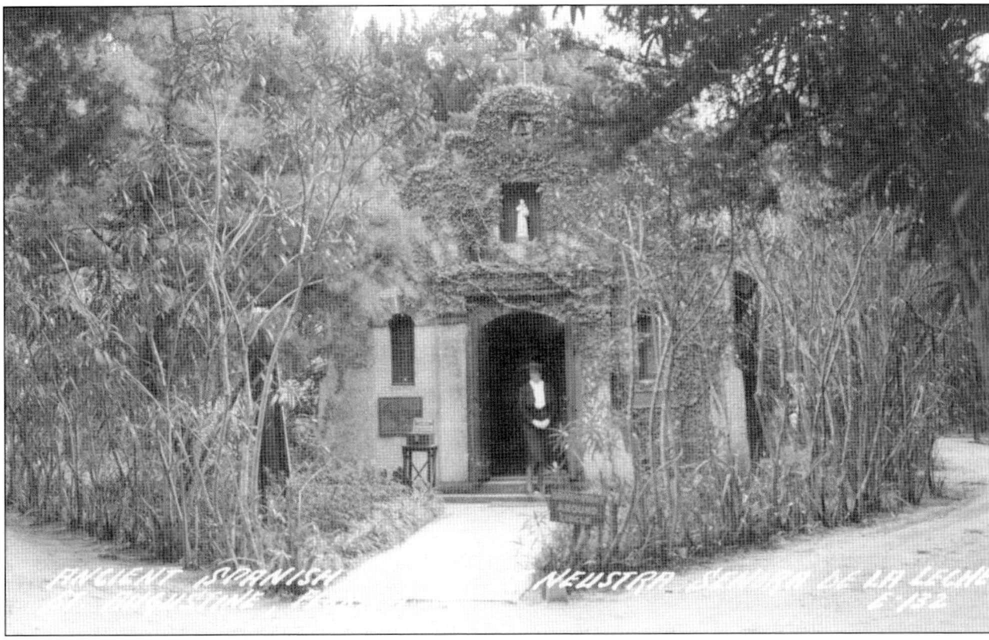

The chapel at the Mission of Nombre de Dios commemorates the first Catholic Mass at the site of the landing of St. Augustine's founder, Pedro Menendez, on September 8, 1565. Prior chapels at the mission were destroyed by British raids and hurricanes. Restoration of the chapel was begun in 1914 by Bishop Michael Curley, with funds provided by Amelia Hardin, widow of Union general Martin D. Hardin. The Hardins moved to St. Augustine in 1893, first living at the Tovar House on St. Francis Street and later at 20 Valencia Street until his death in 1923 at age 85. The chapel was completed in 1925 and dedicated to the memory of the general.

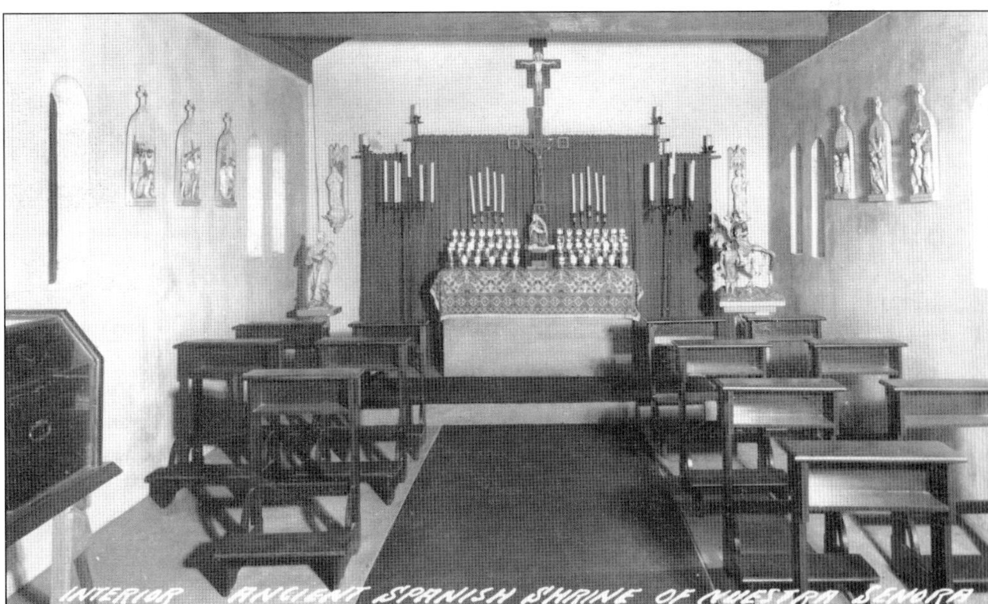

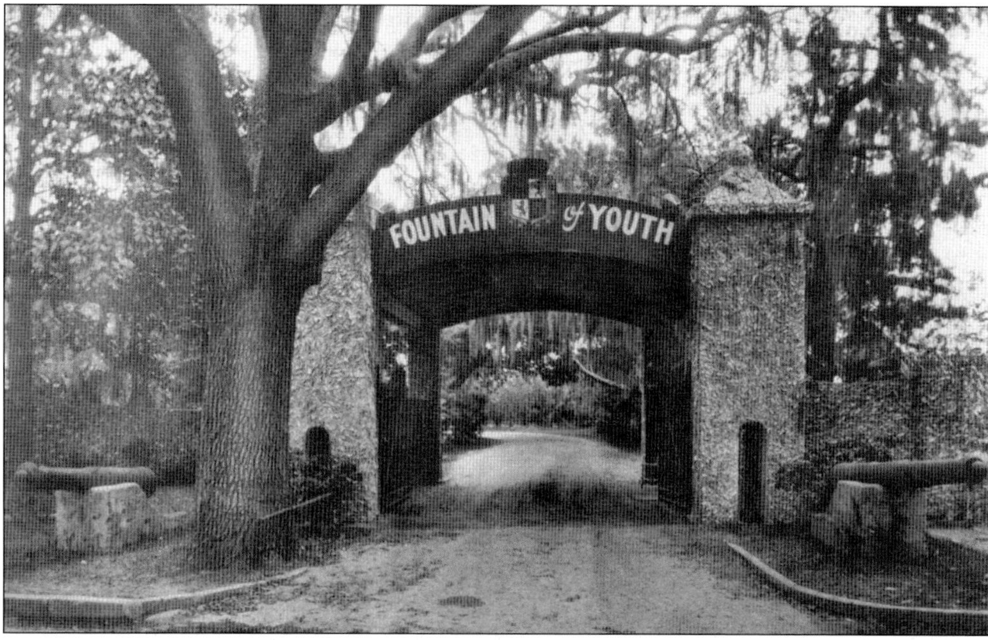

In 1868, English horticulturalist Henry H. Williams, for whom Williams Street is named, purchased 225 acres east of San Marco Avenue. In 1900, the property was sold to the eccentric Louella Day McConnell, who promoted it as Ponce de Leon's Fountain of Youth. After McConnell's death in a 1927 automobile accident, the property was acquired by Walter B. Fraser, of Georgia. He immediately began improving the grounds and erected a tabby wall along Magnolia Avenue. This entrance gate at the east end of Myrtle Avenue led through an avenue of palms to a Mission Revival building that Fraser constructed over the spring and 1513 cross. Recent archaeological findings have identified the property as the location of Pedro Menendez's first settlement of St. Augustine in 1565.

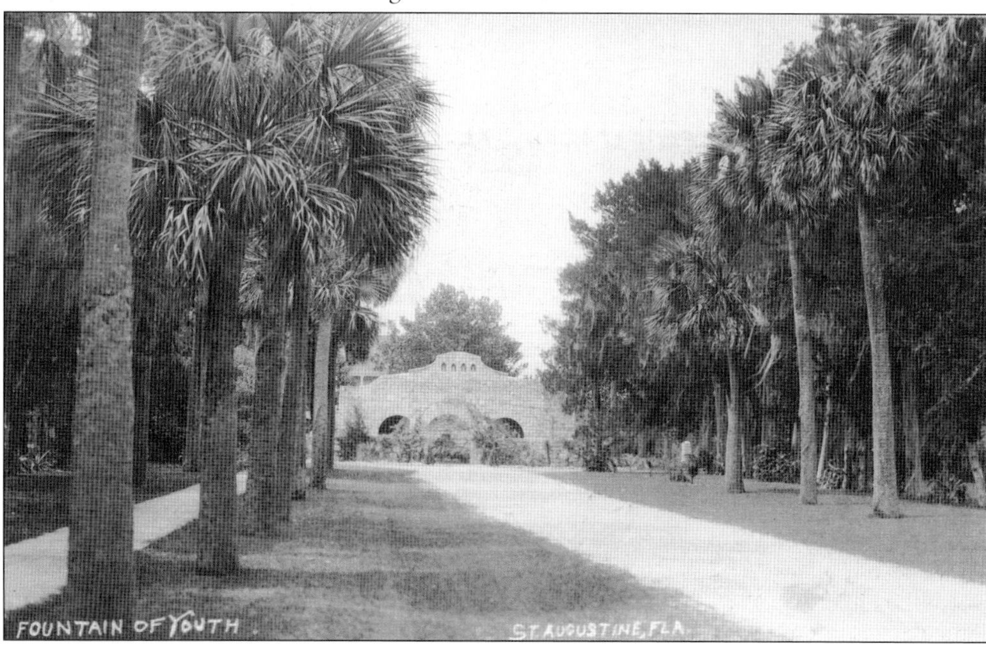

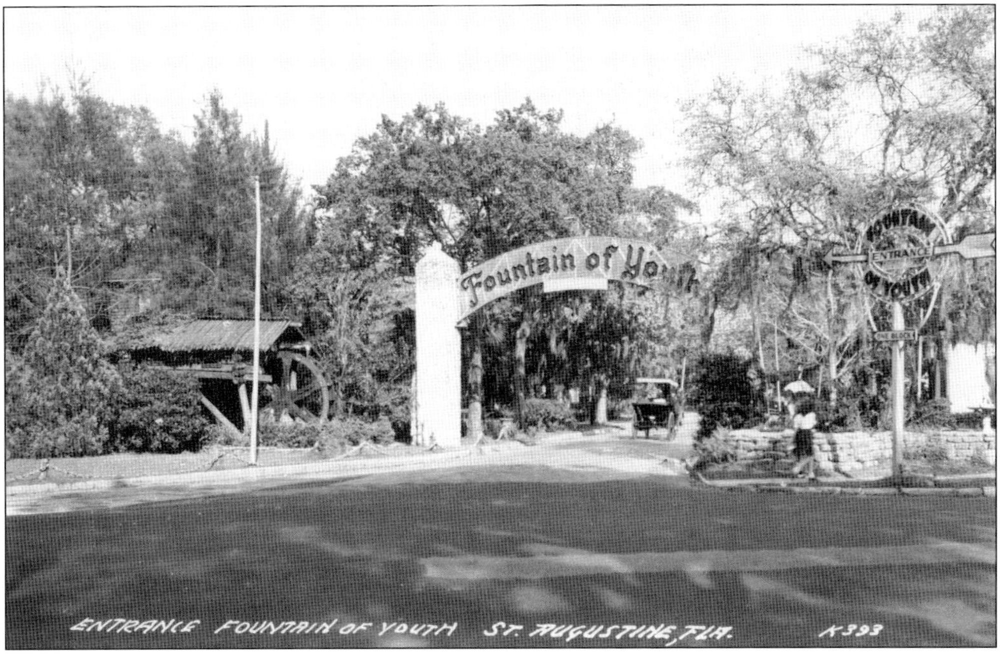

In 1937, the main entrance to the Fountain of Youth was moved from Myrtle Avenue north on Magnolia Avenue to the east end of Williams Street. A large neon sign supported by tabby columns was erected across the west end of Williams Street at San Marco Avenue and a rustic water wheel built on the north side of the entrance.

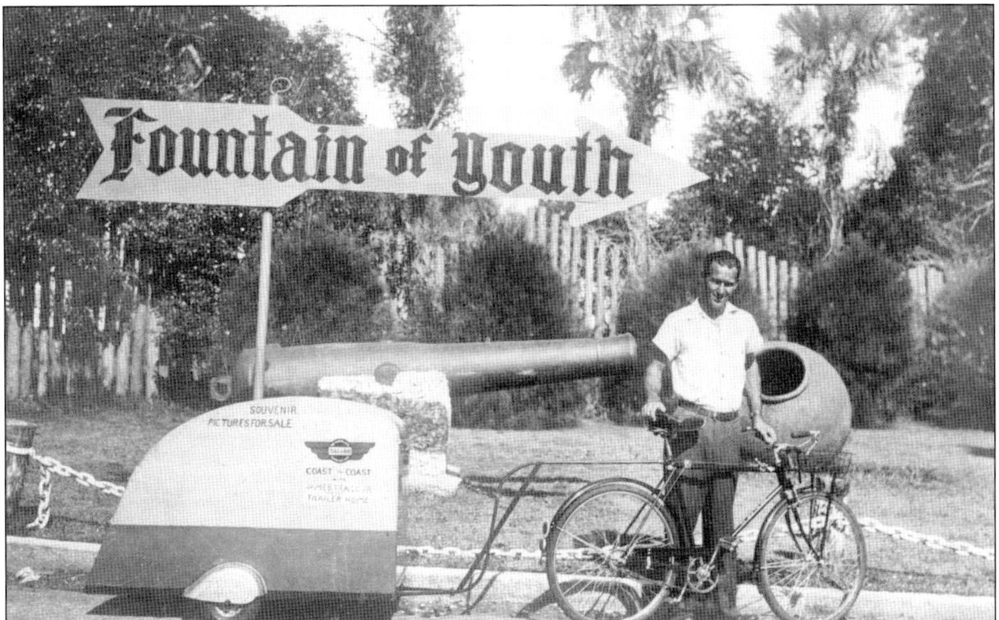

James T. Fagg is pictured on his bicycle in front of San Marco entrance to the Fountain of Youth in this postcard dated April 4, 1941. Fagg contracted polio as a child and began riding a bike to strengthen his legs. In 1939, he designed a small camper trailer for his bike and toured the United States to raise awareness for polio.

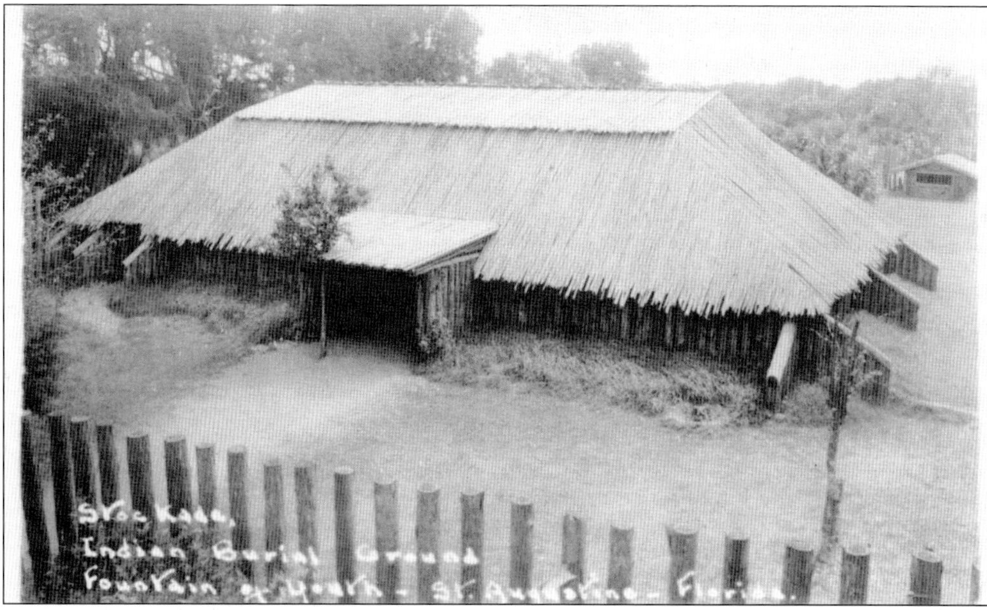

On April 13, 1934, a gardener planting orange trees discovered a human skeleton. Further examination and research by Dr. Matthew W. Stirling, of the Smithsonian Institution, determined that these were burials of Christianized Native Americans. The skeletons were left intact, and a log building in the form of a Timucuan communal house was erected over the site. The "Indian Burial Ground" became part of the attraction. Over the years, further research in the pattern of burials revealed that it was the location of the 1587 Franciscan mission church of Nombre de Dios, the first Christian mission in the United States. Increasing sensitivity to the customs and culture of Native Americans prompted reburial of the remains on December 14, 1991, with a solemn Catholic Mass performed by the Most Reverend Charles J. Chaput, a member of the Prairie Band Pottawatomie tribe.

INDIAN BURIAL GROUND, FOUNTAIN OF YOUTH, ST. AUGUSTINE, FLA. 2505

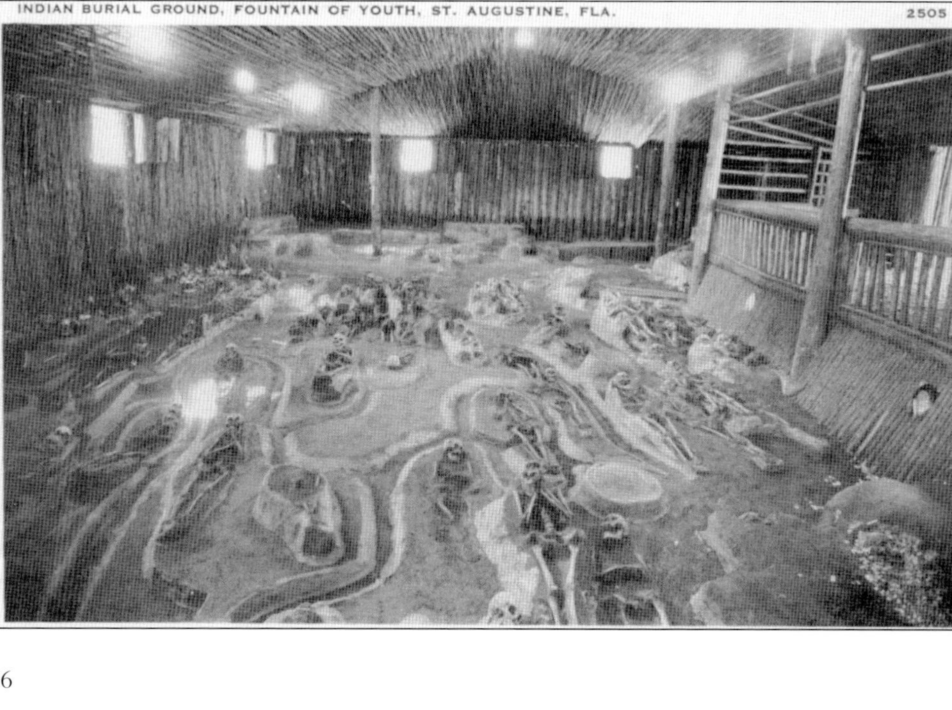

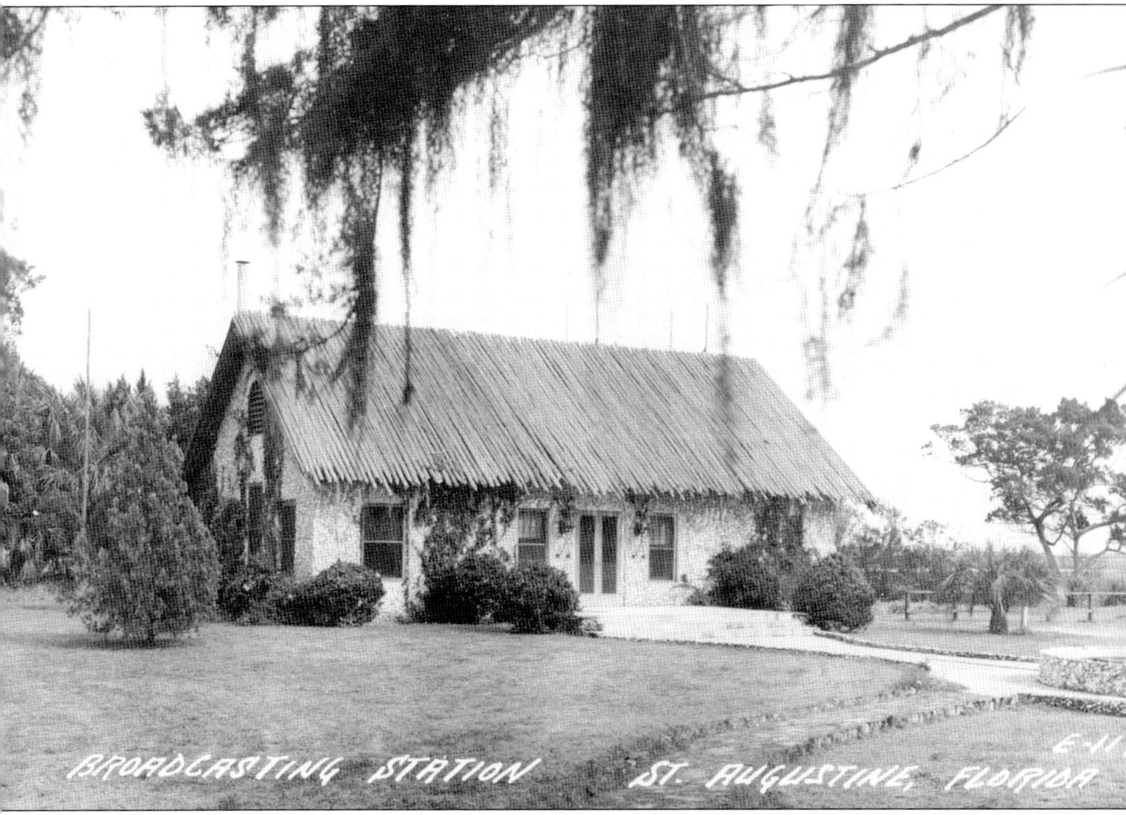

WFOY, whose call letters stand for "Fountain of Youth," was started by Walter B. Fraser, owner of the attraction. Fraser was a prominent local businessman, serving on the City Commission for 20 years, including two terms as mayor. He ran for governor in 1940 and served in the Florida Senate from 1944 to 1948. Fraser passed away in 1972, but his family continues to operate the attraction. The unique tabby building that housed the radio station was located just north of the Fountain of Youth at One Radio Road. The station signed on February 11, 1937, at 1240 on the dial. The signal from its broadcast tower, located at the end of a dock that extended into the marshes of Hospital Creek, was used for years by boats equipped with a radio direction finder (RDF) to guide them into the St. Augustine inlet. The WFOY property was sold in 2002 and is now the location of upscale waterfront condominiums.

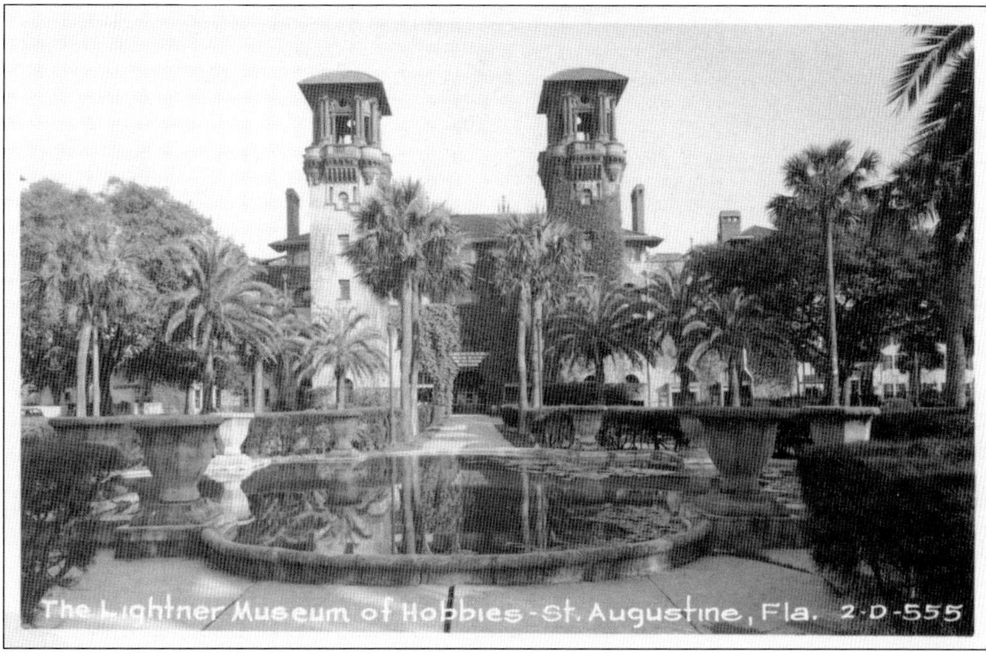

Henry Flagler built the Alcazar Hotel for travelers of more modest means, using the same poured concrete construction as his elegant Ponce de Leon. Opened on Christmas Day 1888, the Alcazar proved so popular that a fourth story was added after the 1891 season. The collapse of the Florida land boom in 1926, followed by the Great Depression, forced the Flagler System to close the hotel in 1932. Except for a few retail shops and offices on its ground floor, the building sat empty until purchased by Otto C. Lightner in 1947 and deeded to the City of St. Augustine. Built in 1948, the bridge in the courtyard replaced an earlier rustic wooden one. Constructed by M. Francis Coate, of Floral City, Florida, the bridge was built from rocks sent to Lightner from all over the world.

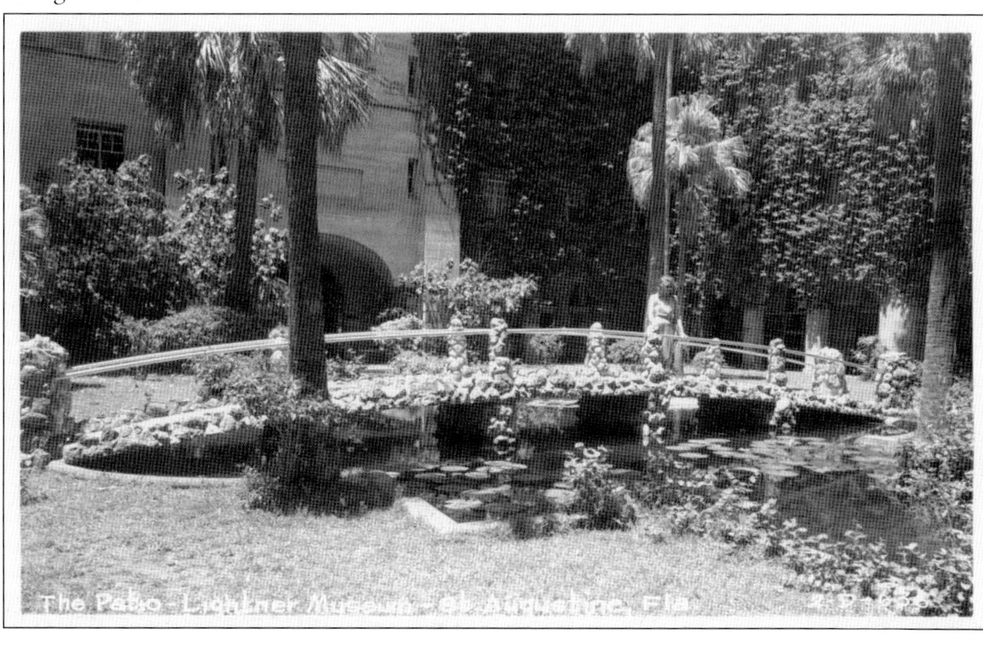

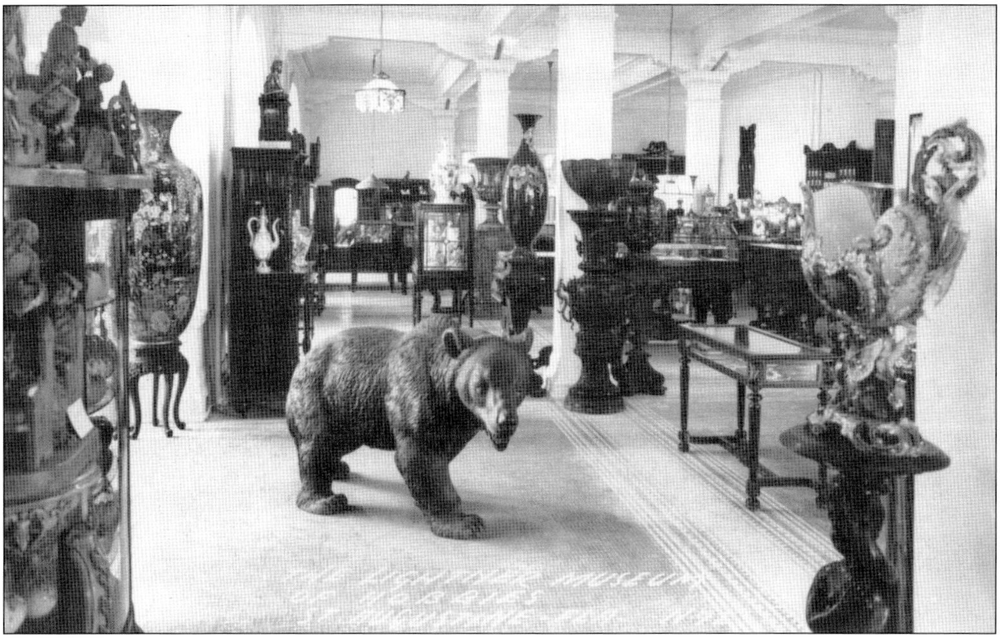

Otto C. Lightner was a newspaperman from Chicago and publisher of *Hobbies—The Magazine for Collectors*, one of the first antique and collectibles magazines. He became fascinated with collecting and began buying other people's collections as well as antiques from Chicago mansions auctioned off during the 1930s. After purchasing the vacant Alcazar, he filled it with his treasures and opened the Lightner Museum of Hobbies in 1948. These two postcards depict some of the objects that were displayed in the former lobby area of the hotel. Much of his "collection of collections" was displayed in the former hotel rooms on the upper floors. In 1971, the Alcazar was renovated to serve as city offices, and the Lightner Museum was magnificently upgraded and relocated to the south portion of the building.

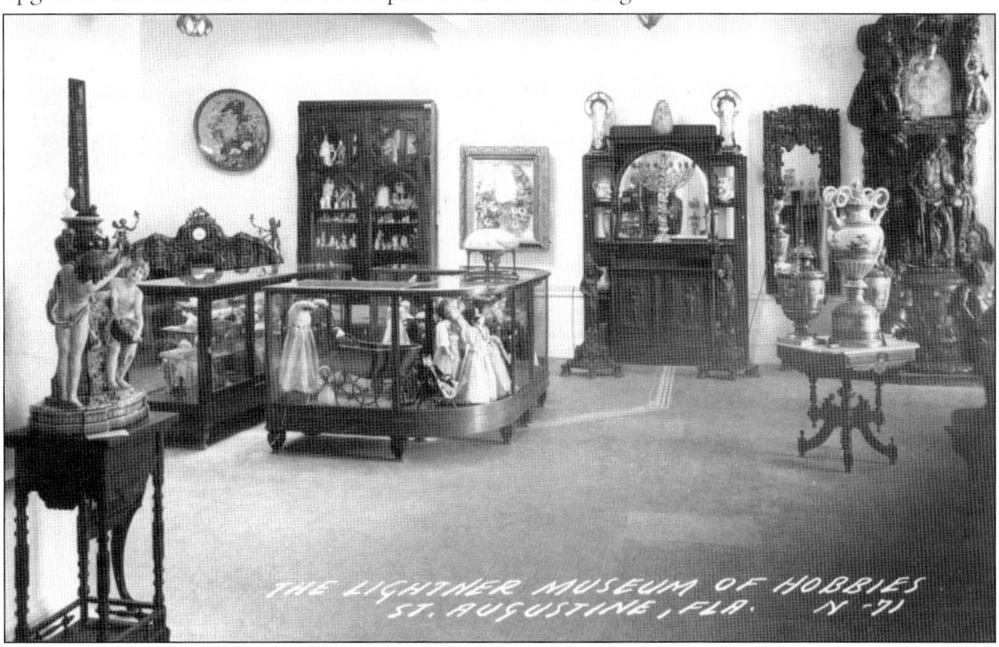

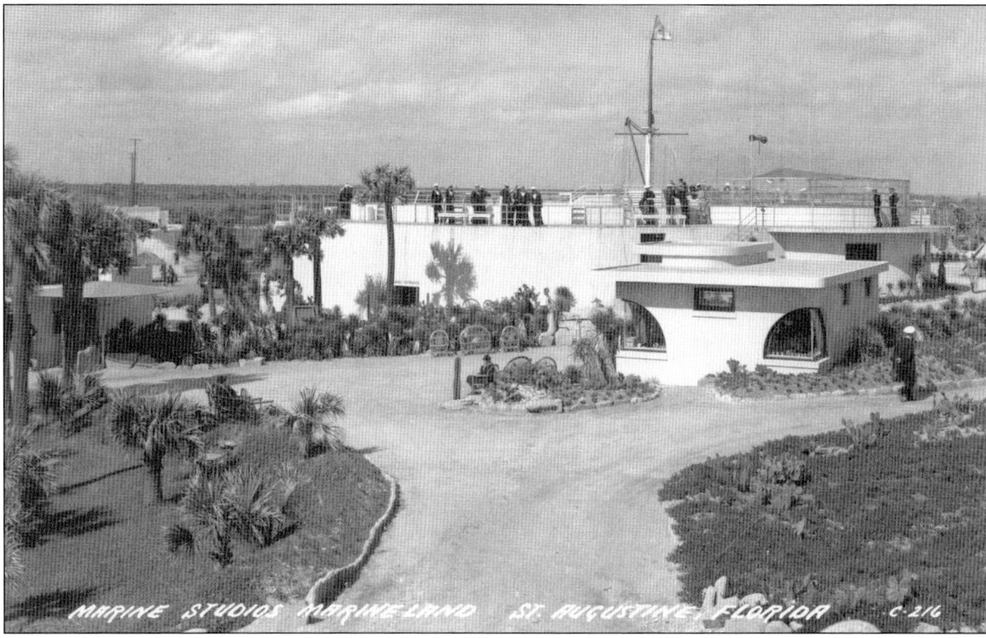

Thousands jammed Route 140 (today's A1A) on June 23, 1938, for the opening of Marine Studios. Located 18 miles south of St. Augustine, the attraction was founded by Cornelius Vanderbilt Whitney, W. Douglas Burden, and Count Ilia Tolstoy. Designed by architect Fred A. Henderich in a nautical Moderne style, the complex was completed in only nine months at a cost of $500,000.

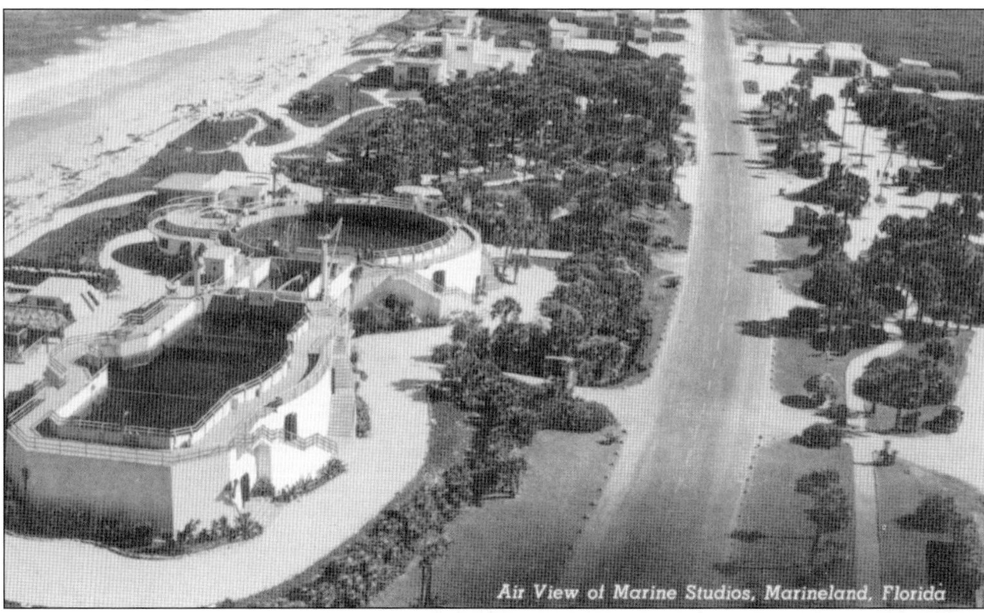

This aerial view of Marine Studios looks southward on Route 140 in the late 1930s. In the foreground are the rectangular and circular oceanariums, gift shop, and landscaped walkways leading to the Dolphin Restaurant and Marine Village Court. To the right of the highway are the parking area and a gas station. The gift shop is the only major original structure that remains today.

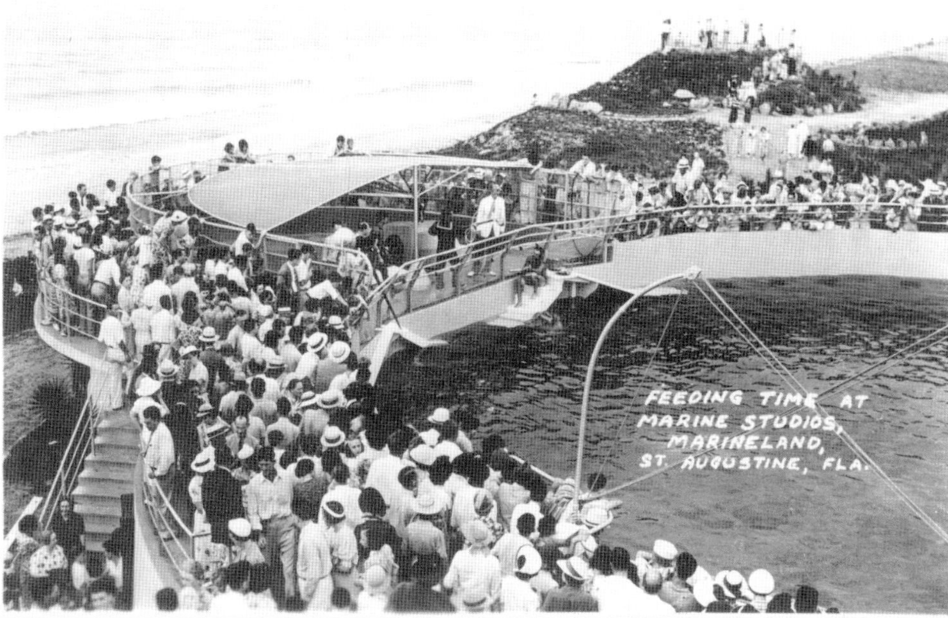

Visitors crowd the top deck of the circular oceanarium at feeding time, as a porpoise (bottlenose dolphin) eagerly awaits his next meal at the platform in front of the canopy. The circular tank was 75 feet in diameter, 12 feet deep, and contained 400,000 gallons of seawater. Originally conceived as an underwater film studio, the tank featured porthole windows on three levels to observe the only bottlenose dolphins in captivity at that time. Marine Studios soon became Florida's most popular tourist spot, but World War II and gas rationing forced the attraction to close from June 30, 1942, to June 1, 1946. Marine Studios, later renamed Marineland, remained popular during the 1950s and 1960s, but attendance suffered after Disney World opened in 1971. The attraction closed in September 2004, and the oceanarium's deteriorated tanks were demolished.

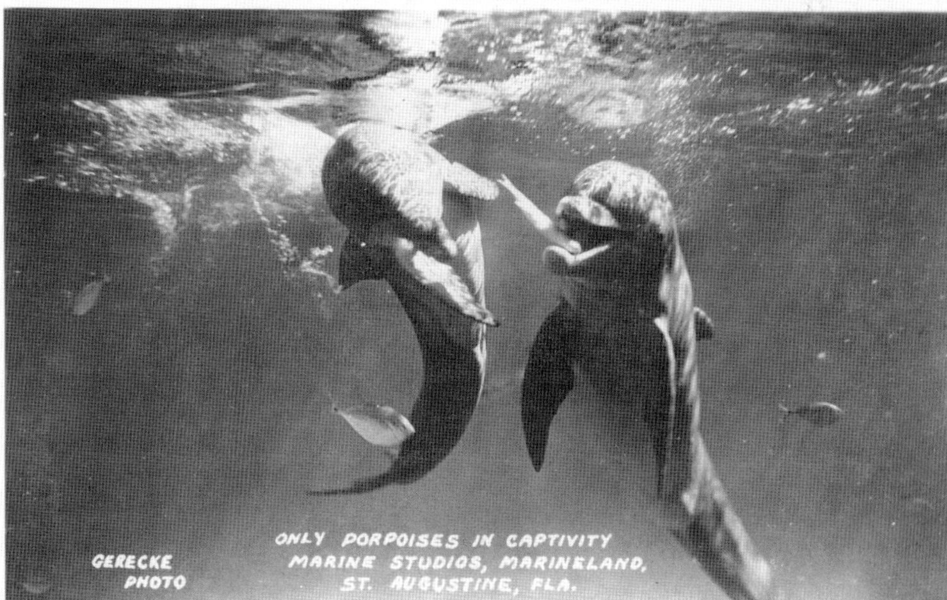

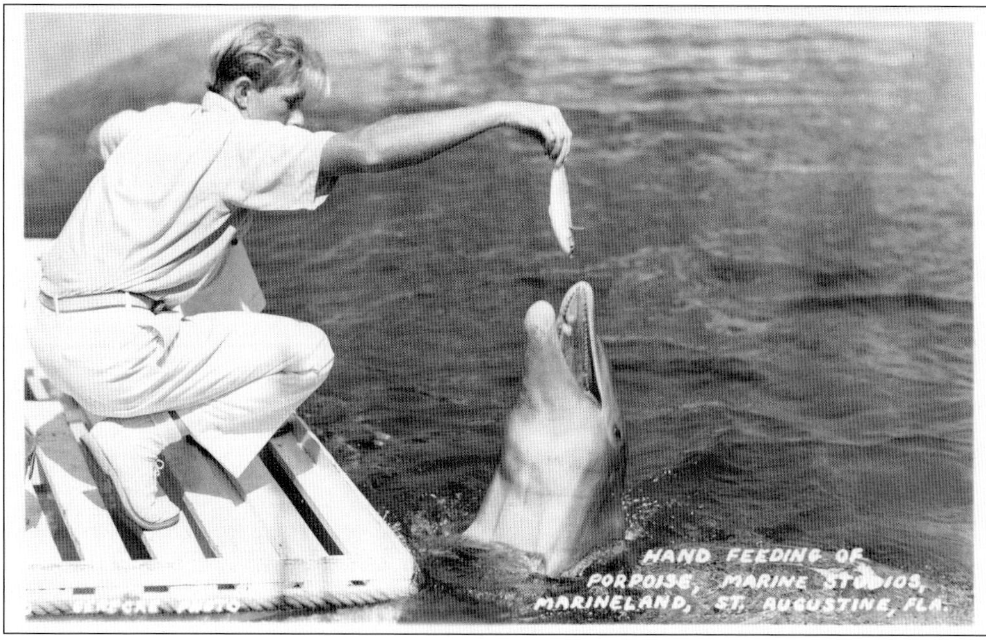

Arthur McBride, Marine Studios first curator at age 23, feeds a dolphin from a platform in the circular oceanarium. McBride discovered much about dolphin behavior through observation and interaction with the mammals. Sadly, McBride was diagnosed with Bright's Disease and died at age 34. The Marineland Dolphin Adventure, owned by the Georgia Aquarium, is now located at the site of the former attraction.

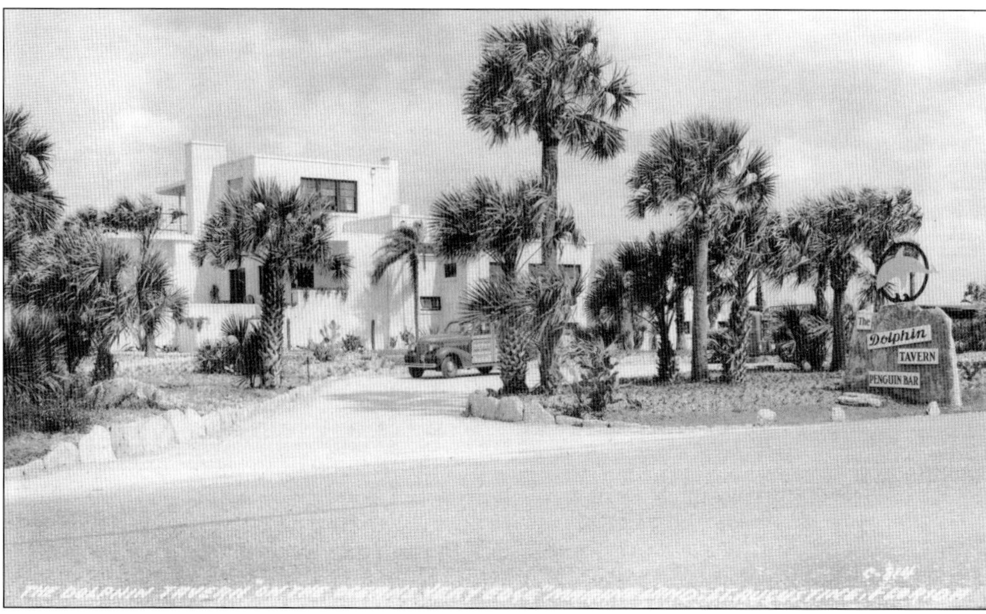

The Dolphin Tavern and Restaurant was located just south of Marine Studios. Norton Baskin, husband of Pulitzer Prize–winning author Marjorie Kinnan Rawlings, managed the restaurant and bar, often visited by noted authors, including Ernest Hemingway. Baskin's brother Tom ran the neighboring Marine Village Court for many years. Both buildings were demolished in the 1970s, replaced by a modern Quality Inn.

Seven

Notable Buildings and Homes

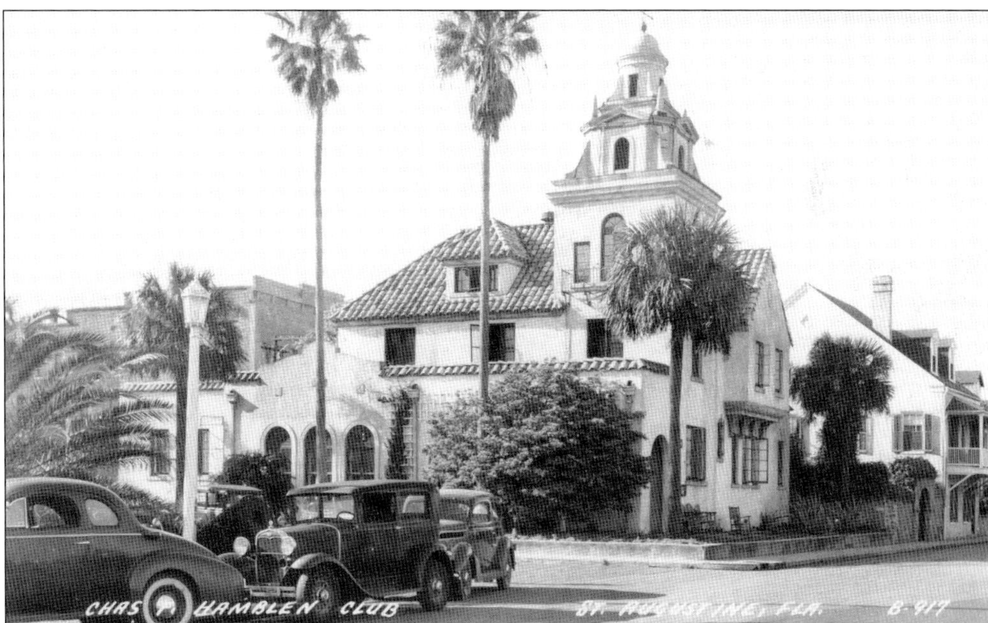

The Hamblen Club on Anderson Circle was once the Victorian-era home of hardware merchant Charles F. Hamblen. Remodeled in Mediterranean Revival style in 1925 by architect Francis A. Hollingsworth, it served for a brief time as a sales office for Davis Shores. The cupola shown in this postcard was damaged during the 1944 hurricane and never replaced. The Hamblen Club later became the longtime home of American Legion Post 37.

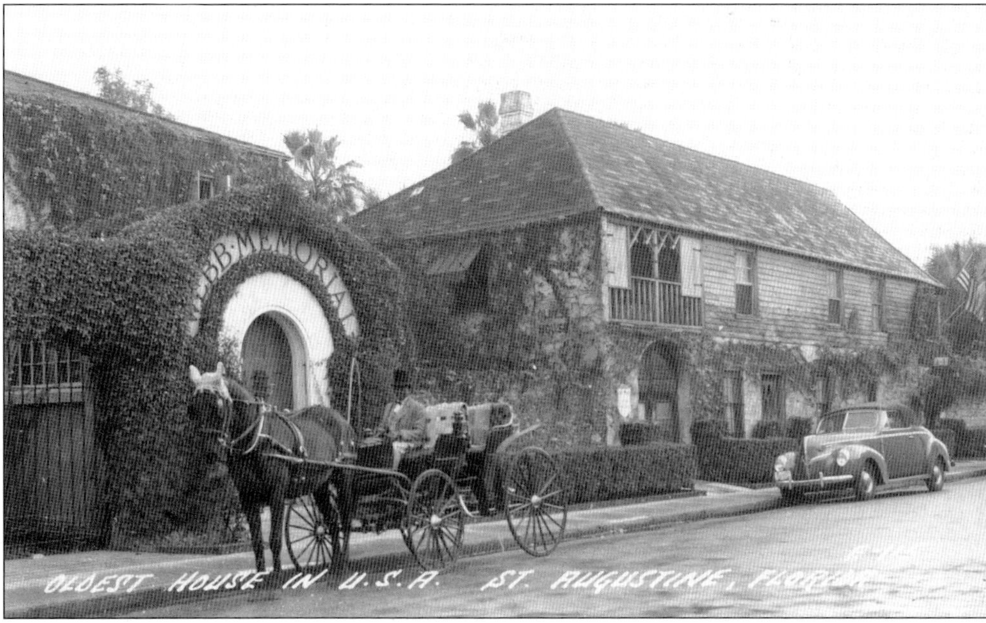

The Oldest House, known today as the Gonzalez-Alvarez House, at 14 St. Francis Street, dates from the early 1700s and is the oldest surviving Spanish Colonial dwelling in Florida. The above postcard shows a 1940 Ford convertible parked in front of the house and a sightseeing carriage at the Webb Memorial Building, constructed in 1925. The carriage horse is wearing a fly guard over his ears, crocheted by a docent at the Oldest House. In the garden view, the round tower at left was added in the 1880s when Dr. Charles Carver owned the house. Purchased by the St. Augustine Historical Society in 1918, the tower and other Victorian additions were removed in 1959–1960 when the society partially restored the house to its original Spanish Colonial appearance. (Below, O'Neill Collection.)

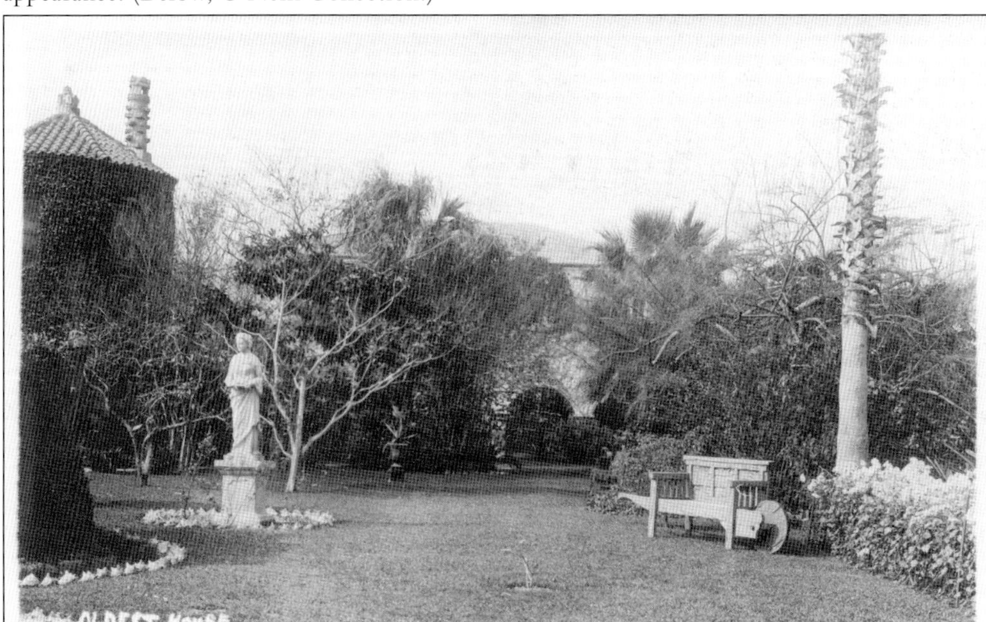

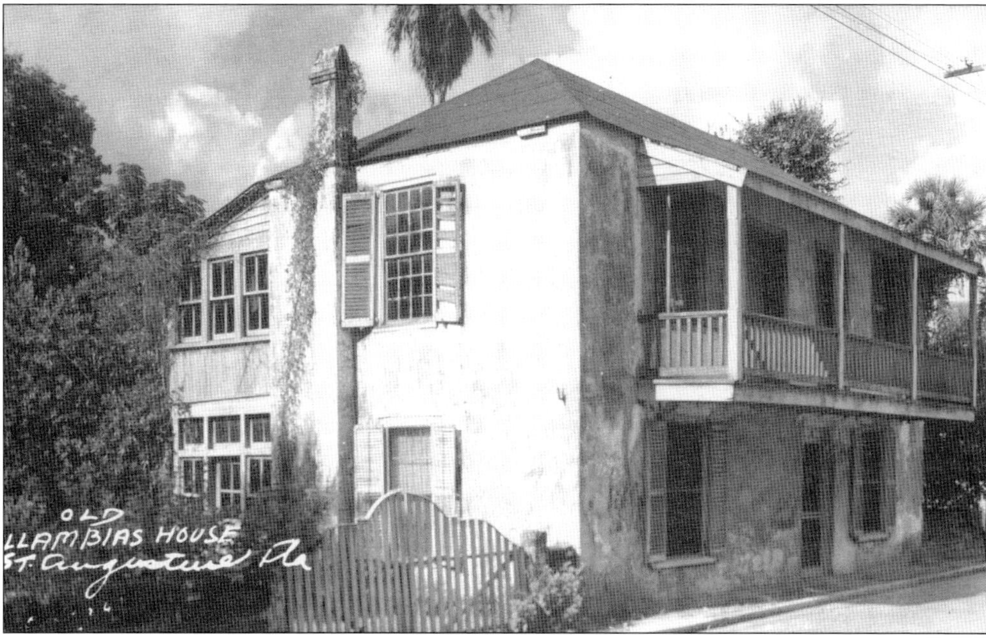

The Llambias House at 31 St. Francis Street dates from around 1750. In 1854, it became the property of the Llambias family, who owned it for the next 65 years. During the 1920s and early 1930s, it was a gift shop and tearoom. In 1938, the house was purchased by the Carnegie Institute with the aid of the St. Augustine Historical Society, who oversees the home today.

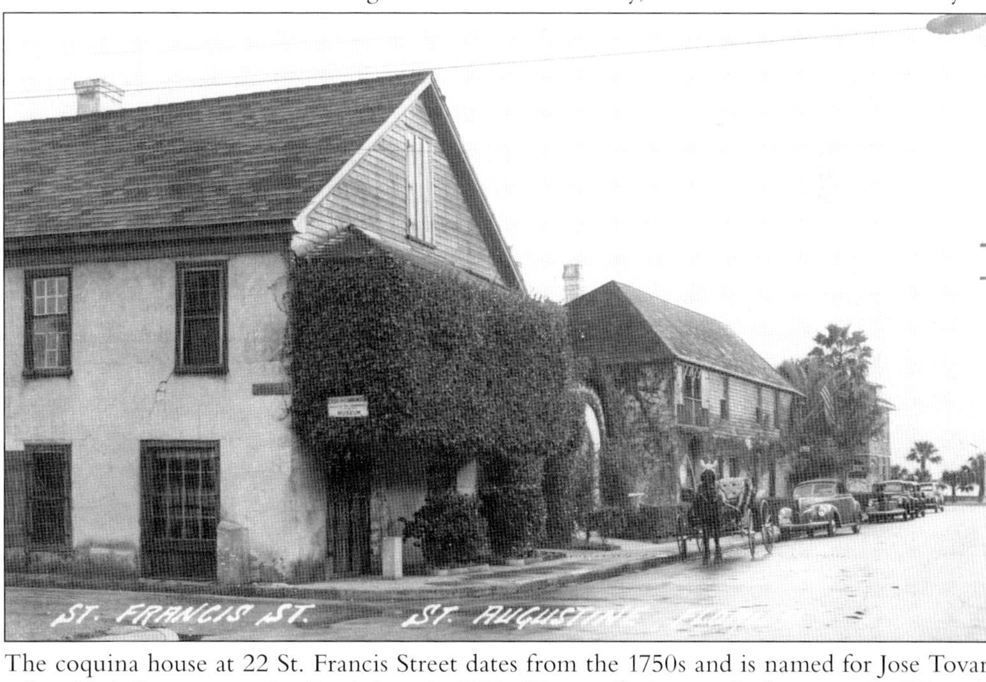

The coquina house at 22 St. Francis Street dates from the 1750s and is named for Jose Tovar, a Spanish infantryman who lived there in 1763. The small sign on the house reads, "Casa de Cannonosa—House of the Cannonball Museum," named for a cannonball embedded in its eastern wall. Owned by the St. Augustine Historical Society since 1918, the house is part of its Oldest House Museum Complex.

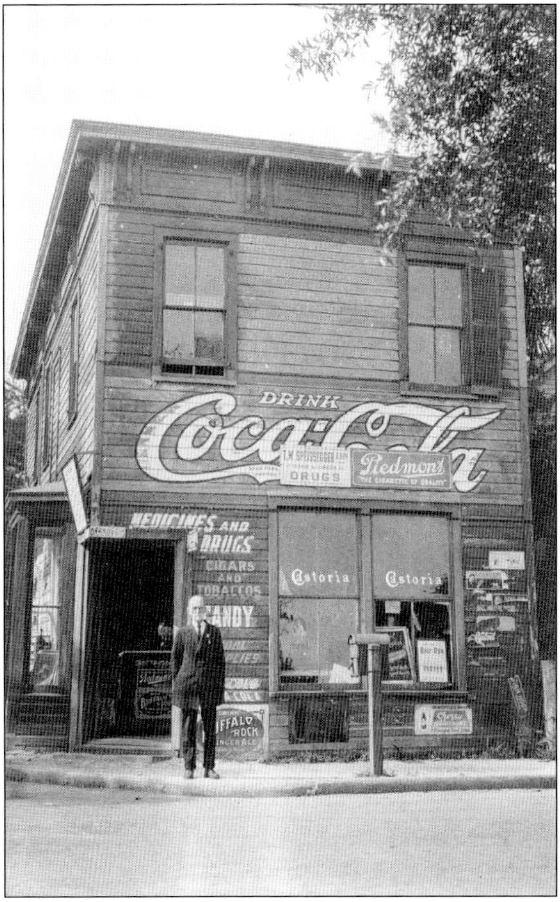

Thomas W. Speissegger, a Civil War veteran from Charleston, South Carolina, operated a drugstore at 46½ Bay Street. After his business was destroyed in the fire of 1887, he moved to a new two-story wooden building at 31 Orange Street. The store was later operated by his son Thomas Julius Speissegger, pictured here standing at the corner of Orange and Cordova Streets. After Julius's death in 1935, his nephews Richard Alton and Milton Sterling Speissegger continued to operate the store until the 1960s, when it became a tourist attraction, the Oldest Drugstore. Nicknamed "Spike's," the store's penny candies were popular with children from the nearby Orange Street School. (Left, SAHS.)

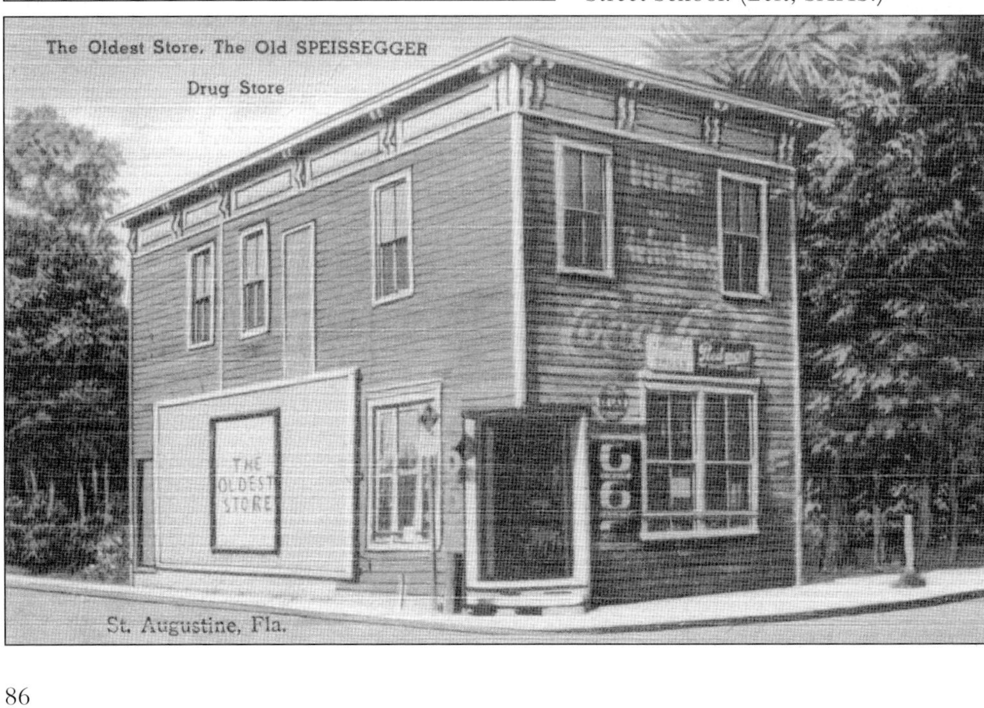

The coquina house at 54 St. George Street was built between 1803 and 1814. In 1900, it was sold to James P. Dodge, a jeweler who named his business Dodge's Old Curiosity Shop. It retained the Old Curiosity Shop name through the years, as seen in this c. 1940 postcard when it was the Barlow Gift Shop. Now known as the Parades-Dodge House, the building still houses a gift shop.

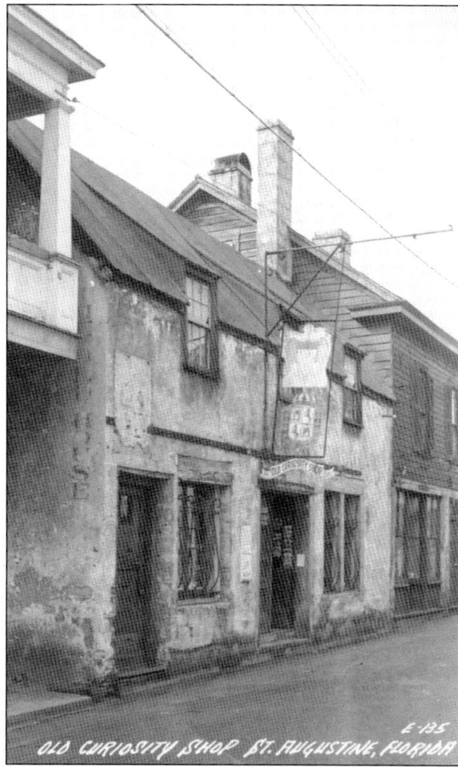

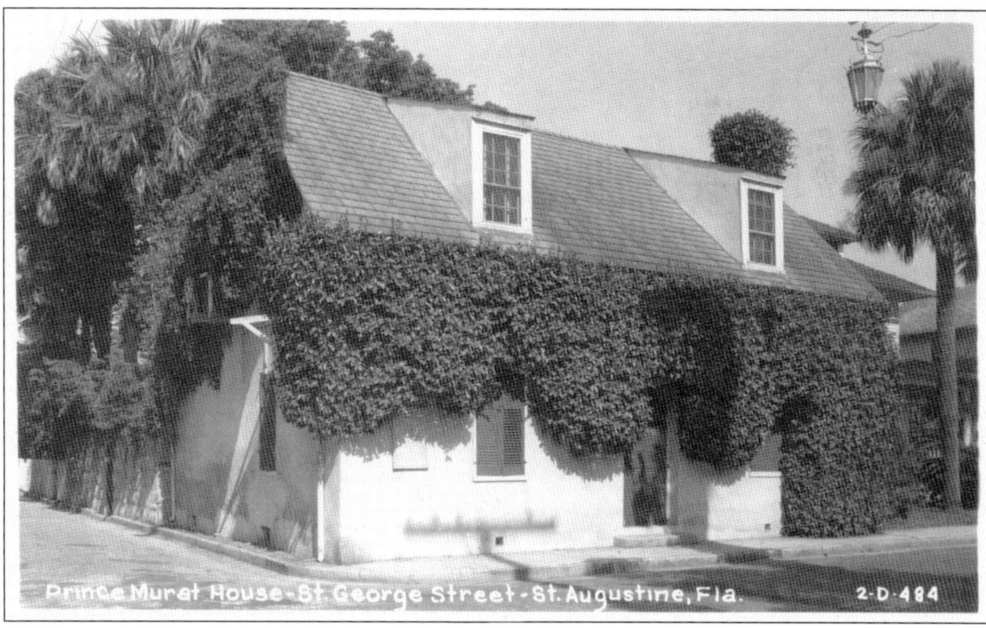

The coquina house at the corner of St. George and Bridge Streets was built around 1815 and named for Prince Achille Murat, who visited there in the 1820s. Operated as a coffee house in the late 1930s, it was purchased in 1941 by Kenneth Dow, who lived there for over 40 years and donated the house to the Museum of Arts and Sciences in Daytona. The house is now part of the Collector Luxury Inn and Gardens.

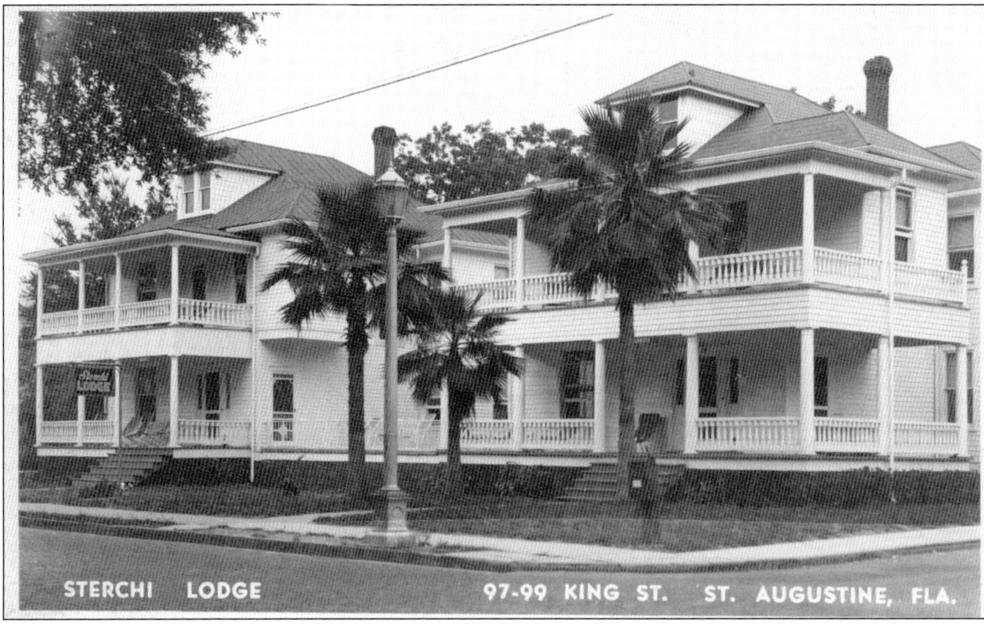

These large homes were located at 97 and 99 King Street. During the late 1930s and 1940s, 97 King Street was occupied by the Helen Watson and William B. Parkhill families, and 99 King Street was the residence of Clinton B. "C.B." May. In the late 1940s, the homes became the Sterchi Lodge and were later demolished to build a modern motel. Today, the post office and its parking lots sit on this site.

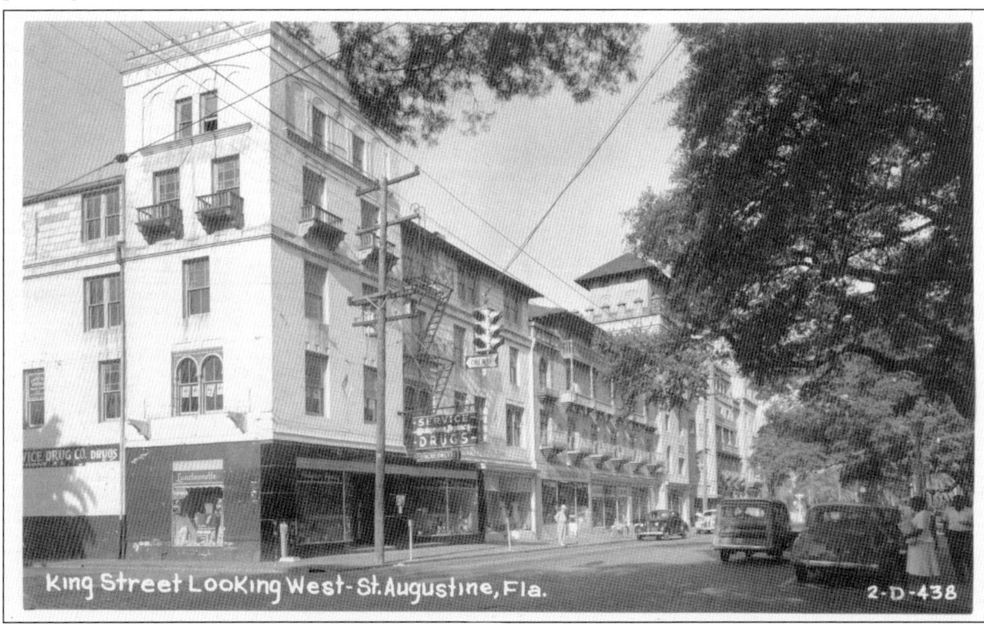

Constructed in 1887–1888, the Lyon Building copied the Moorish Revival style and poured concrete construction of Villa Zorayda. Named for Walter Lyon, who had operated a grocery store on that corner, the building had retail space on the ground floor and furnished rooms above. From 1918 through the 1940s, this busy corner of King and St. George Streets was the location of Service Drugs, operated by Stanley L. Padgett.

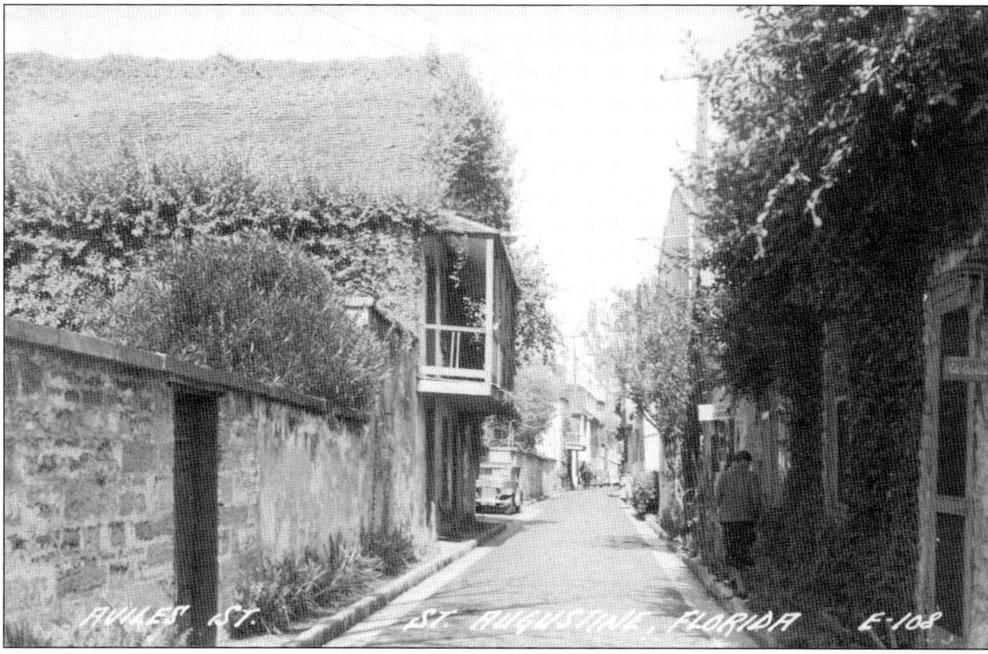

The balcony at left is the O'Reilly House at 32 Aviles Street, and this coquina house is one of the oldest in St. Augustine. Fr. Miguel O'Reilly, an Irish priest in the service of the Spanish crown, bought the property in 1785, and it became the parish rectory. The house is now owned by the Sisters of St. Joseph, who opened it as a house museum in 2003.

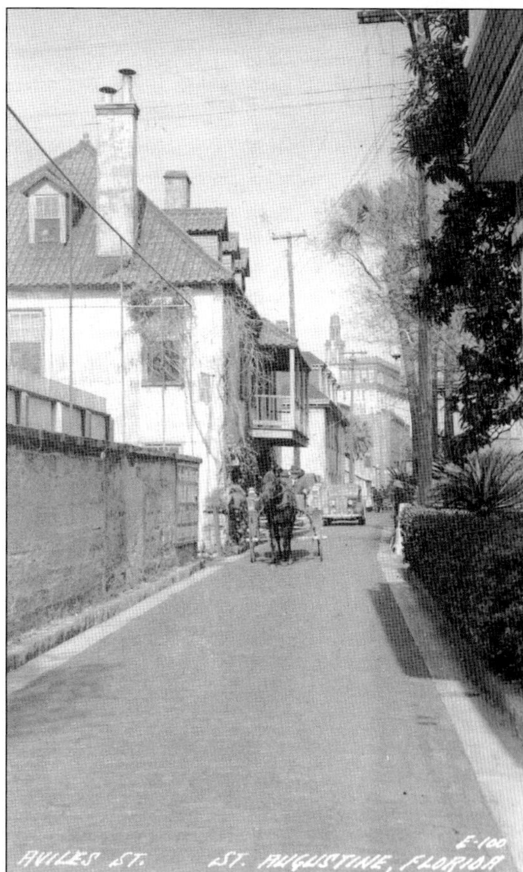

Andres Ximenez built the coquina house at 22 Aviles Street around 1798, and Louisa Fatio later operated it as a boardinghouse. During the 1930s and 1940s, it housed Ruthana Weavers rug shop and several artists' studios. The National Society of the Colonial Dames of America in Florida acquired the Ximenez-Fatio House in 1939 and now operate it as a house museum.

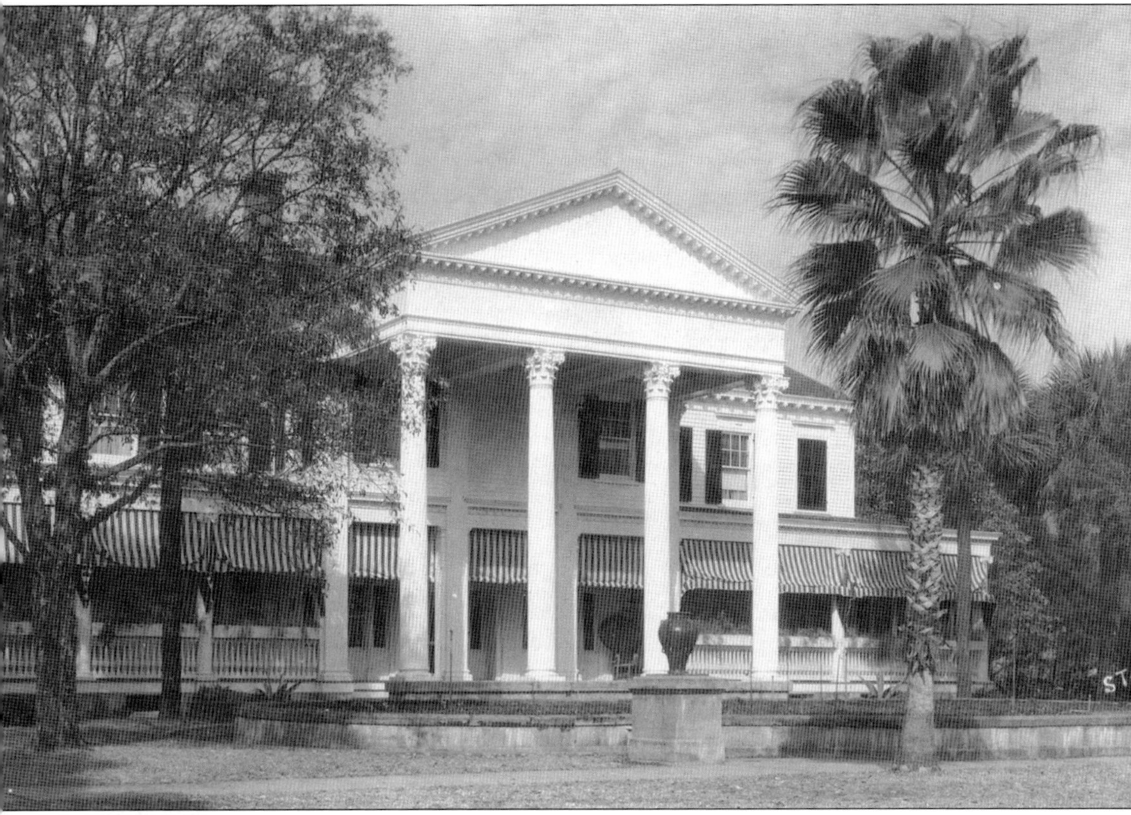

Henry Flagler's home, Kirkside, was located at 40 Valencia Street, just west of Memorial Presbyterian Church, and its grounds occupied the entire block bordered by Valencia, Riberia, and Carrera Streets. Built in 1892–1893 by McGuire and McDonald, the same builders Flagler used for his Ponce de Leon Hotel, the 15-room mansion had marble floors and silver faucets. After Flagler's death in 1913, the house was later occupied by his third wife's niece Louise Wise Lewis. After sitting empty for four years, in 1942 Kirkside was leased to the University Foundation to provide a low-cost space for Christian education, with St. Augustine's Dr. Wilma E. Davis as a faculty member. The school closed in 1949, and the following year, Kirkside was demolished and the property divided into residential building lots. Today, the mansion's stately columns grace the Kirkside Apartments at 55 Riberia Street. (SAHS.)

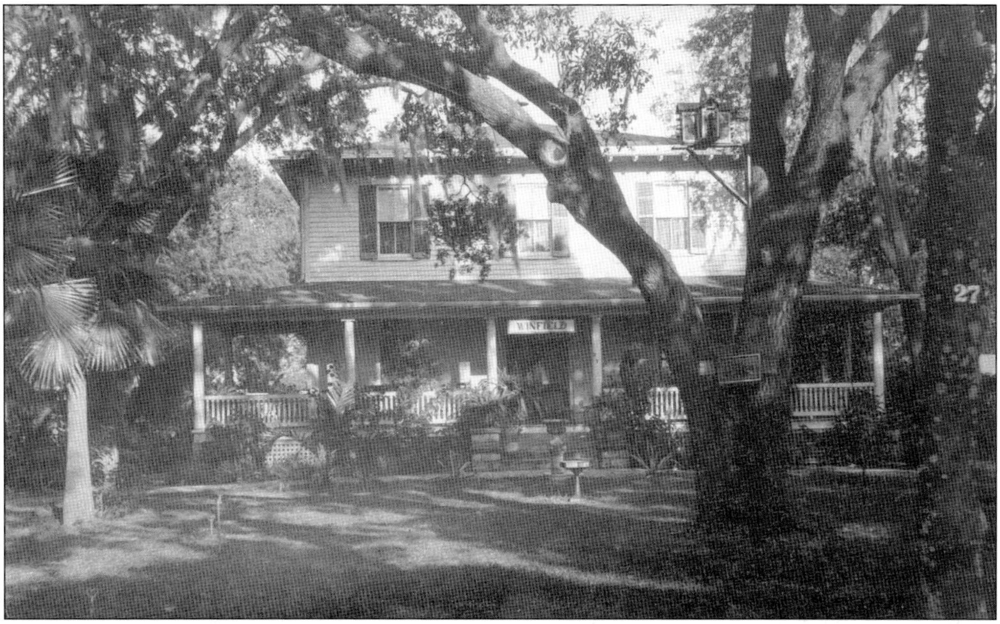

The home at 27 Riberia Street was built between 1885 and 1894. It was once the residence of R.T. Goff, a superintendent with Florida East Coast Railway and later the home of Adrian L. Joynes, manager of the Southern Bell Telephone and Telegraph office. During the 1930s, it was the residence of William C. and Elizabeth B. Winfield, as evidenced by the name sign hanging over the door.

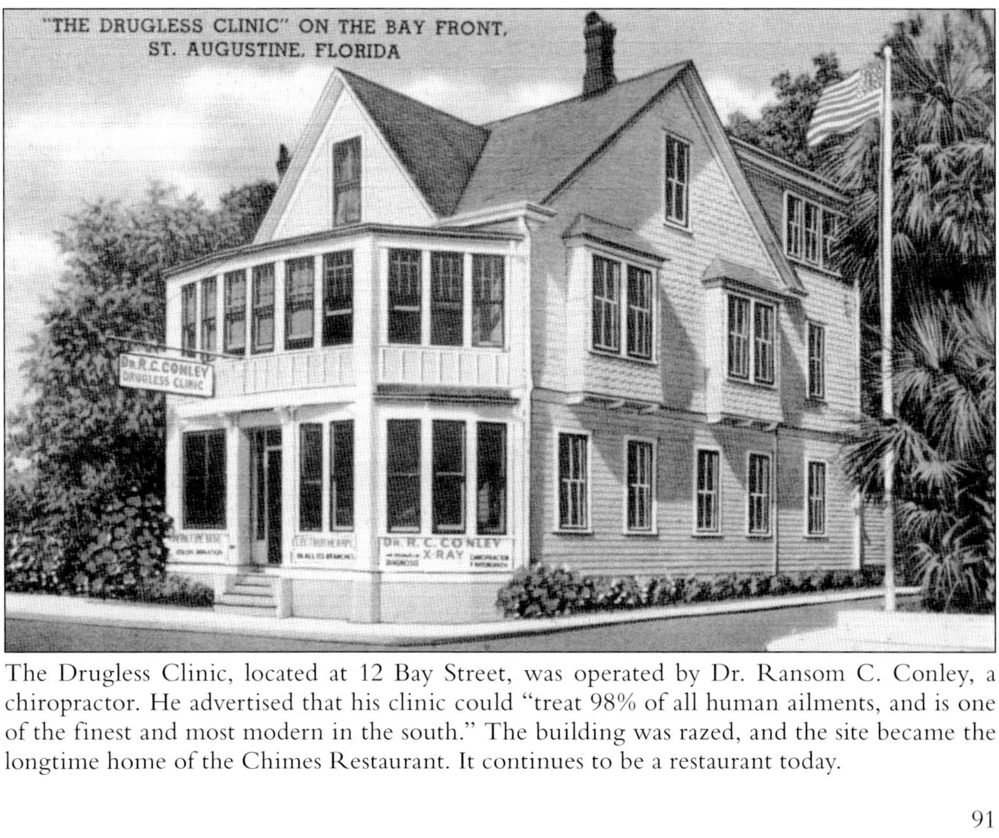

The Drugless Clinic, located at 12 Bay Street, was operated by Dr. Ransom C. Conley, a chiropractor. He advertised that his clinic could "treat 98% of all human ailments, and is one of the finest and most modern in the south." The building was razed, and the site became the longtime home of the Chimes Restaurant. It continues to be a restaurant today.

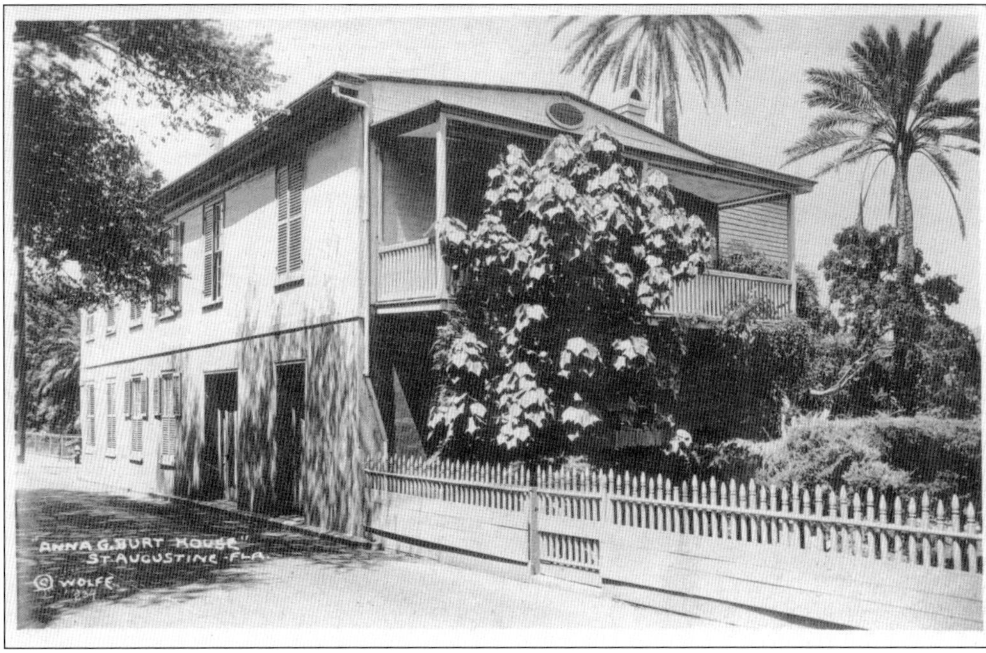

The house at 143 St. George Street was constructed around 1750 as a residence for the royal treasurer, Juan Esteban de Pena. Dr. Seth Peck purchased the home in 1837 and added a wooden second story. The Peck family lived in the house until 1931 when Peck's granddaughter Anna Burt willed the house, furnishings, and artwork to the City of St. Augustine. This was at the height of the Great Depression, and the city almost refused the gift because it would lose the property tax income. The Woman's Exchange agreed to pay an annual rent on the property and show it as a museum. These two views of the house and gardens were taken by local photographer Philip A. Wolfe.

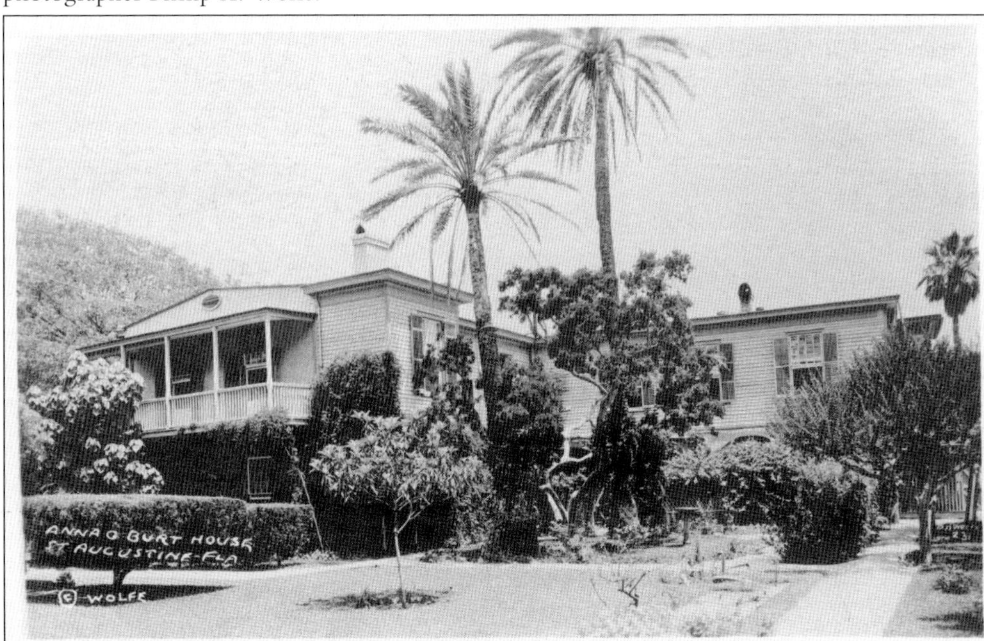

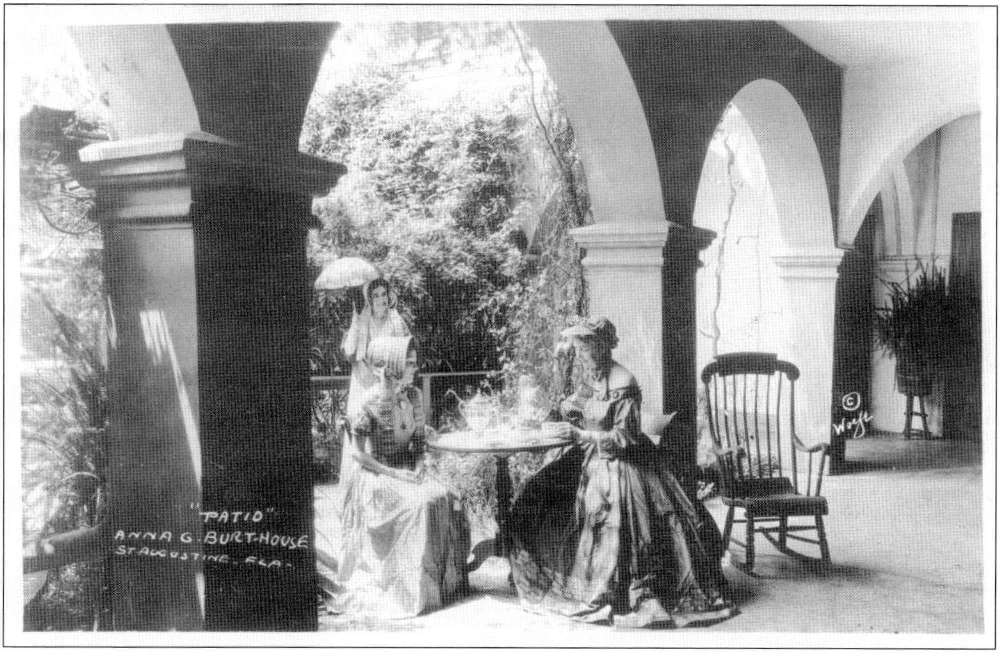

These postcards, also made by Philip A. Wolfe, were photographed on May 1, 1932, the day the Woman's Exchange opened the house for tours, with members acting as costumed guides. In the above postcard, seated on the right at the table, is Elizabeth ("Bessie") White, chairman of the Woman's Exchange board from 1938 until her death in 1964. Also seated at the table is Priscilla Knight, daughter of William A. and Ann Knight, owners of Three Oaks estate at 175 Oneida Street. Standing behind the table is Nina Hawkins, editor of the *St. Augustine Evening Record* until 1953. She served as publicity chairperson and historian of the Woman's Exchange until her death in 1972. The standing woman in the other postcard is unidentified. (Right, O'Neill Collection.)

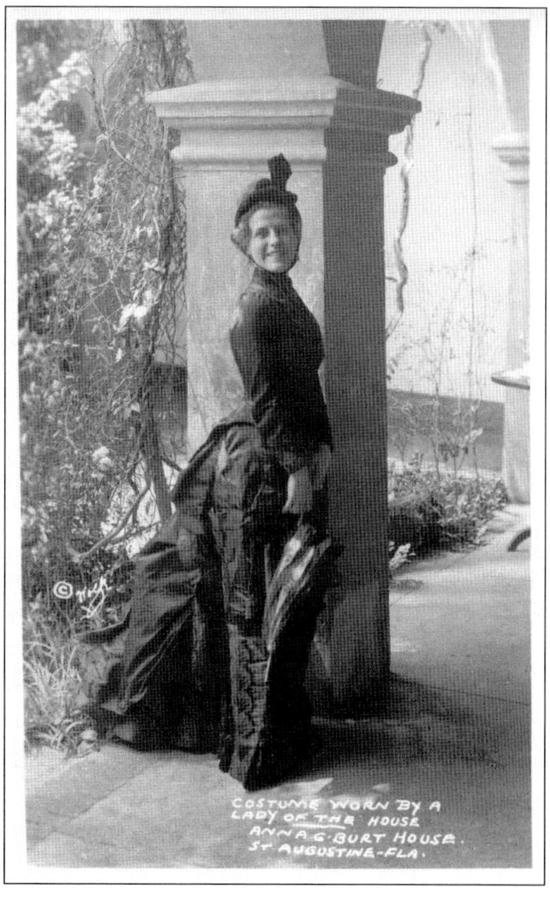

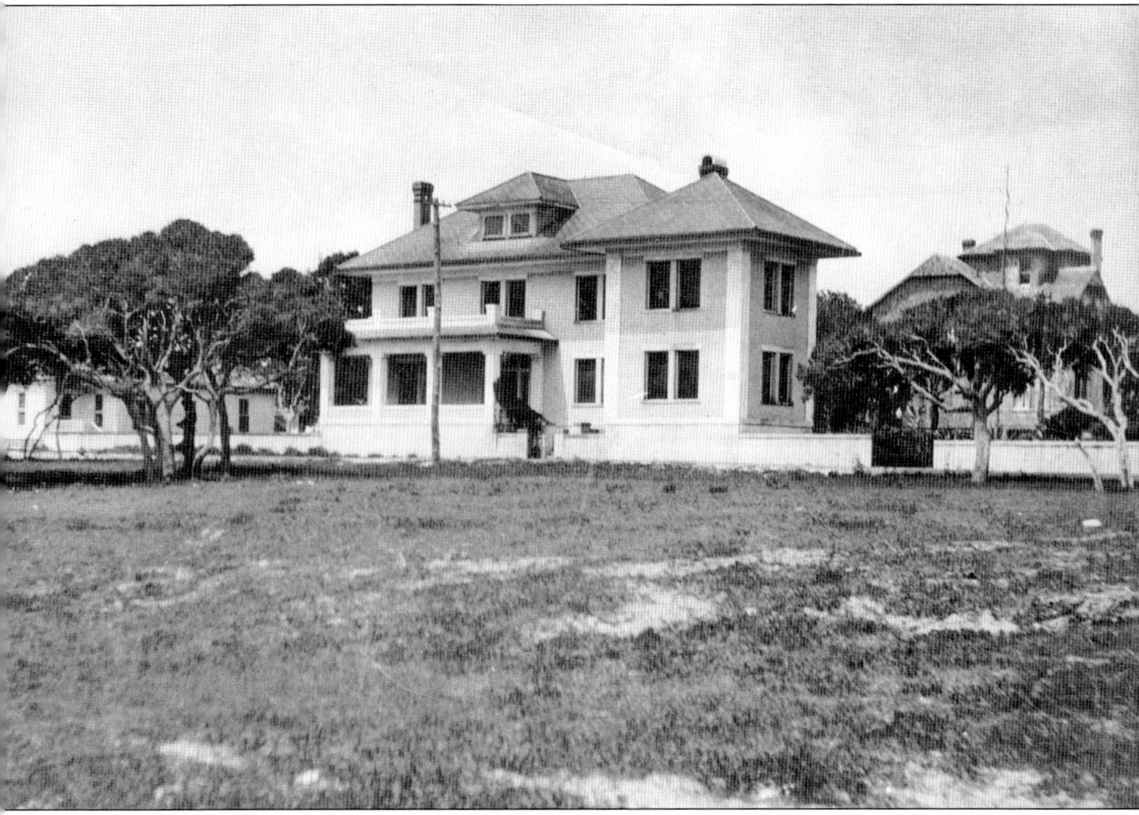

The 2.5-story home at 60 Lighthouse Avenue was built in 1912 by Utley J. White, a developer of the Lighthouse Park area. White died in 1917, and in 1923 his widow sold the home to H.W. Davis, owner of a men's clothing store on King Street. The property also included land across the street, kept vacant to preserve the waterfront view. After Davis's death in 1953, his daughter Dr. Wilma E. Davis donated the home to the trustees of the Preacher's Relief Fund of the Florida Conference of the Methodist Church. The home was divided into apartments where Methodist ministers or their widows could live for free. Dr. Davis retained an apartment in the house for many years. It became a private residence again in 1988, and the owner has gradually renovated the interior to its original condition. (SAHS.)

Eight

STREET SCENES

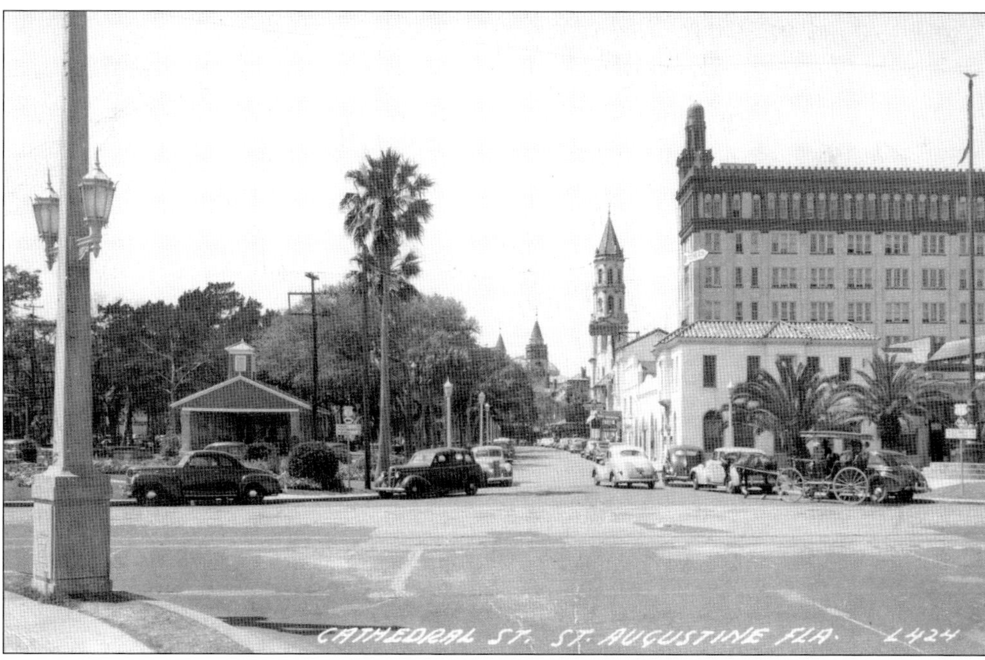

Looking west from the foot of the Bridge of Lions, the First National Bank building on Cathedral Place is at the far right. The bank failed in 1929 but reopened in the early 1930s as the Exchange Bank, with Herbert E. Wolfe as president. Just east of the bank is the Vaill Block, retail stores built by Capt. Edward E. Vaill after his St. Augustine Hotel burned in 1887.

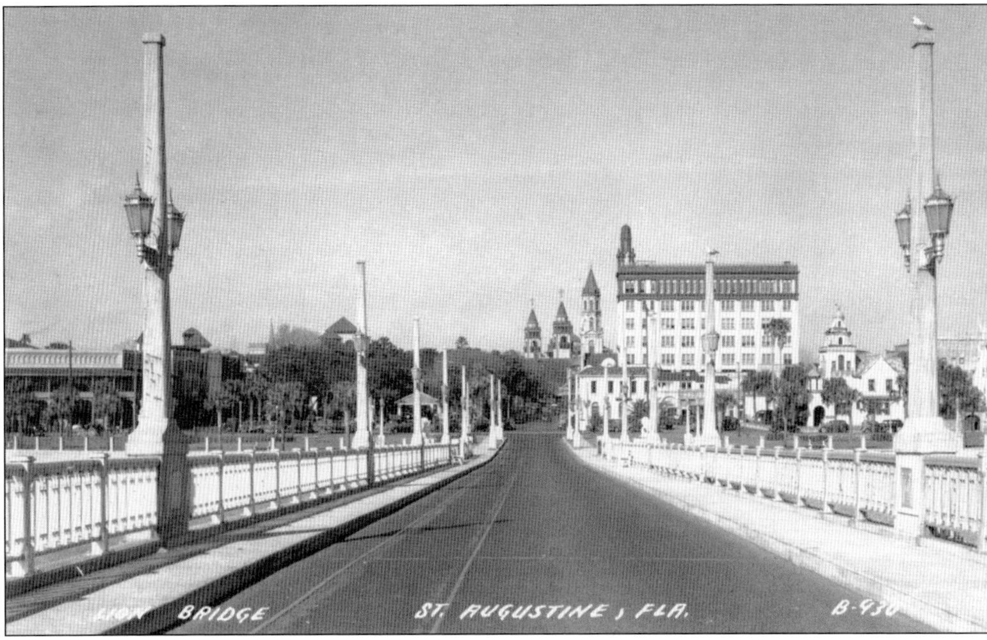

This view of St. Augustine's beautiful skyline looks west from the Bridge of Lions, built from 1925 to 1927 by the City of St. Augustine. Financed by a million-dollar bond issue, bridge tolls would be collected until 1933. An electric trolley ran to Anastasia Island and St. Augustine Beach until 1930, and its tracks are still visible in the bridge's eastbound lane in this postcard from the early 1940s.

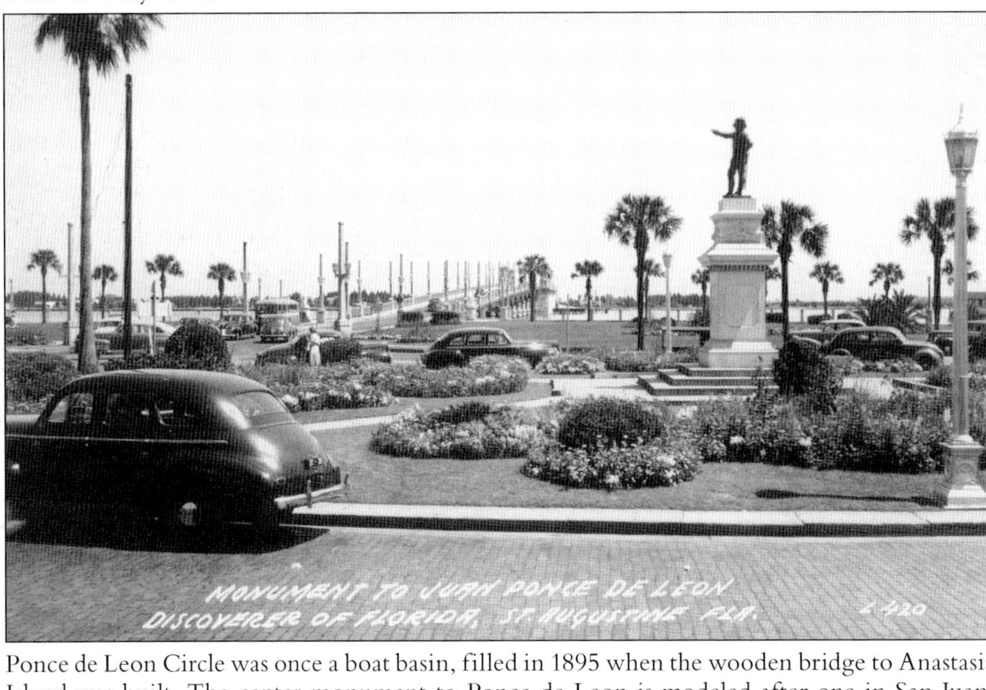

Ponce de Leon Circle was once a boat basin, filled in 1895 when the wooden bridge to Anastasia Island was built. The center monument to Ponce de Leon is modeled after one in San Juan, Puerto Rico. It was a gift to the city from Dr. Andrew Anderson and unveiled by him on Armistice Day, November 11, 1923.

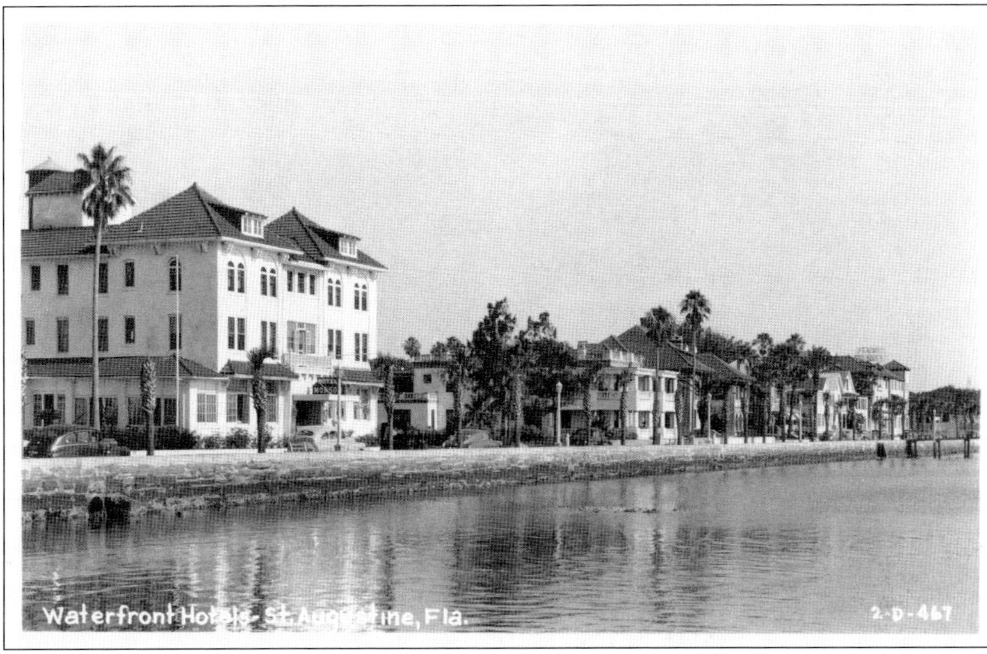

Looking south from the Bridge of Lions to Fort Marion, the Monson Hotel is on the left. The smaller building at center is the Matanzas Apartments, built in 1914 by Goold T. Butler. The Mediterranean Revival building featured four large apartments with open porches overlooking the bay. Now the Casablanca Inn, it is noted for its magnificent lighting display during St. Augustine's annual Nights of Lights.

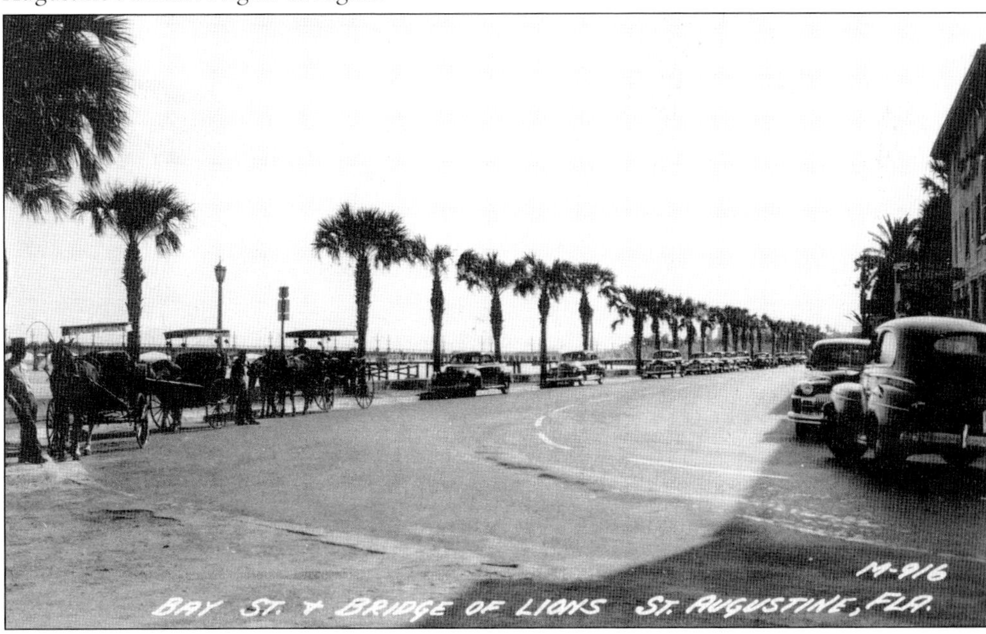

This is the curve where Fort Marion Circle met Bay Street. On the far right is the Hotel Bennett, demolished in 1961 when Fort Marion Circle, now Castillo Drive, was widened and moved southward to create a parking lot for the Castillo de San Marcos. Sightseeing carriages are parked along the seawall and still occupy that same location today.

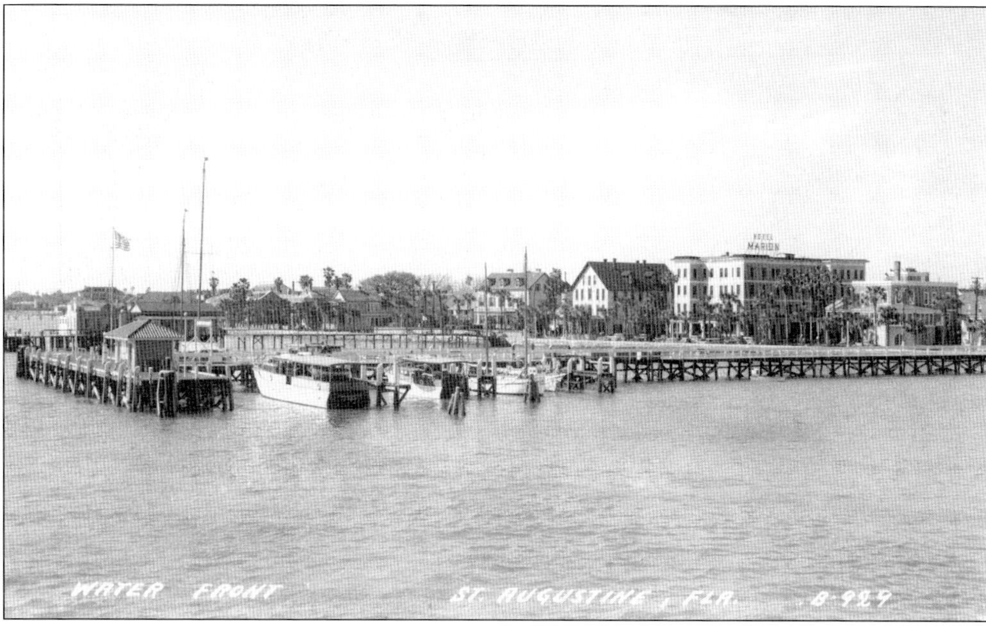

Looking south from the Bridge of Lions, this postcard shows the City Yacht Pier with Corbett's Dock just behind. George W. Corbett floated his seafood house to the dock in front of the Ocean View Hotel in 1925 when the Bridge of Lions was built at his original location at the foot of Cathedral Place. Corbett's Dock later became the longtime home of the Santa Maria Restaurant.

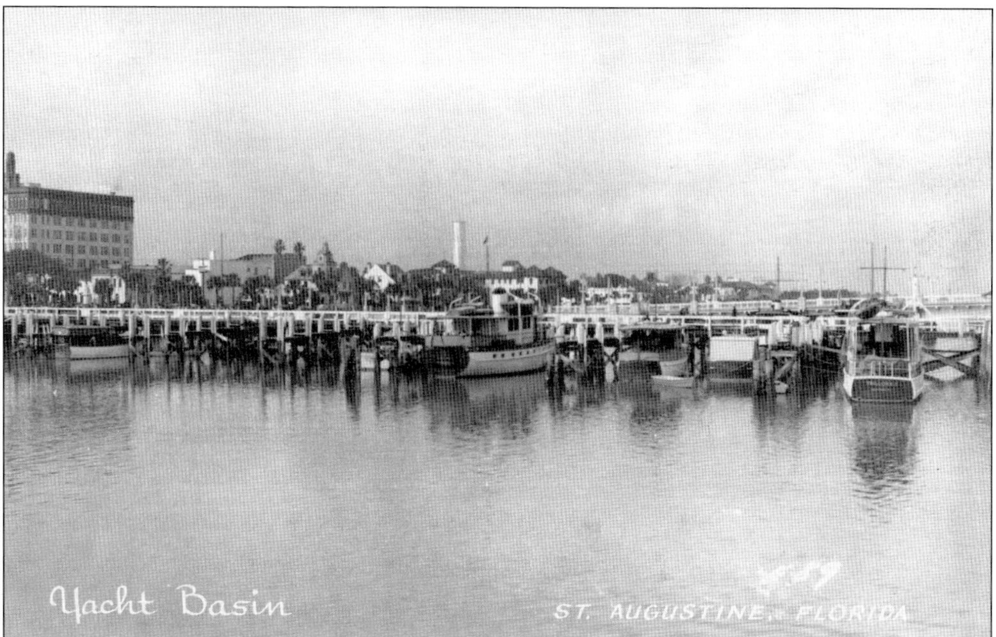

This view looking north from Corbett's Dock shows a variety of boats moored at the City Yacht Pier, built in the late 1920s. At the far left is the Exchange Bank building with the city water tower in the center of the photograph. Located on Hypolita Street at Tocques Place, the water tower was taken down in 1965, and the site is now a parking lot.

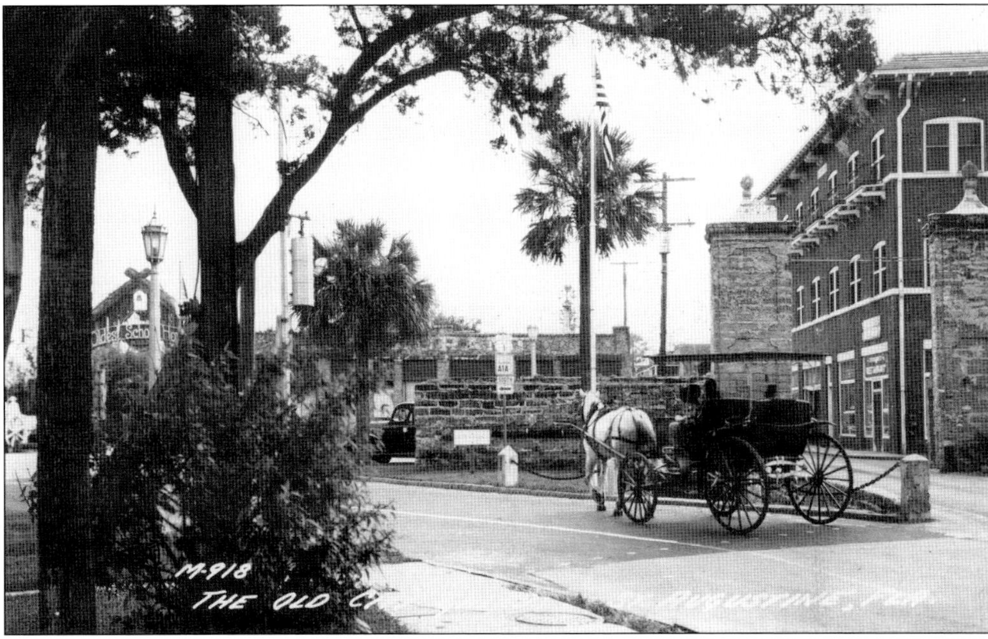

This view is looking through the City Gate toward the three-story brick Byrne Building with Grissom's City Gates Restaurant shown at the center of the gate. The building was constructed around 1923 by brothers Corrigan and Jimmie Byrne to house their Jordan Motor Car agency on the ground floor; there were apartments above. The building was demolished in the late 1950s.

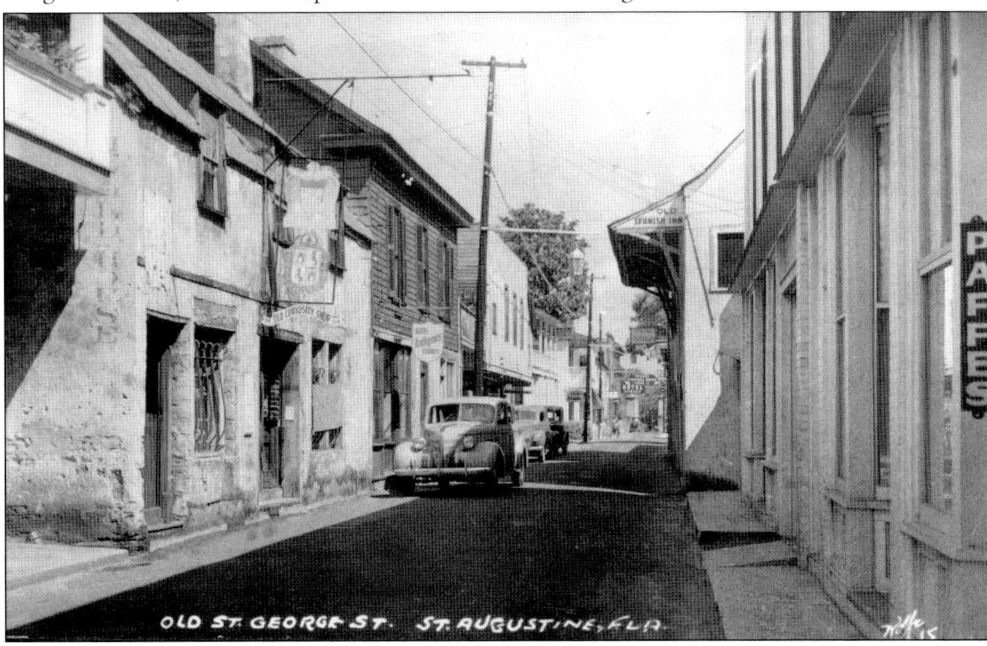

This postcard of St. George Street by Philip A. Wolfe shows the middle of the block north of Cuna Street. Located in the row of shops on the right was Henry C. Paffe's printing business, later run as a stationery and card shop by his widow, Marie. The site is now a restaurant in the Colonial Quarter, located in the reconstructed frame home of Menorcan carpenter Francisco Pellicer. (O'Neill Collection.)

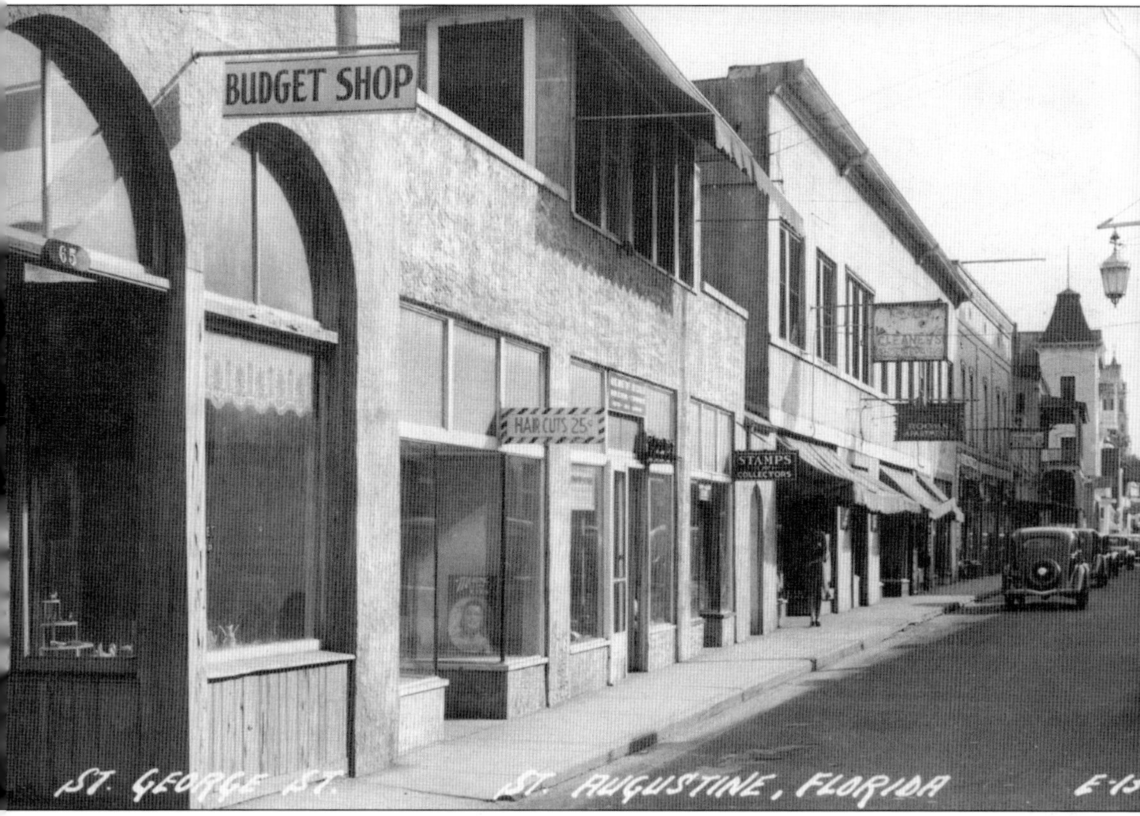

Looking south on St. George Street, the commercial buildings at left were constructed in front of the Lorillard Villa, built in the 1880s as a winter residence for tobacco heir George Lorillard. A small sign between the two awnings marks the entrance to the Lorillard Villa Rooms and Apartments at 73 St. George Street. Operated in the early 1930s as the Cosy Inn by Dora Tarlinsky, it was later taken over by her daughter and son-in-law, Lena and Benjamin Lichter. The house was demolished in the 1950s, and the buildings along St. George Street are now the location of Mi Casa Café and the Florida Cracker Café. In the distance is the mansard-roofed tower of Weinstein's Grocery, located on the corner of Hypolita Street. Traffic on St. George Street was one-way going south with parallel parking on the west side of the street, requiring much skill in the days of behemoth autos with no power steering.

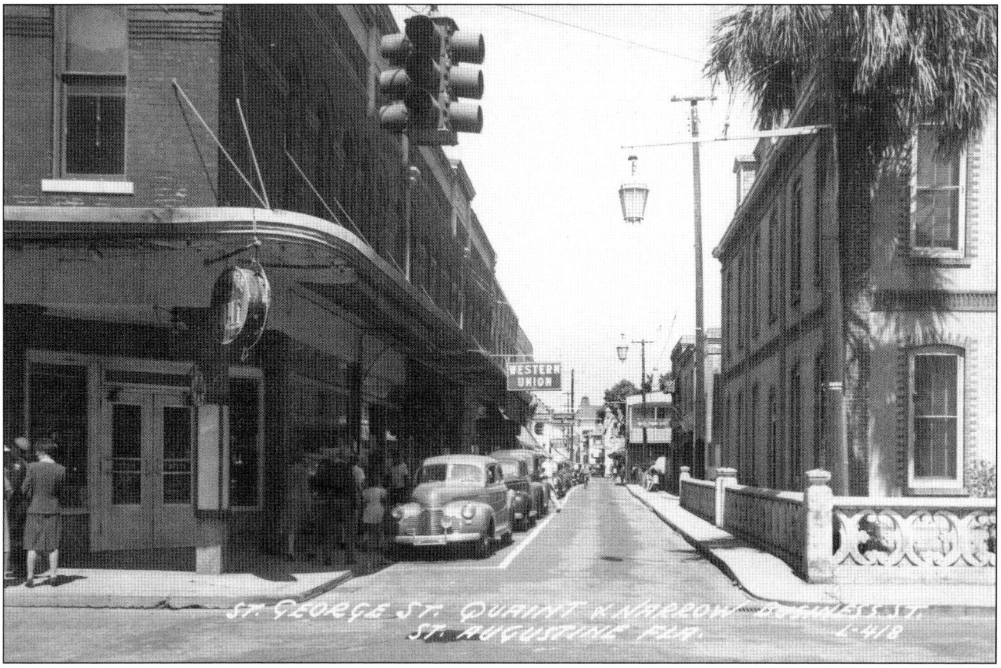

This view looks north on St. George Street from the intersection of Cathedral Place. On the right is the Cathedral Rectory, and at left is the Bishop's Building, with the entrance to the Neptune Grill at a 45-degree angle. The Bishop's Building would be demolished in 1960 and is now a parking lot for the Bank of America. (O'Neill Collection.)

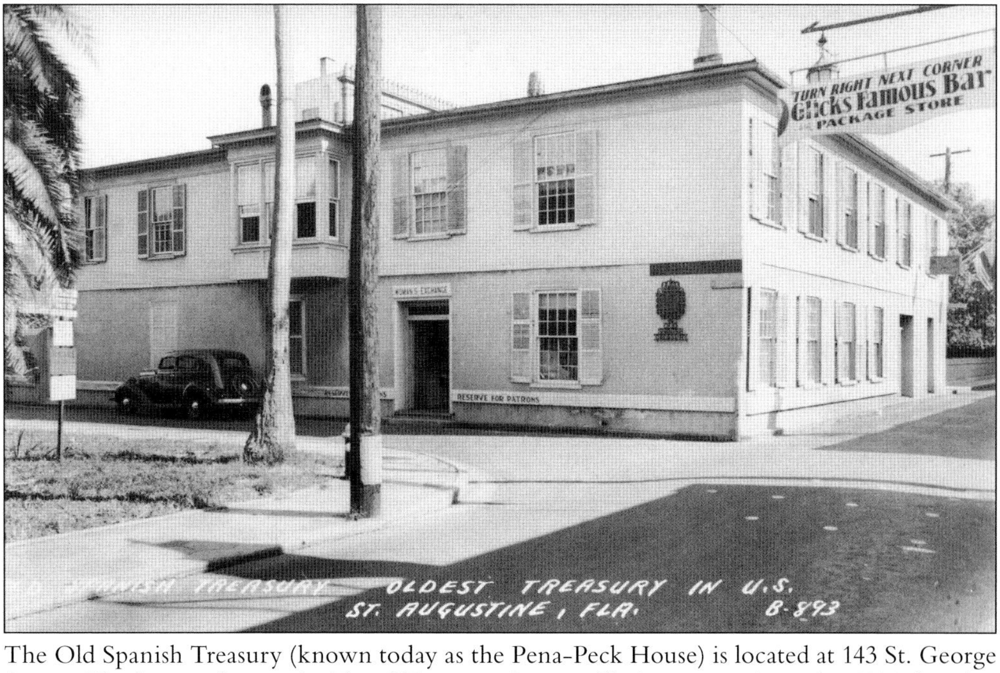

The Old Spanish Treasury (known today as the Pena-Peck House) is located at 143 St. George Street. The lot on the north side of Treasury Street still sits empty since the 1914 fire that destroyed the Florida Hotel on that site. The sign over the street points the way to Glick's Famous Bar at 52 Cathedral Place, owned by brothers Max and Irving Glickstein.

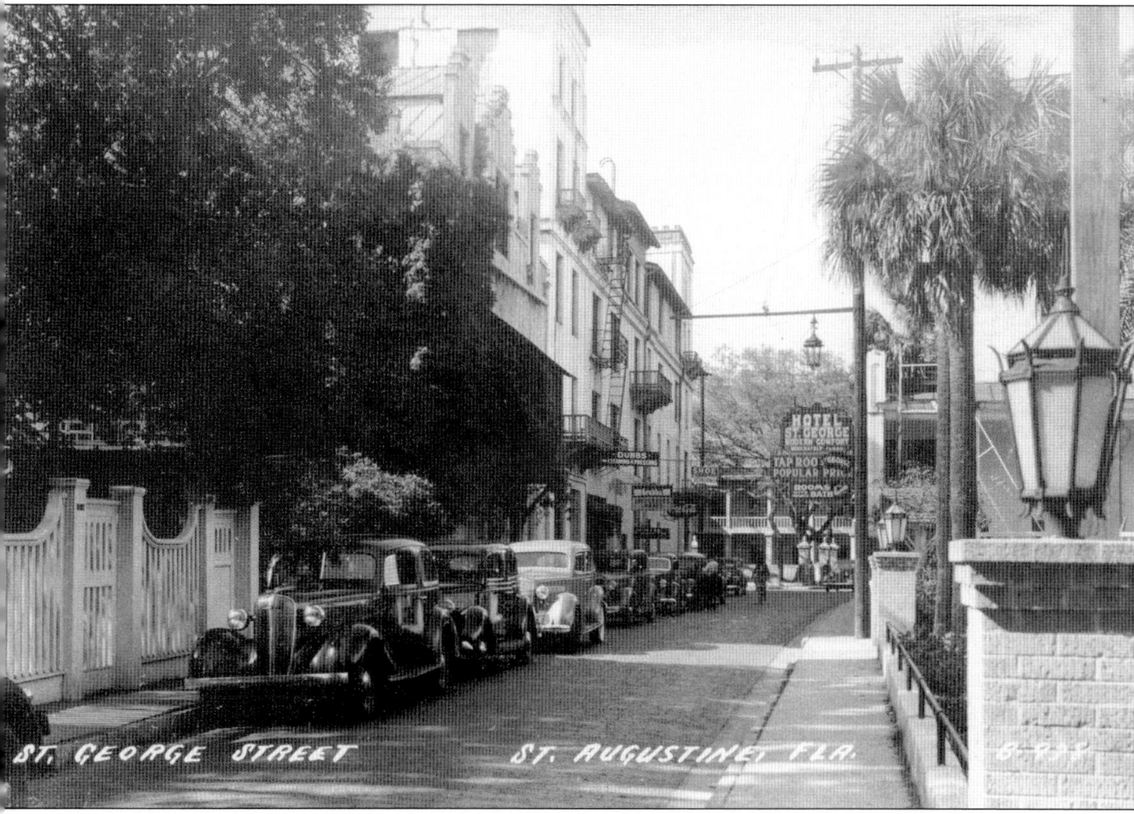

Looking north on St. George Street from Artillery Lane, the St. George Hotel at right was purchased by Trinity Parish Episcopal Church and demolished in 1942. It is now the site of the church's parish hall. At left, partially obscured by trees, is one of the city's oldest homes, the Horruytiner House, then occupied by James S. Lindsley and his mother, Bessie, widow of Dr. Horace Lindsley. The fence at left marks the entrance to the home and office of physician Walter D. Webb. Formerly the residence of Holmes Ammidown, developer of Palm Row, the house would be demolished in the mid-1950s for the Park and Shop lot, always referred to as the "Webb Lot" by locals. Now the valet parking lot for the Casa Monica Hotel, the lot's small entrance office still remains.

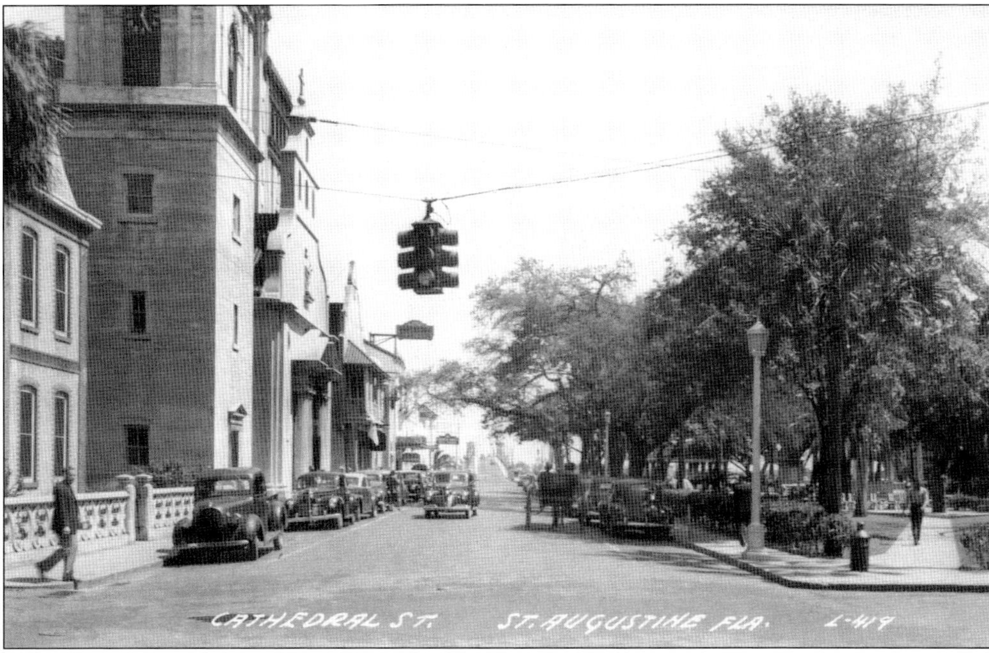

Looking east on Cathedral Place from the corner of St. George Street, the Bridge of Lions is seen in the distance. The sign just below the traffic light is hung from the Matanzas Theatre, which opened in early 1939. The facade of the theater stills survives as an art gallery, but the auditorium was demolished in 1967 to make way for a bank parking lot.

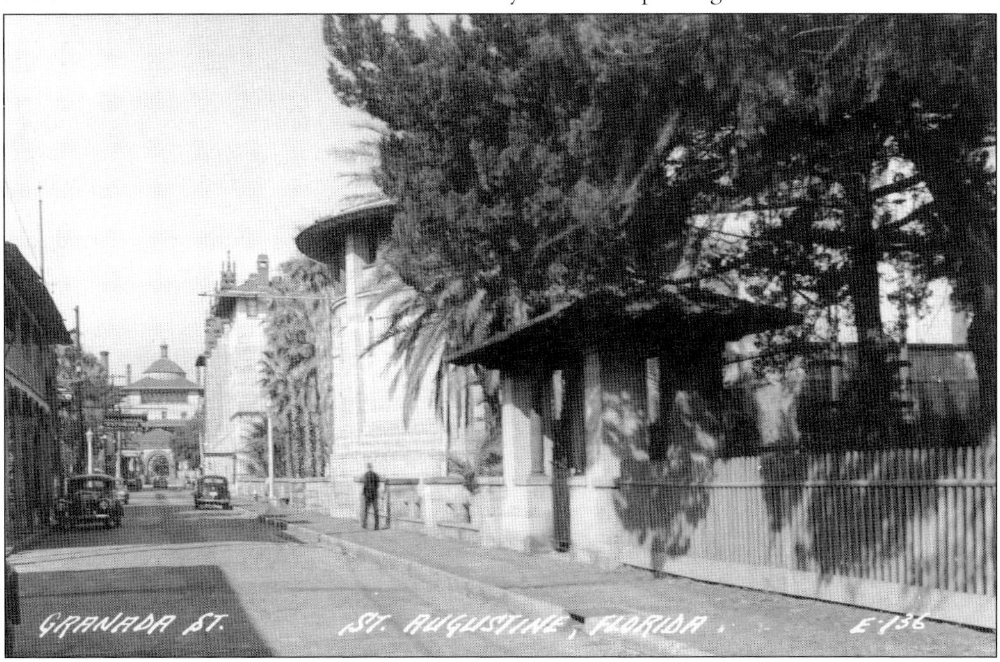

This view looks north on Granada Street, near the intersection of Bridge Street. On the right, the circular wall surrounds the pool at the rear of the Alcazar Hotel, which closed in 1932. The wooden fence is gone, but the tile-roofed gate still remains and marks the entrance to a parking lot. In the distance is the entrance to the Ponce de Leon Hotel.

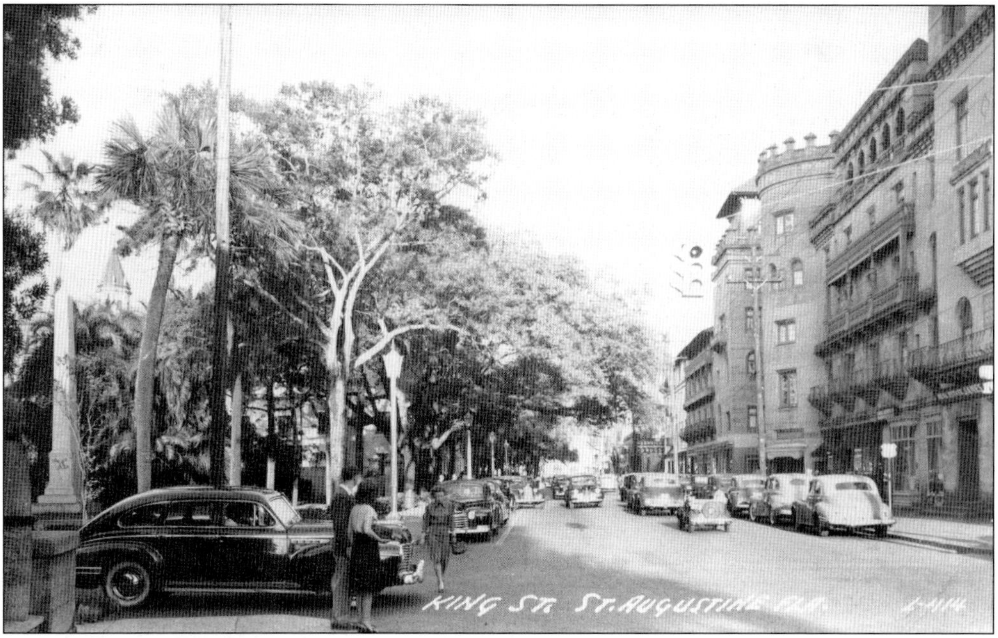

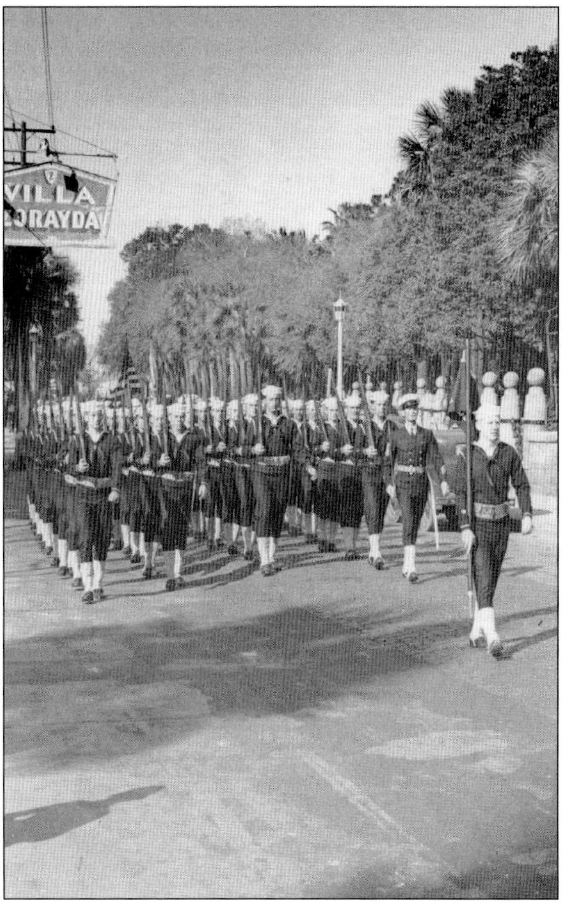

Looking east on King Street from the intersection of Cordova Street, the former Cordova Hotel is on the right. A sign on the building advertises the James A. Colee Real Estate Agency, which occupied the 69 King Street location for many years. At left is the park west of the post office with its monument to Confederate general William Wing Loring, who spent his early years in St. Augustine.

Coast Guard trainees march eastward on King Street in front of the Villa Zorayda. At right is the wall surrounding the palm grove on the west side of the Hotel Ponce de Leon. The hotel was taken over by the Coast Guard during World War II and housed up to 2,500 trainees at any one time. (SAHS.)

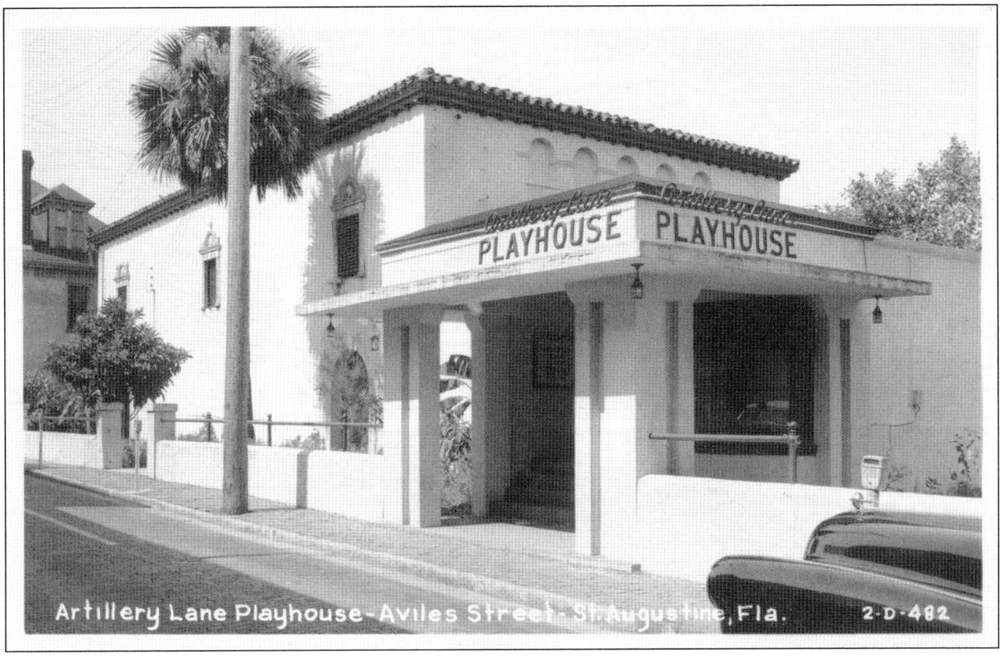

The building at 6 Aviles Street, at the corner of Artillery Lane, was constructed in the mid-1920s as a sales office for Davis Shores and housed a large-scale model of the projected development. It was later used as a bowling alley and in the late 1940s was remodeled into the Artillery Lane Playhouse. It was demolished in 1955 to construct new retail stores along King Street.

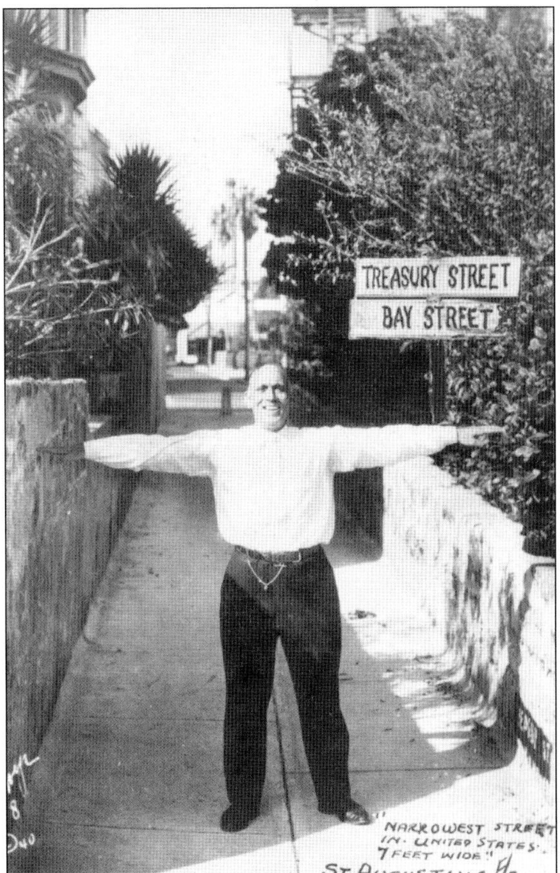

Treasury Street has been depicted in thousands of postcards as the "Narrowest Street in the United States." Named for the Old Spanish Treasury (today's Pena-Peck House) on the corner of St. George Street, the pedestrian-only portion of the street between Bay and Charlotte Streets is only seven feet wide. The low wall at right surrounded a garden at the Monson Hotel, and a portion of it still survives today.

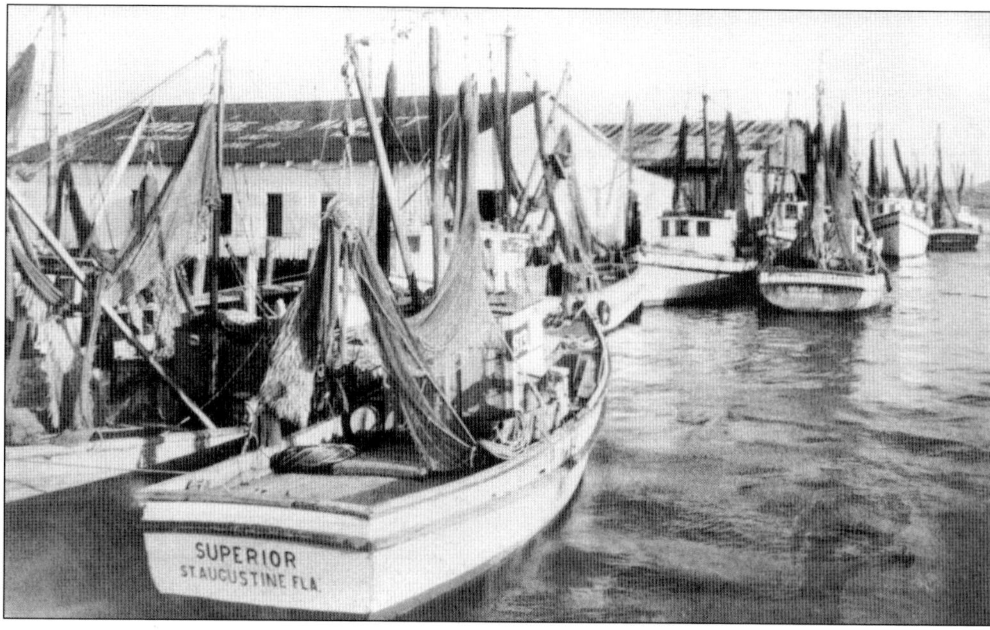

Riverside Fish Market was located on the east side of the San Sebastian River, just south of the King Street bridge, and was owned by brothers John R. and Felix A. Salvador. Their father, Sollecito "Mike" Salvador, together with his brothers-in-law Salvadore Versaggi and Antonio Poli, moved their shrimping operations from Fernandina in the early 1920s. By the 1940s, shrimping had become one of the town's largest industries. During World War II, several shrimp boats were commandeered to use as coastal patrol boats. The many servicemen stationed here during the war got their first taste of St. Augustine's famous fried shrimp, further increasing the demand for the tasty crustacean. (Above, Connahey Collection; below, Hird Collection.)

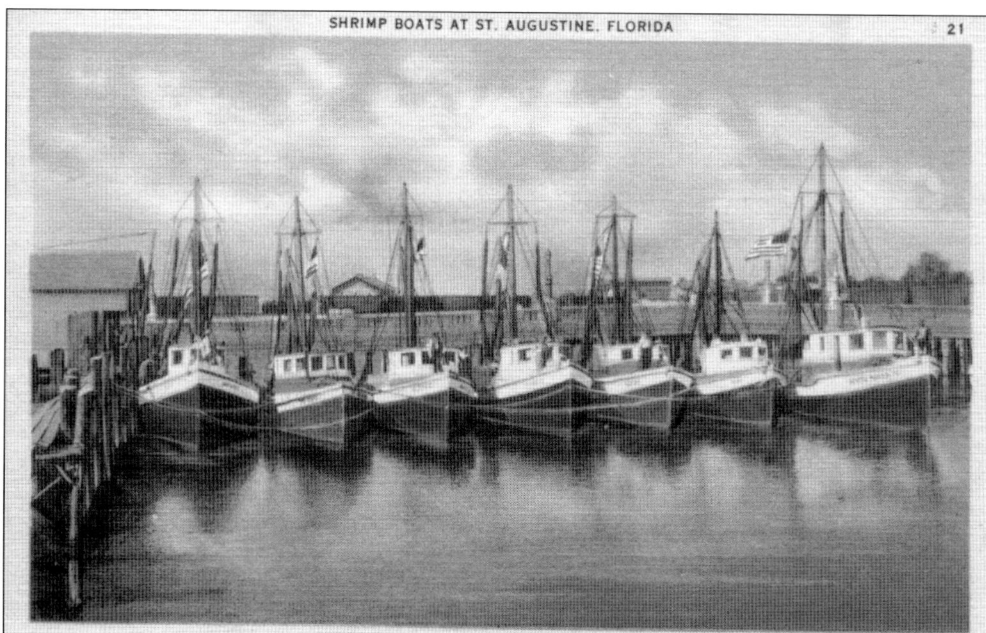

Constructed in 1887–1888 by Buckingham Smith, the Casa Monica Hotel was a failure after only four months in operation. It was purchased by Henry Flagler in 1888 and renamed the Cordova Hotel. When remodeled in 1962 for the St. Johns County Courthouse, these lovely balconies along Cordova Street were removed. After the courthouse moved to larger quarters, the building became a hotel again in 1999 under its original name, Casa Monica.

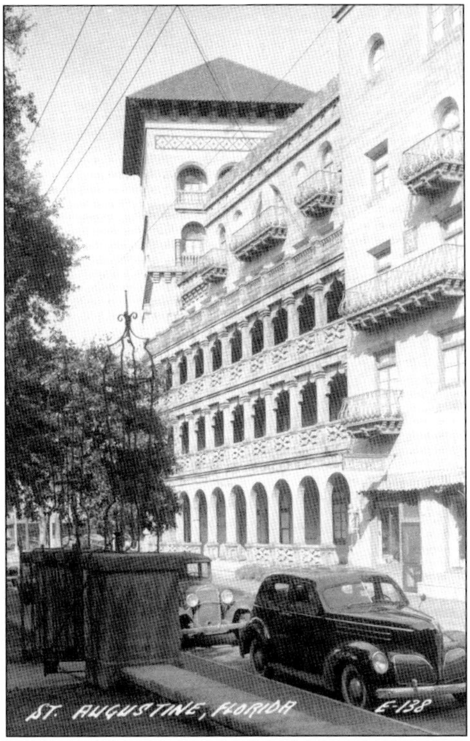

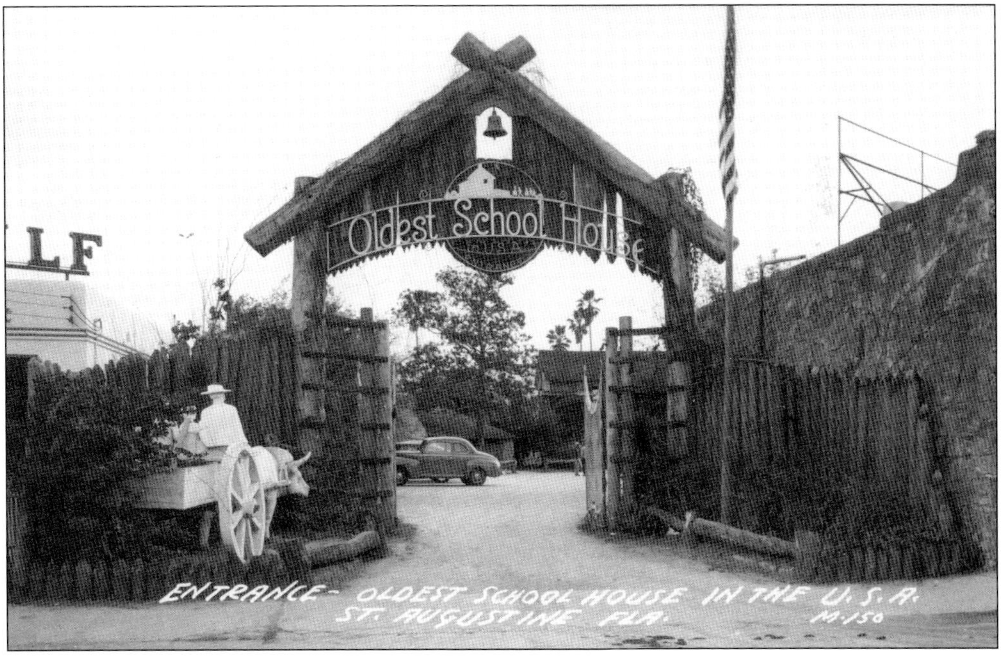

The entrance to the Oldest School House parking lot was at the east end of Orange Street. Just left of the entrance is the oxcart sculpture commissioned in the late 1930s by Walter Fraser, then owner of the attraction. When Fort Marion Circle was rerouted and widened to become Castillo Drive in the late 1950s, the oxcart was relocated to Ripley's Believe It or Not! and still resides there today.

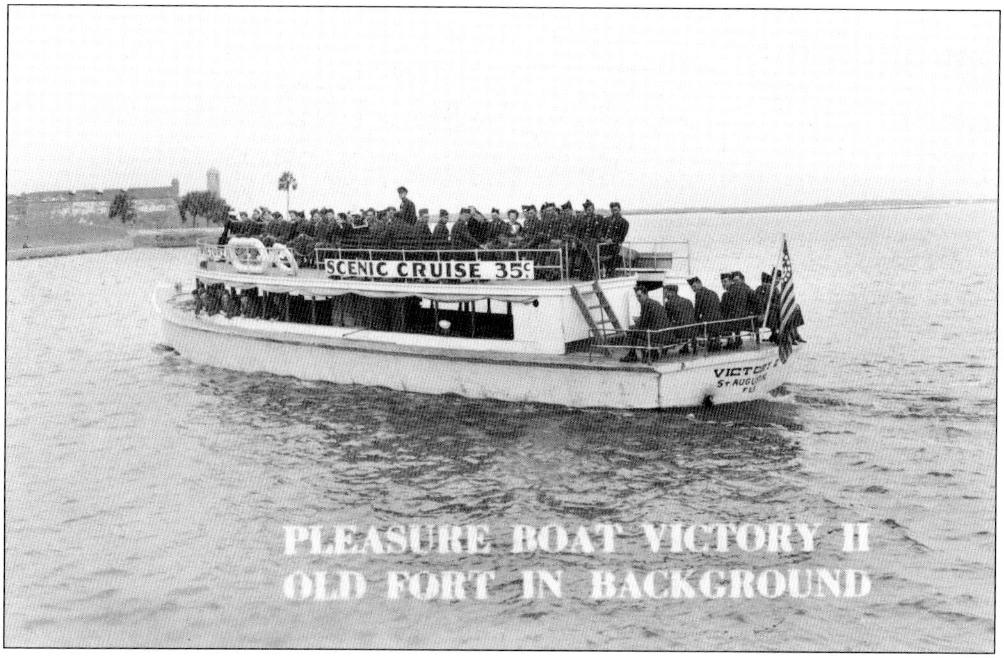

Francis Usina's sightseeing boat *Victory II* is loaded with servicemen for a harbor cruise during World War II. Launched in 1917, the *Victory II* was used to ferry passengers to outings at Usina's North Beach. In the late 1930s, the *Victory II* became a sightseeing boat and after 1942 operated from its own dock at the foot of Hypolita Street. (Usina Collection.)

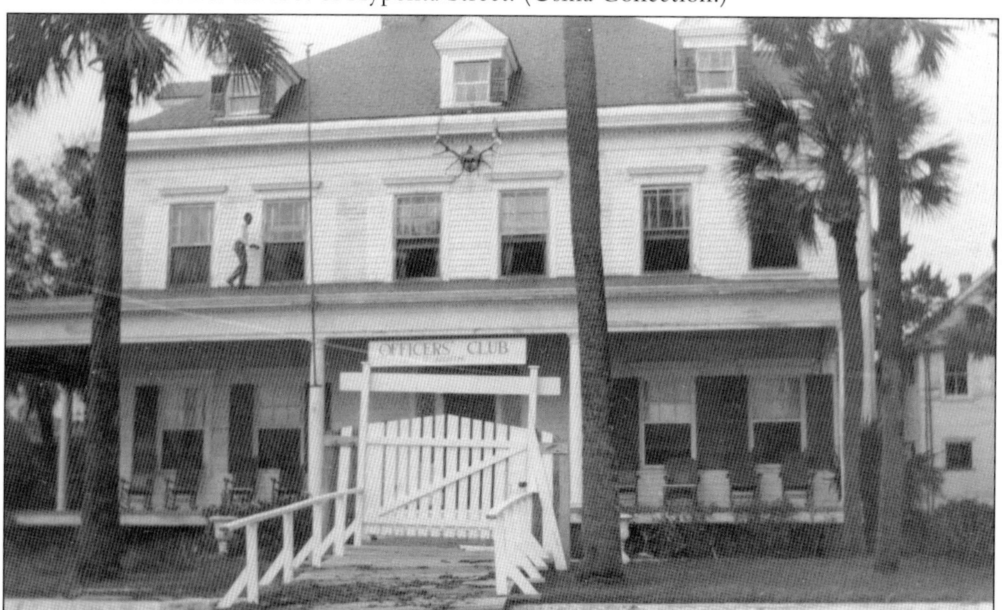

Floodwaters from the hurricane of October 19, 1944, pushed the dock for the Usina's *Victory II* sightseeing boat into the front yard of the Elks Club, which served as the Officer's Club during World War II. The home at 20 Bay Street was the former residence of Mary Gibbs Smethurst and later occupied by Bartolo Genovar. It became the Elks Club in the early 1930s. (SAHS.)

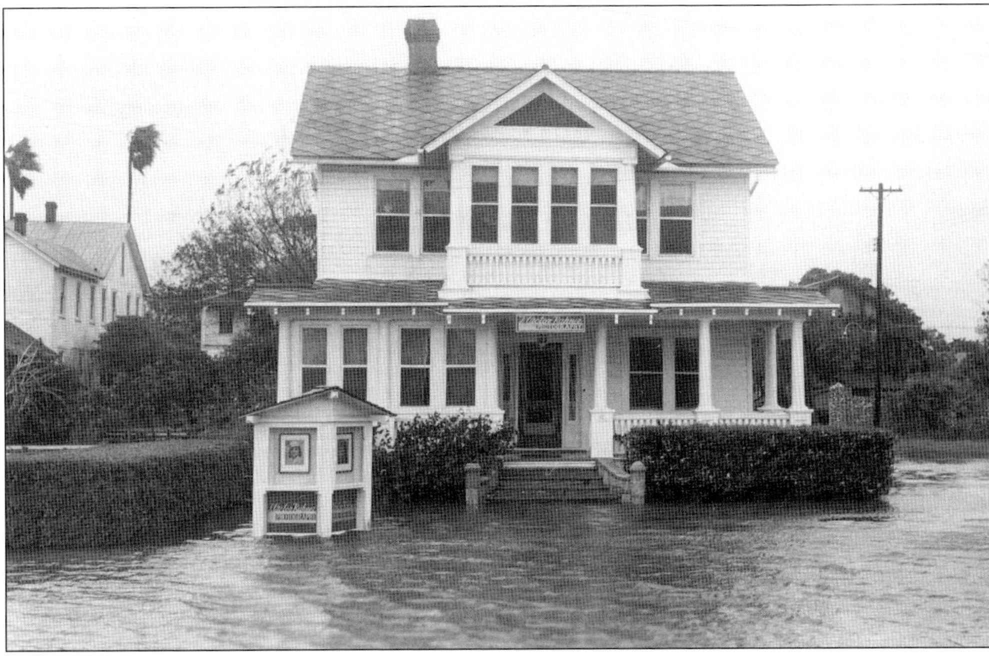

F. Victor Rahner (1899–1984) was a St. Augustine native who began studying photography at age 10. He started his own studio in 1924 and became one of the town's leading photographers. This is his home and studio at 12 Fort Marion Circle (today's Castillo Drive) during the 1944 hurricane. His son Tom Rahner can be seen at an upstairs window on the left. (SAHS.)

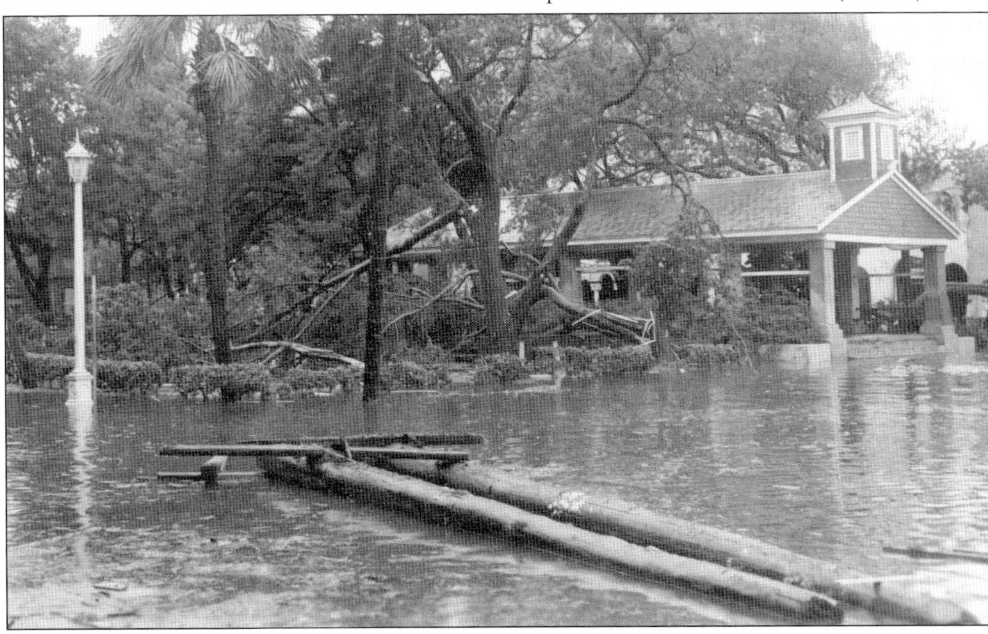

F. Victor Rahner took a series of photographs during the 1944 hurricane, including this one showing damage in the plaza. A fallen utility pole lies in Bay Street, while downed trees and limbs have fallen near the slave market. Coast Guard trainees housed at downtown hotels helped with recovery efforts, as floodwaters reached a level not seen again until Hurricane Matthew in 2016.

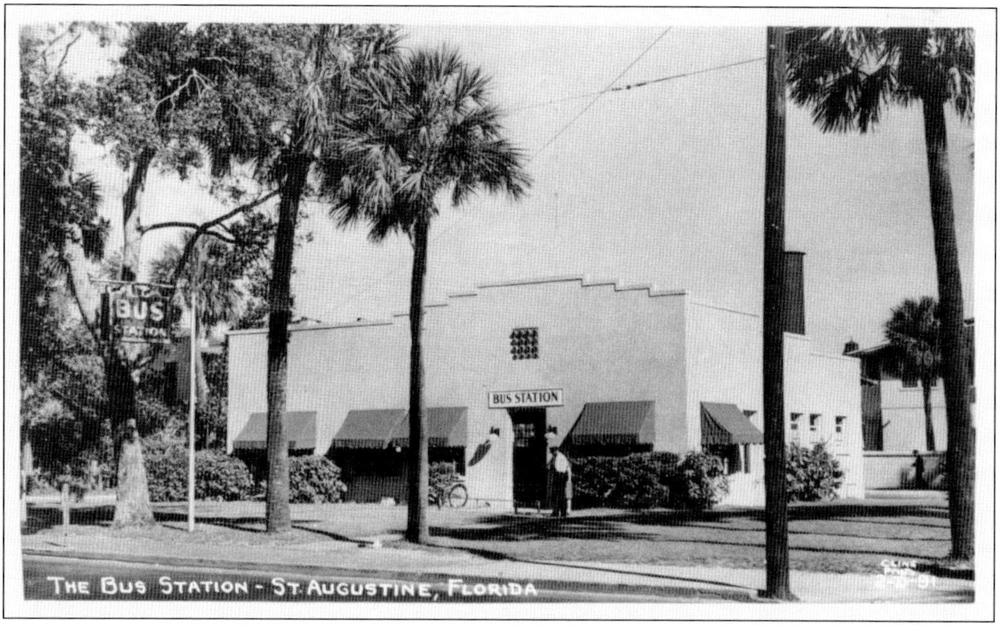

On January 1, 1946, the Greyhound Corporation bought the Florida Motor Lines, which had operated from a small station in the "triangle" formed by Bay, Marine, and Cadiz Streets. Greyhound built a new station at 61 Cordova Street that featured a circular drive to unload passengers at the rear of the station. The bus station later moved to Malaga Street, and its Cordova Street location is now the Thompson-Baker Agency.

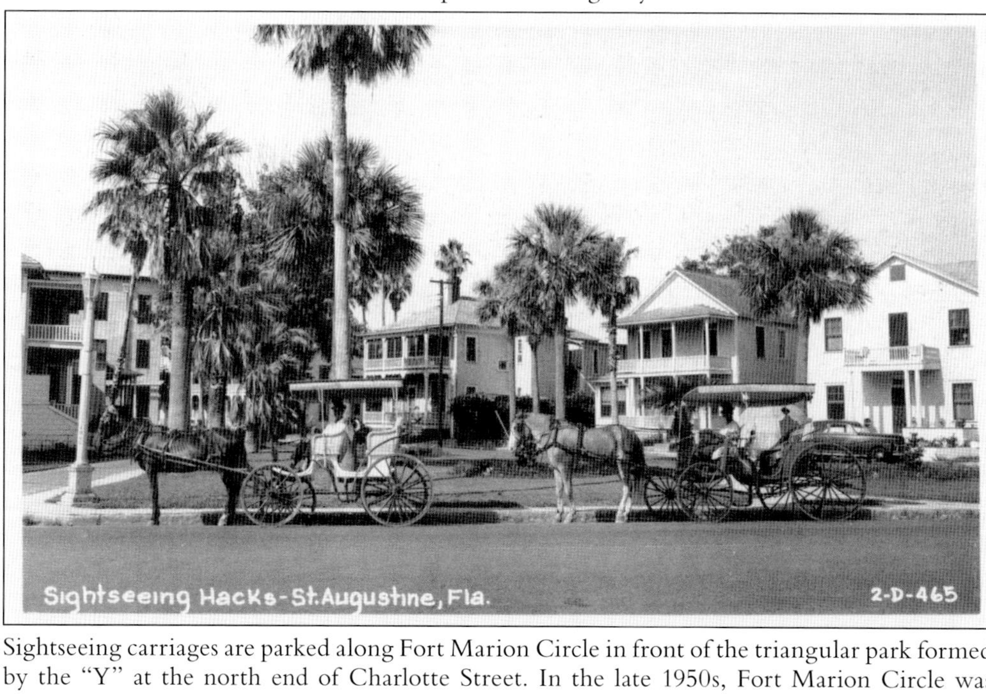

Sightseeing carriages are parked along Fort Marion Circle in front of the triangular park formed by the "Y" at the north end of Charlotte Street. In the late 1950s, Fort Marion Circle was widened and rerouted southward to create a larger parking lot for the Castillo de San Marcos. The homes seen in the background along Charlotte Street were demolished and Fort Marion Circle renamed Castillo Drive.

Nine

Islands and Beaches

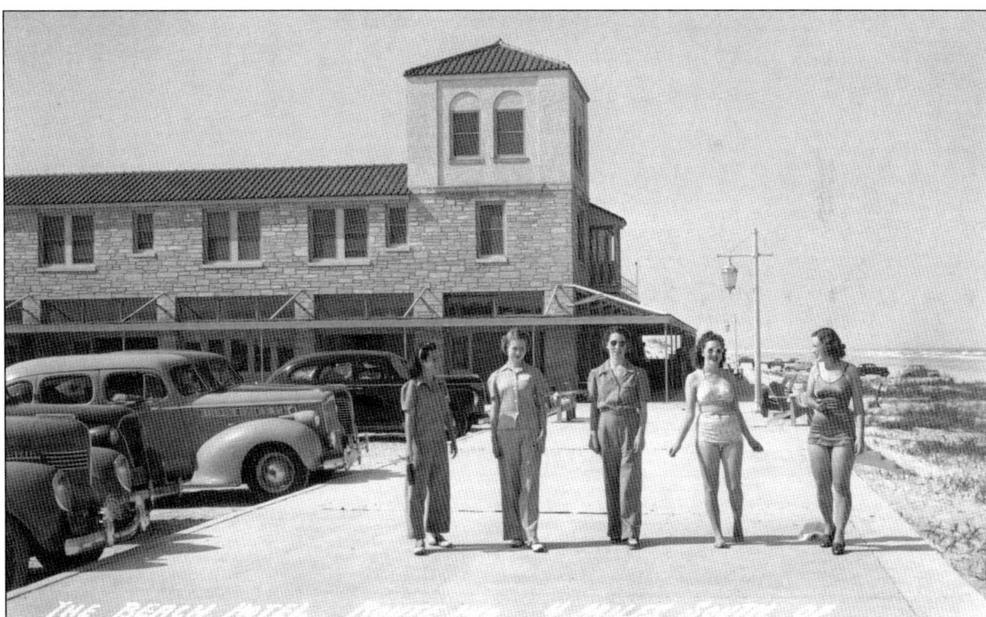

Five young women stroll along the boardwalk at St. Augustine Beach. Funded by the Works Progress Administration, St. Johns County constructed a 1,344-foot fishing pier, seawall, and boardwalk flanked by two coquina buildings. The complex opened in July 1939, but the pier was severely damaged by an October tropical storm. The northern building, shown in this photograph, was demolished in the 1980s, but its twin to the south still remains.

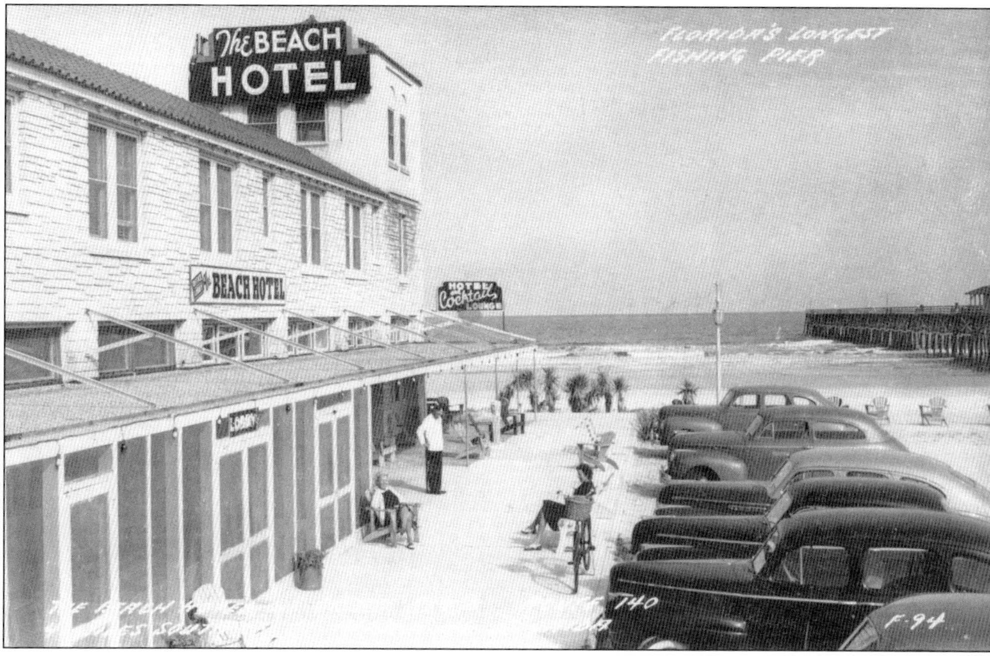

The building north of the pier contained the Beach Hotel, which featured rooms, apartments, a cocktail lounge, and a penthouse in the tower section behind the sign. In 1940, Elmer Davis signed a long-term lease to operate the hotel and pier complex, but the country's entry in World War II the following year curtailed recreational activities at the beach. (Connahey Collection.)

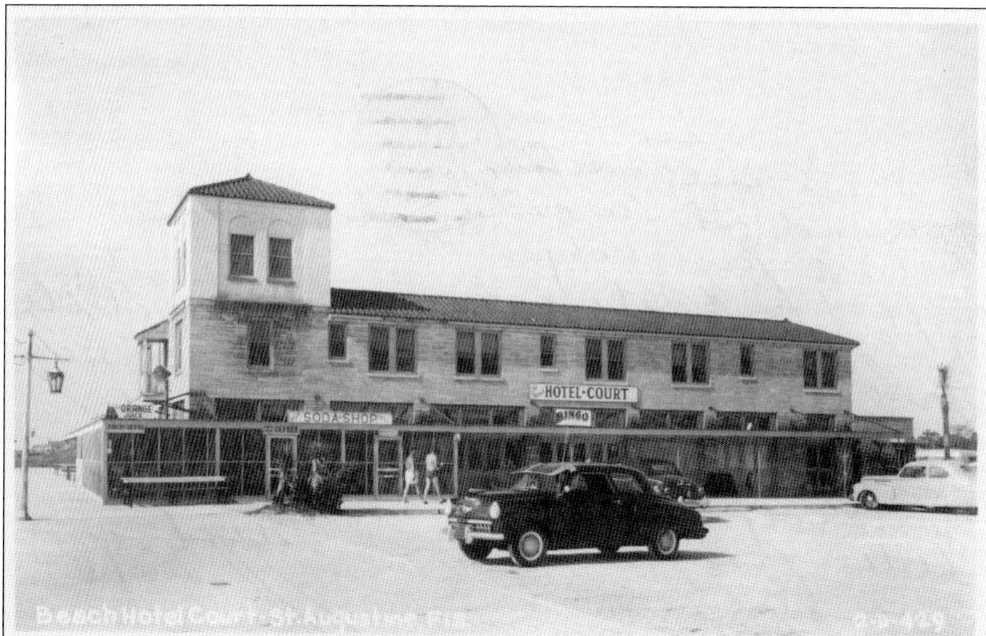

The south building at the pier featured a snack bar with hotel rooms on the second floor. Coquina used to construct both buildings was hauled from a reopened quarry just east of Old Beach Road. The City of St. Augustine Beach was incorporated in 1959 and used the south building as its town hall until 2001. It is now a community cultural center.

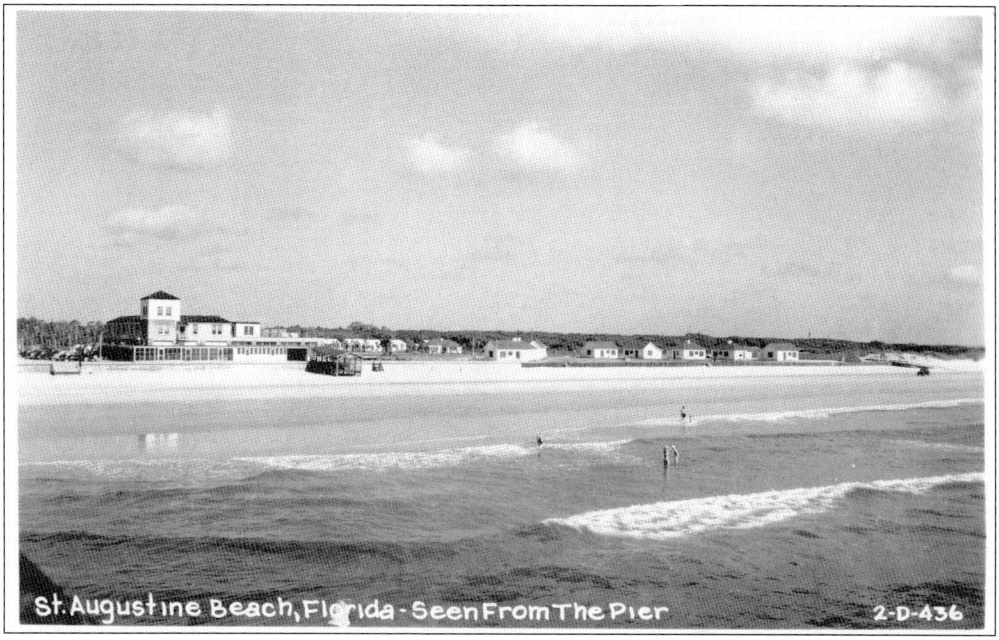

Looking north from the St. Augustine Beach pier, the Beach Hotel is on the left. To the right of the hotel are the cottages of the Ocean Manor tourist court, owned by local realtor and state senator Verle A. Pope. The beach ramp seen just north of the cottages is at the east end of Pope Road, named for him.

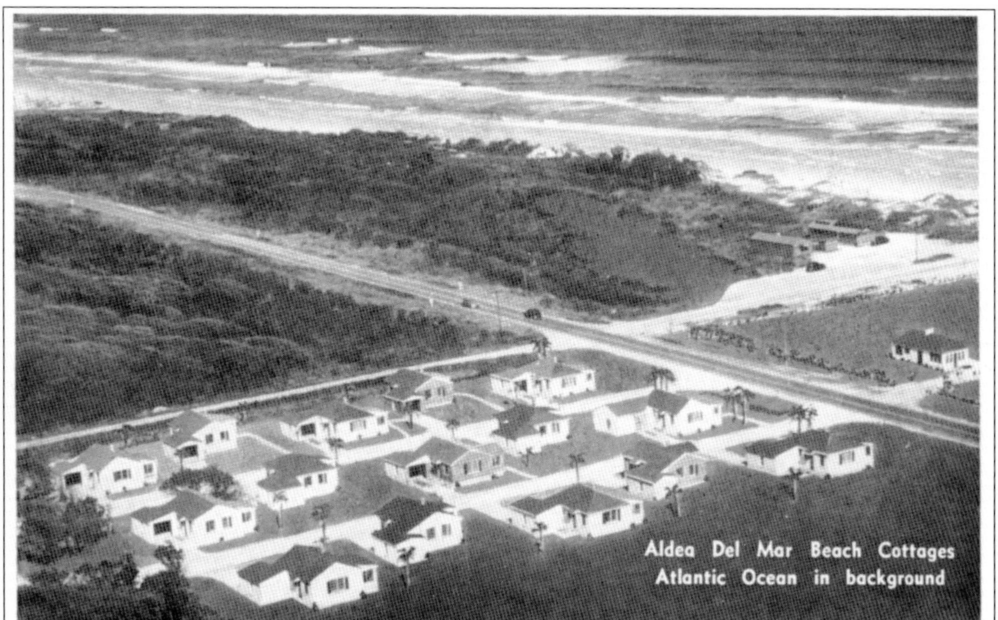

Located on A1A at Pope Road, Aldea del Mar—"Village by the Sea"—was built in 1947, and its cottages later converted to private homes. The land north of Pope Road, once part of a military reservation, became Anastasia State Park in 1949. Due to beach erosion, A1A north of Pope Road was relocated to the west, and that portion of the road seen in this postcard is completely washed away.

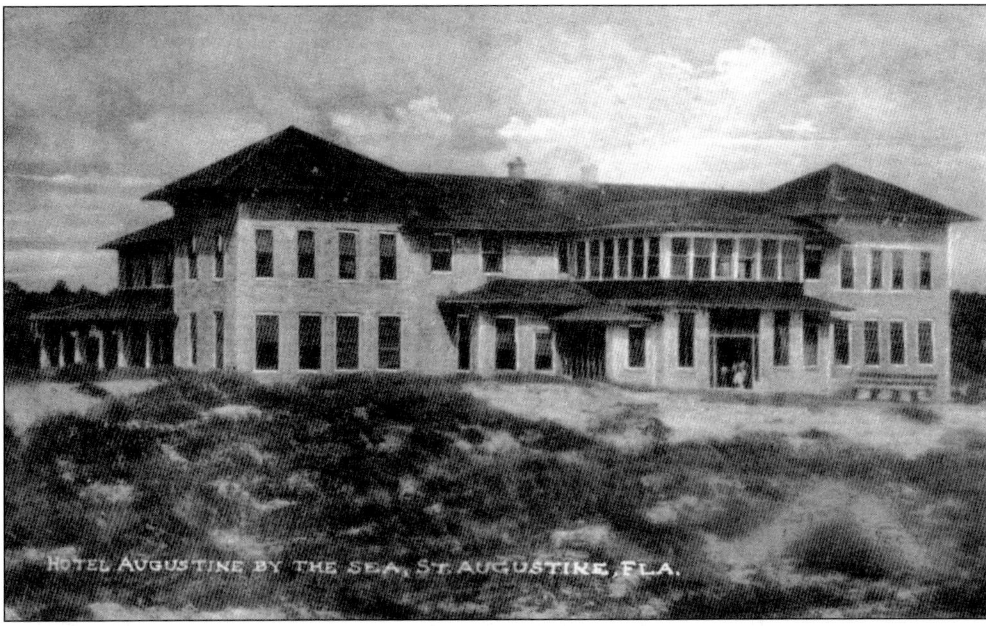

Located between Fourth and Fifth Streets at St. Augustine Beach, the Hotel Augustine by the Sea was built around 1915 as the Assembly Beach Hotel, part of the summer Chautauqua of the Mission Society of the Methodist Church. Over the years, the hotel has had many owners and name changes, the last being the Villa Gay Hotel before it was demolished to make way for Island South Condominiums.

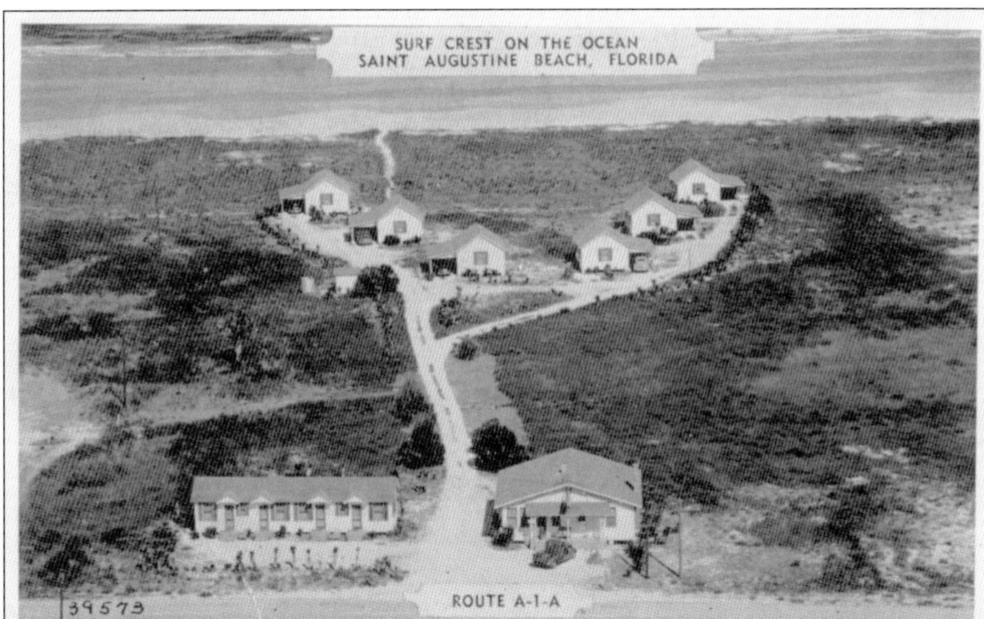

Built in the mid-1940s, the Surf Crest Cottages were located on A1A in St. Augustine Beach, about half a mile south of A Street. The house on the highway had formerly been a bathhouse, with an open center hallway and changing rooms on both sides. The location is now Surf Crest Village Condominiums at 838 A1A Beach Boulevard.

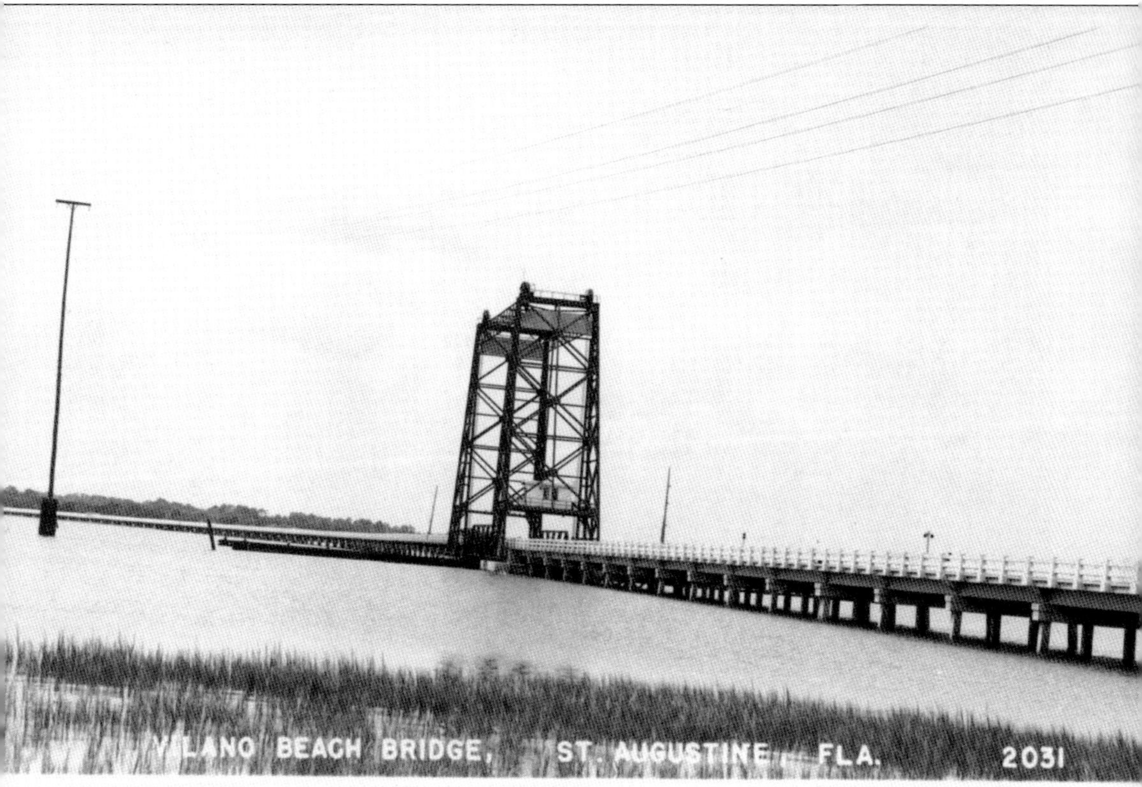

On the night of June 13, 1938, fire destroyed the eastern end of the wooden Vilano Beach bridge, built in the mid-1920s. A temporary single-lane bypass was constructed around the burned portion, and the eastern end was replaced with a concrete and steel structure that connected to the existing draw. Steel shortages during World War II delayed replacement of the bridge's western portion and draw until 1947. During the year of construction, the State of Florida contracted Francis Usina to operate his *Victory II* as a passenger ferry between Riverside Fishing Camp and the Usina's dock on Bay Street. The state also brought in some Word War II landing craft to ferry cars between slips near present-day St. Augustine Marina at Vilano and docks just north of the Bridge of Lions. The new bridge opened September 18, 1948, and remained in use until 1995, when it was replaced by the high-rise Francis and Mary Usina Bridge.

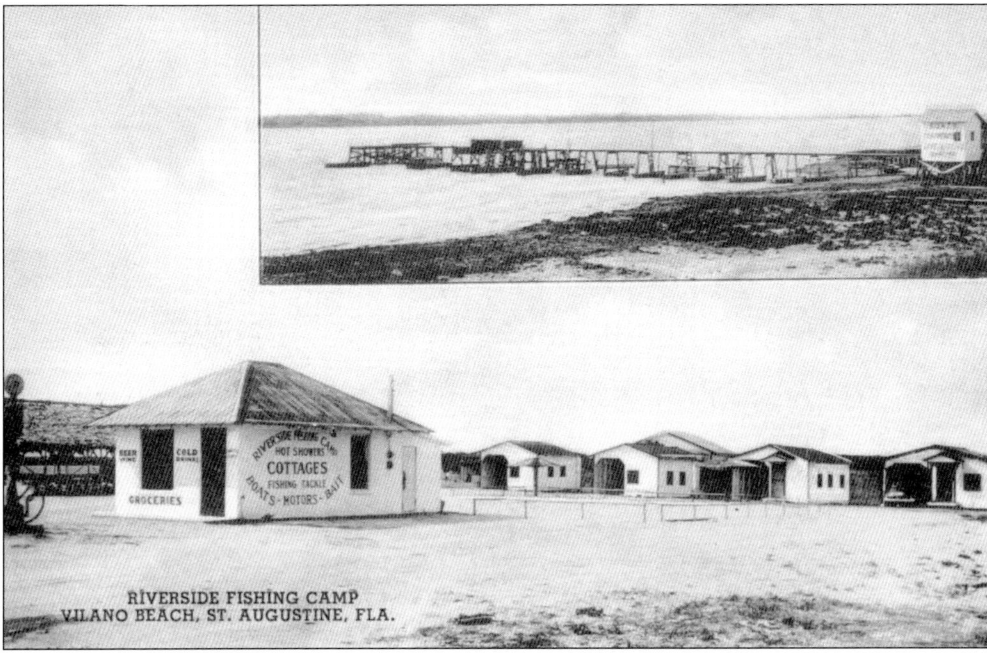

Riverside Fishing Camp was located on the north side of A1A at the east end of the Vilano Beach Bridge. The above postcard shows Riverside Cottages, operated in 1937 by Christobal Rogero. The business was soon taken over by Rogero's nephew Phillip J. Manucy Jr., who owned it until his death in 1976. Manucy expanded the operation with a larger store and featured a gas station, bait shop, and rental boats along with the cottages. Always known by locals as "P.J.'s," the fishing camp is now the location of Beaches Restaurant, but the old store still remains at 200 Vilano Road. (Above, O'Neill Collection.)

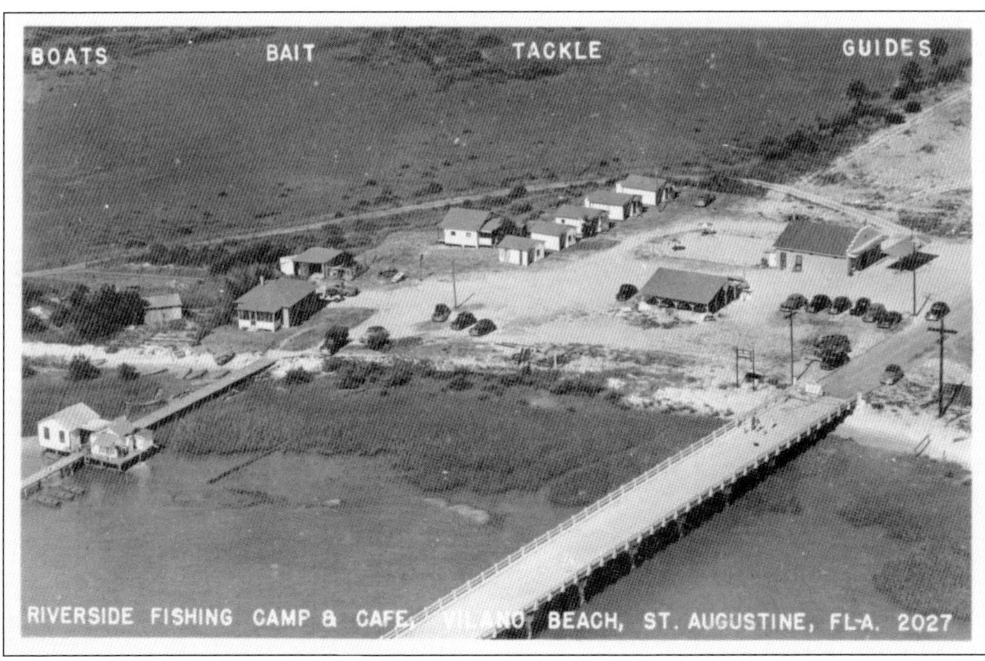

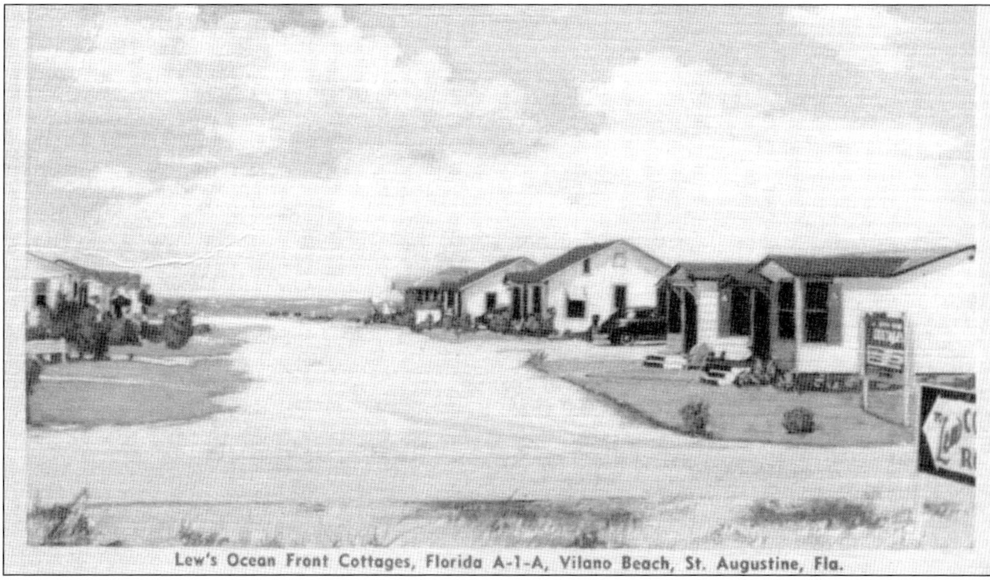

Lew's Oceanfront Cottages were located on A1A, three blocks north of the intersection of Coastal Highway and Vilano Road. Jacob Arthur Lew (1877–1937) owned the Lew Shop and Lew Building on Cathedral Place and was a large property owner in town; Lew Boulevard is named for him. His widow, Annie, ran the cottages at Vilano in the 1940s. After her death in 1950, ownership passed to Lew's nephew Harold Wayne.

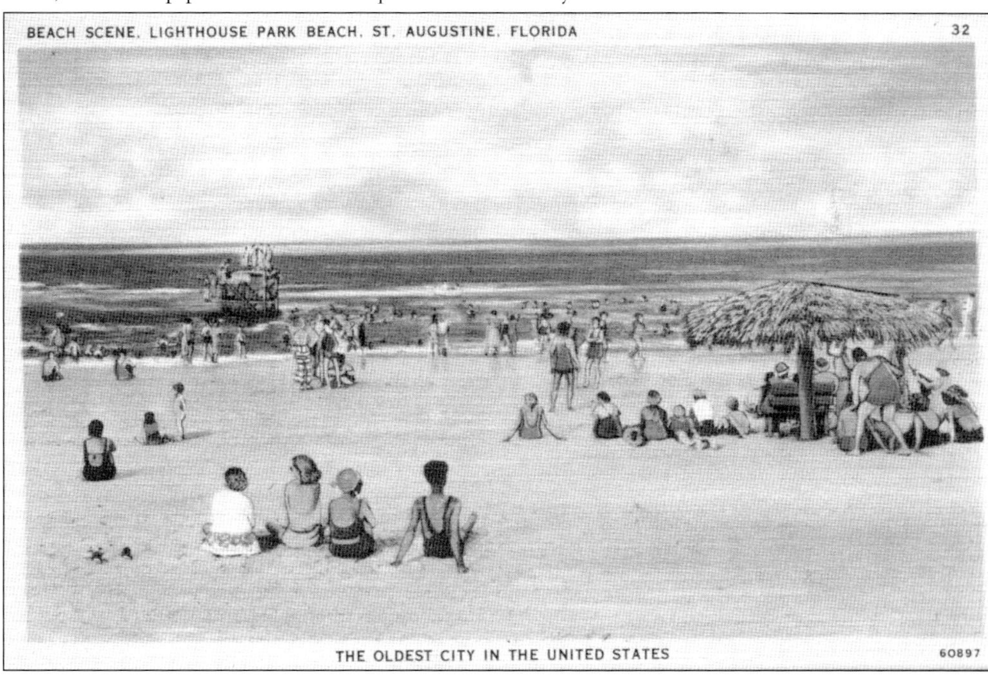

Prior to its relocation in 1940, the St. Augustine Inlet ran in a southeasterly direction, along what is today known as Salt Run. Lighthouse Park, a public beach in front of the lighthouse, featured thatched-roofed cabanas, a swimming area, a fishing pier, and a small restaurant called the Sea Gull. The dredging of this new inlet, lined with stone jetties, caused the old inlet to silt up and eventually close.

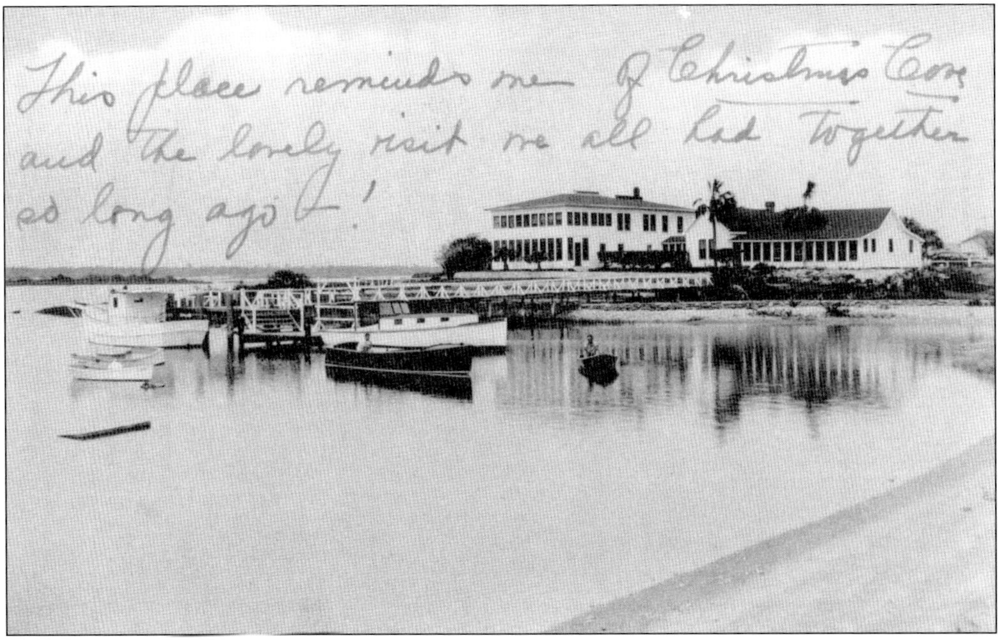

Summer Haven is 18 miles south of St. Augustine on the south side of the Matanzas Inlet. Founded in the 1880s by families from Palatka and Crescent City, it is likely Florida's first summer beach resort. This view looking north along the Summer Haven River around 1940 shows the Cove Tavern and Cottages, then owned by G.W. Noell. It has now been converted to a private residence.

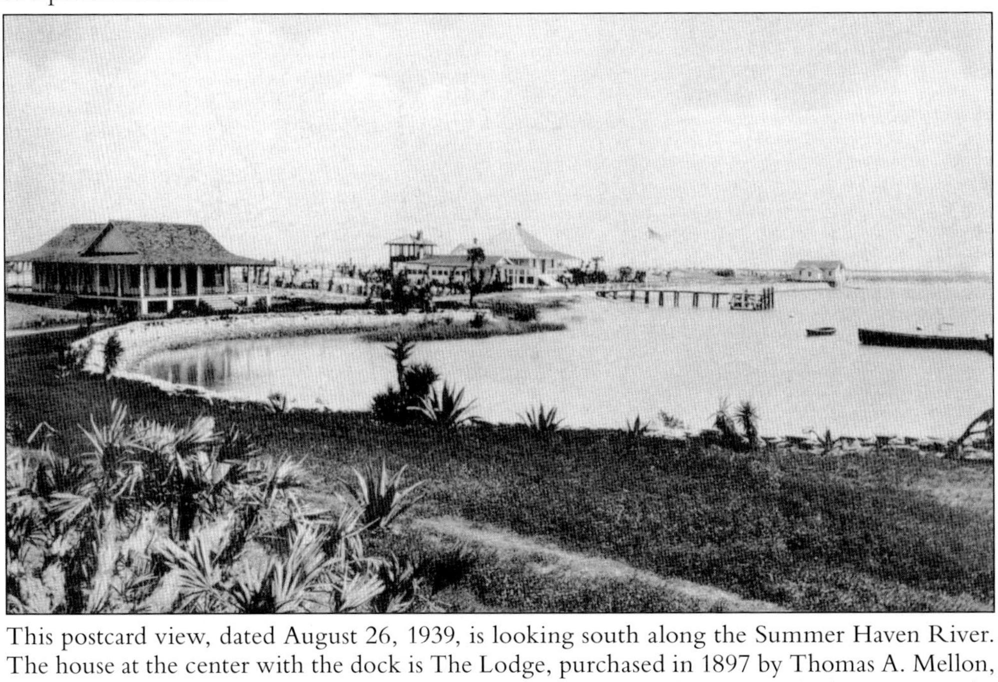

This postcard view, dated August 26, 1939, is looking south along the Summer Haven River. The house at the center with the dock is The Lodge, purchased in 1897 by Thomas A. Mellon, one of the heirs to the Pittsburgh Mellons' banking and industrial fortune. The house just to the left with the sun deck is The Hut, also a Mellon property. Both houses are currently vacation rentals. (O'Neill Collection.)

Ten

Artists' Postcards

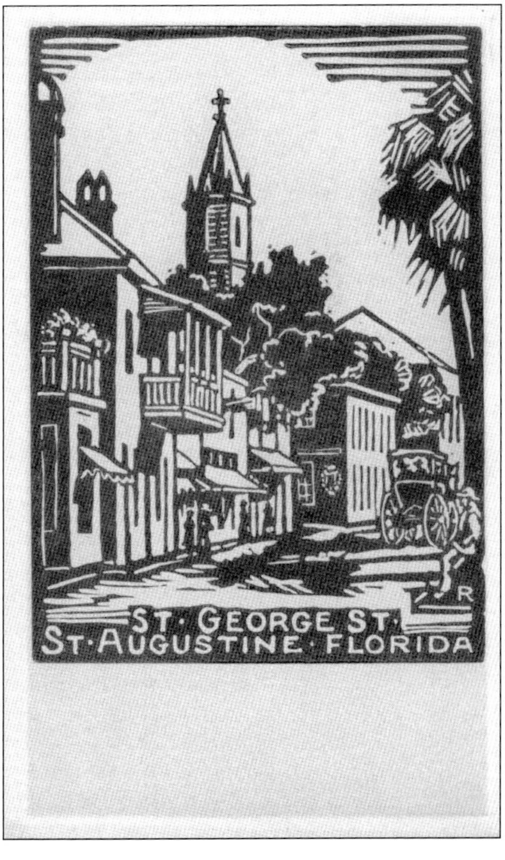

Celia Gregor Reid (1895–1956) was one of the town's most important artists and instrumental in founding the St. Augustine Arts Club in 1931. A versatile artist, she specialized in printmaking, decorative tiles, and jewelry. Her woodcut postcard of St. George Street looks south from Hypolita Street, with the Sanchez House at 105 St. George Street in the left foreground.

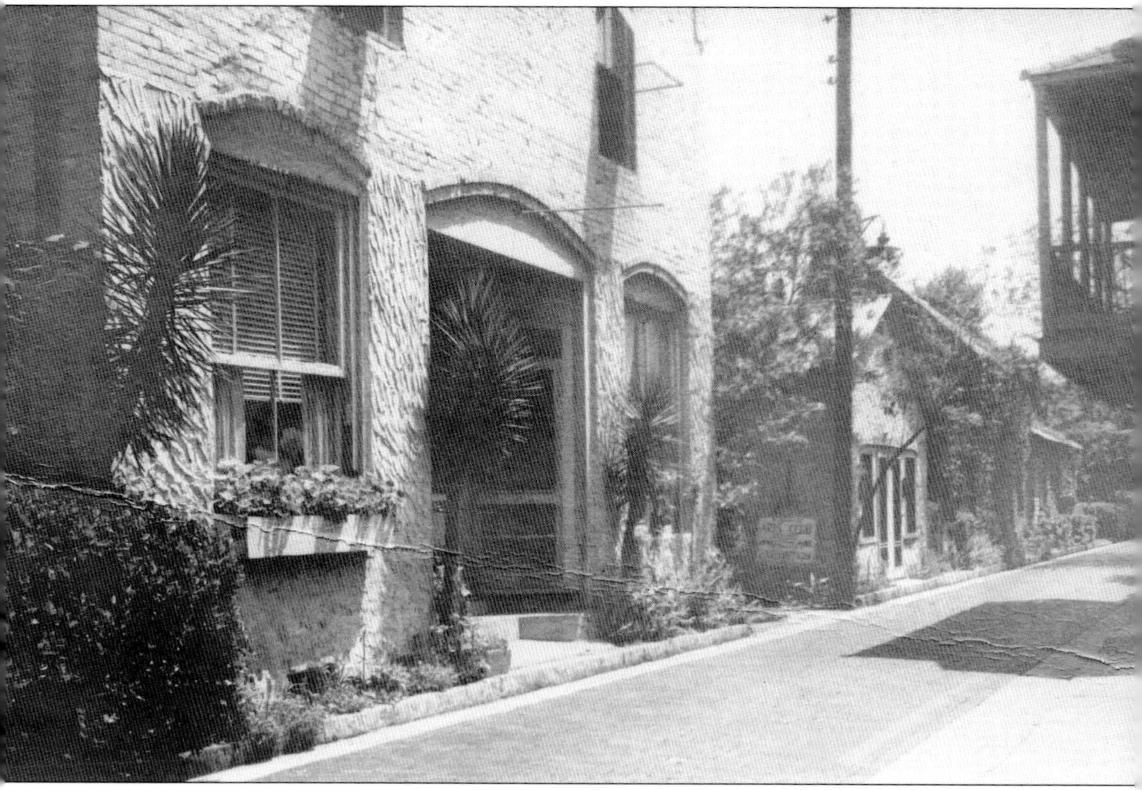

In the late 1930s, this Artists' Studio Building at 29 Aviles Street housed some of St. Augustine's most prominent painters, including Victor Casenelli, John Hare, and George F. Castleden. In January 1942, Arts Club leased the building directly behind this one at 230 Charlotte Street from Robert Oliver, husband of artist Edith Walker Oliver, and it remained the club's home until 1948. The small sign at the side of the house at 31 Aviles Street reads, "Arts Club Exhibition," with an arrow pointing down Baya Lane to direct visitors to the club's location. The buildings at 29 Aviles Street and 230 Charlotte Street have both been demolished and are now a small park with a marker for the Cofradia coquina well that once stood on the property. The balcony of the O'Reilly House can be seen at right. (Hird Collection.)

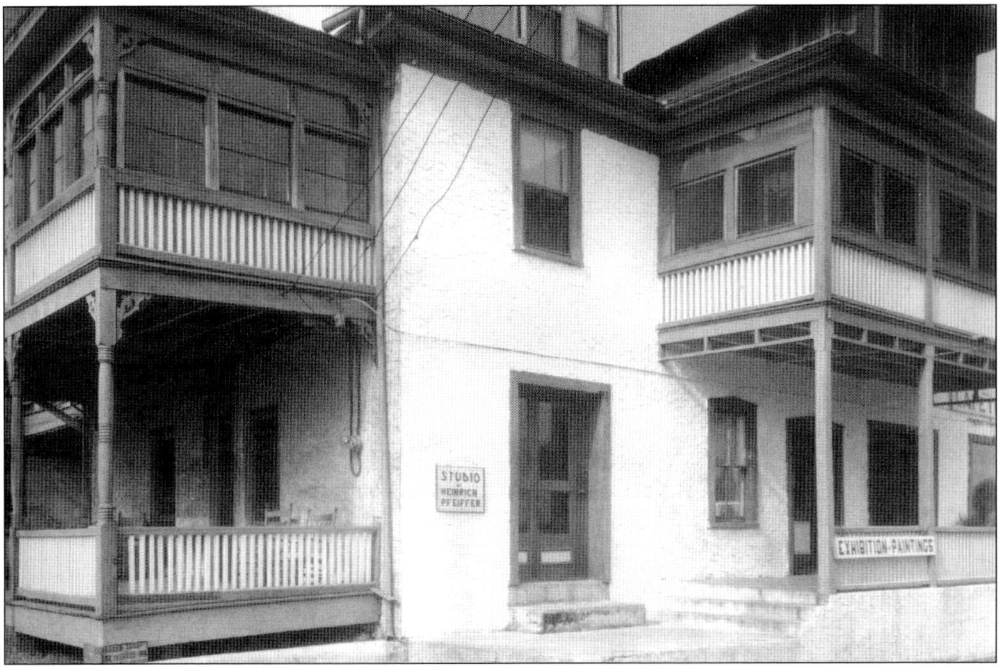

Shown in this 1937 image by Frances Benjamin Johnston, the Worth House at 16 Marine Street was then the studio of artist Henrich Pfeiffer (1874–1960). Born in Pennsylvania, Pfeiffer came to St. Augustine around 1920 and was one of the mainstays of the Arts Club. In 1961, the Worth House was dismantled and reconstructed across Marine Street and is now the home of O.C. White's Restaurant. (SAHS.)

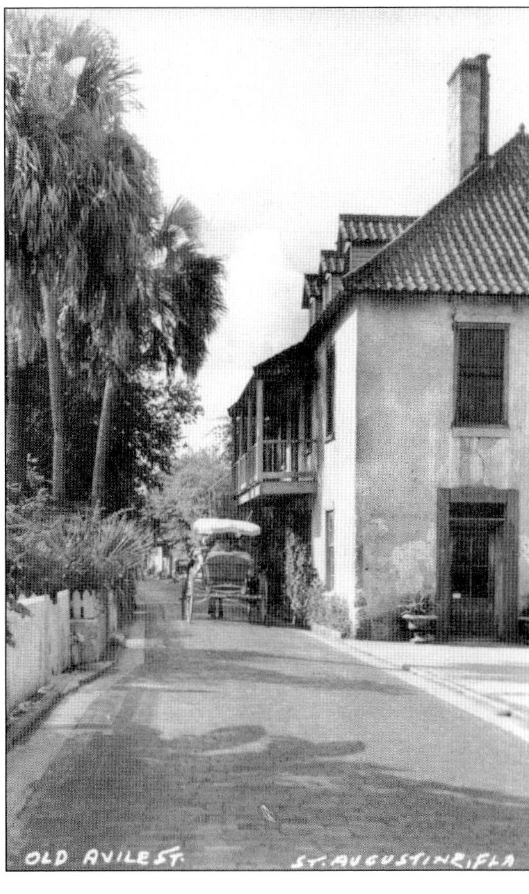

Artists were drawn to the quaint, old-world charm of Aviles Street, and it became the hub of a winter art colony. Tod Lindenmuth and his wife, Elizabeth Boardman Warren, first came to St. Augustine in 1934 and maintained a winter studio in the Fatio House at 22 Aviles Street, pictured here. They were soon joined by other artists from Provincetown, Gloucester, and Rockport, Massachusetts. (O'Neill Collection.)

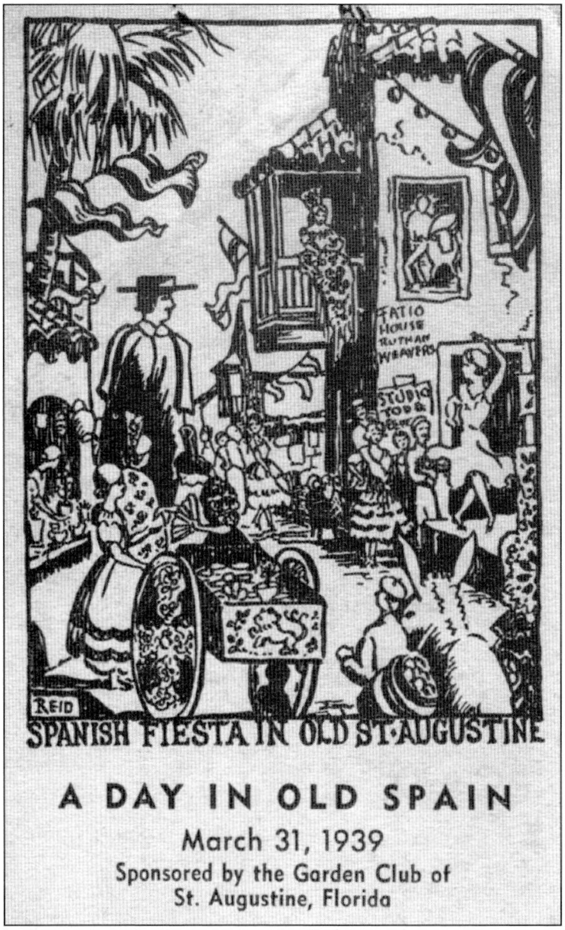

Celia Reid designed many of the posters for Arts Club events and the decorations for St. Augustine's street festivals. Her postcard advertises A Day in Old Spain, held on Aviles Street on March 31, 1939. Sponsored by the Garden Clubs of St. Augustine, the festival was a mini-revival of the Ponce de Leon Festival, last held in 1930. Reid's woodcut depicts the Fatio House on Aviles Street, home of many artists' studios at that time. The back of the postcard describes the festival's activities, which included *gigantes y cabezudos*—giants and big heads—costumes that were used for many years. The Aviles Street festival later became the Days in Spain, sponsored by the St. Augustine Jaycees. Reid's other woodcut postcard advertises the Old Curiosity Shop at 54 St. George Street (known today as the Dodge-Paredes House).

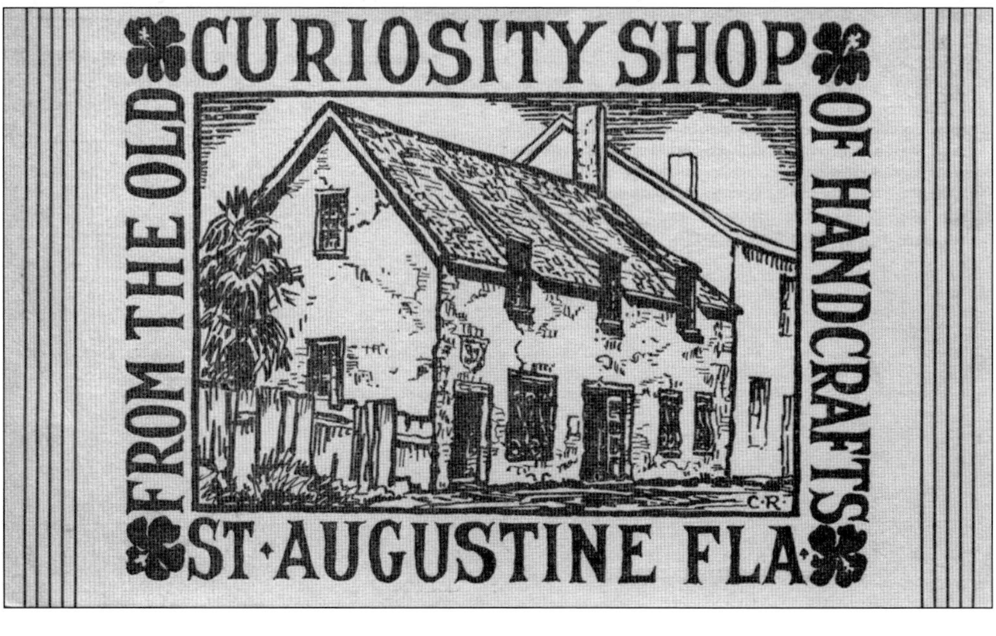

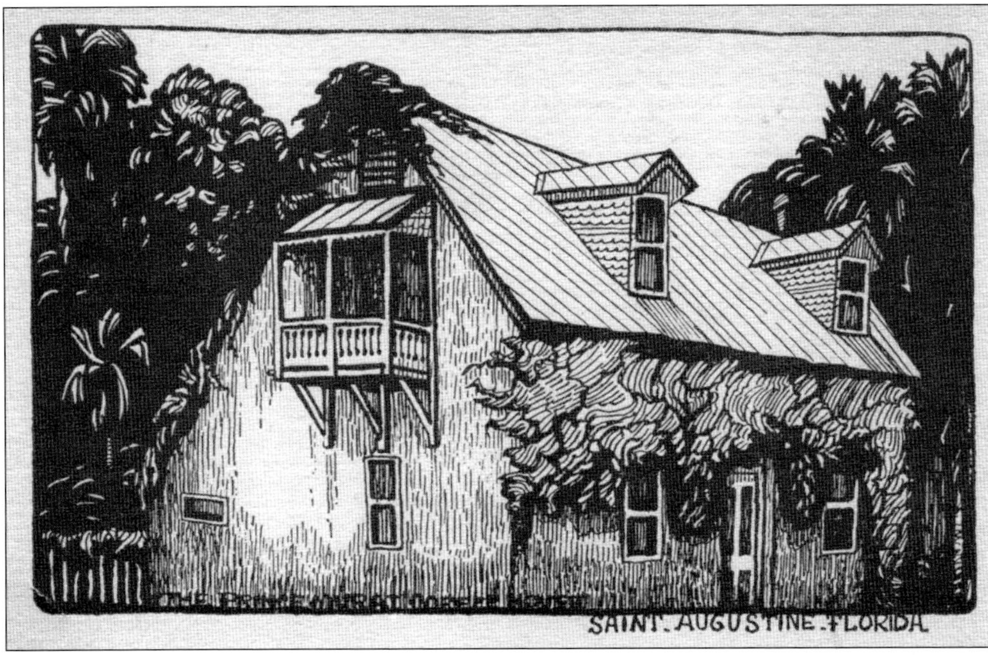

Hildegarde Muller-Uri (1894–1990) was the daughter of Henry S. Muller, owner of the Hotel Marion on Bay Street. Trained by Heinrich Pfeiffer, she lived and worked at her father's hotel, where she sold her artwork to the guests. A prolific artist specializing in woodcuts, she was one of the mainstays of the Arts Club, forerunner of today's St. Augustine Art Association. Her postcard above depicts the Prince Murat House, located on the northwest corner of St. George and Bridge Streets, when it was a coffee house in the late 1930s and early 1940s. At right is a charming view of Aviles Street, with the Fatio House at left. (Right, Whetstone Collection.)

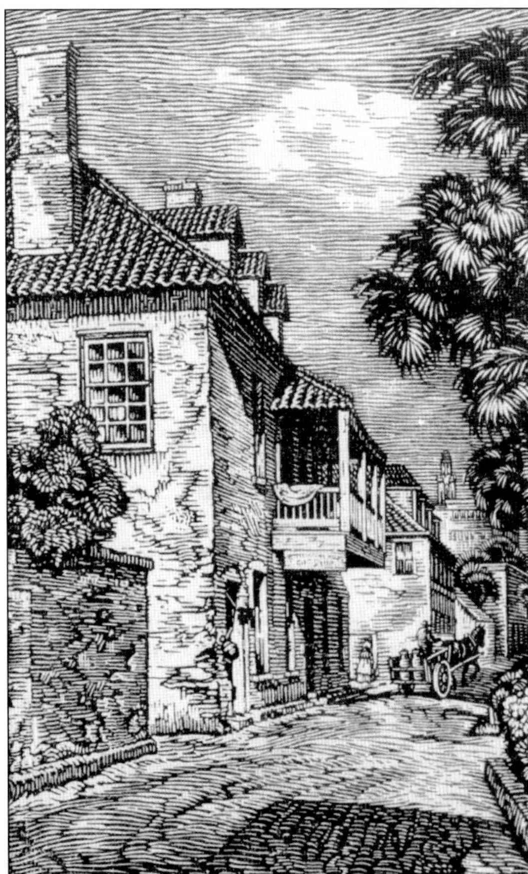

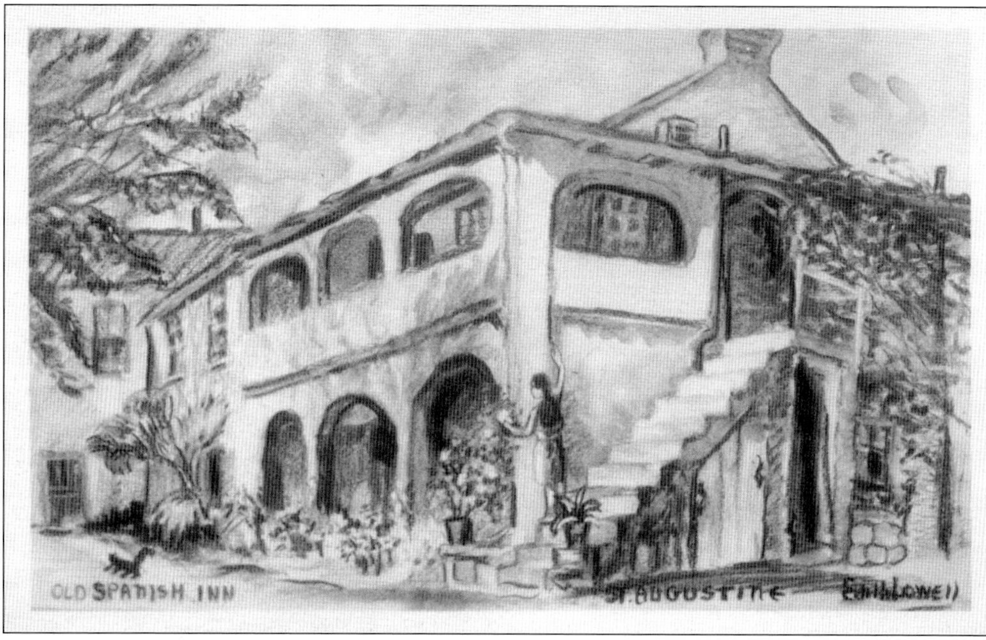

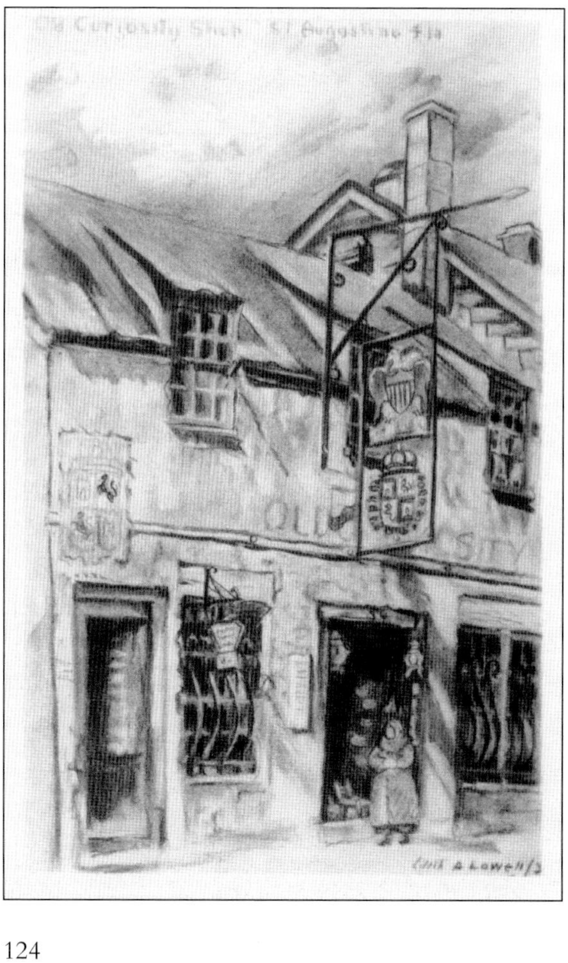

Edith Allen Lowell was a member of the Rockport Art Association and friend of Tod Lindenmuth and Elizabeth Boardman Warren. As she had done in Rockport and New York City, she created a series of postcards of different views of St. Augustine. Shown here are the rear courtyard of the Old Spanish Inn, today's DeMesa-Sanchez House, at 43 St. George Street, and the Old Curiosity Shop, or Paredes-Dogde House, at 54 St. George Street.

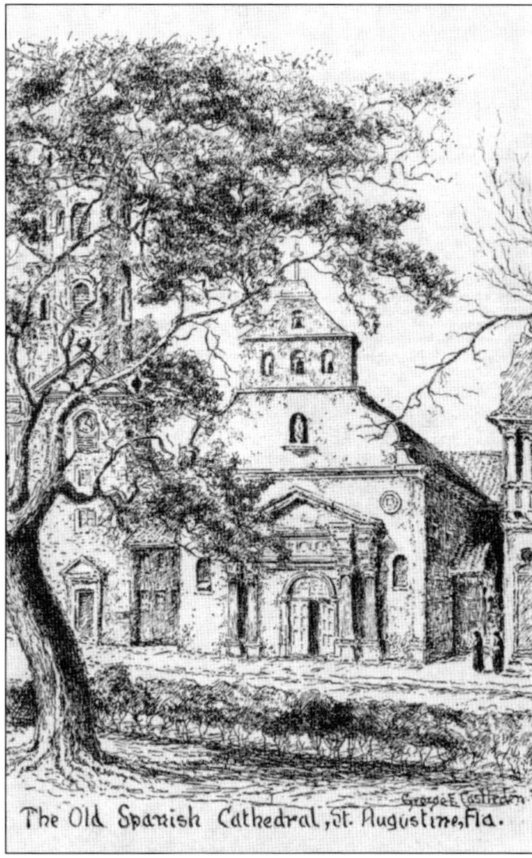

George Frederick Castleden was born in Canterbury, England, in 1861 and first came to the United States in 1903. He later became a prominent New Orleans artist and was a winter resident here during the late 1930s. He did a series of postcards of St. Augustine, including the Old Spanish Cathedral and Old Spanish Treasury, pictured here.

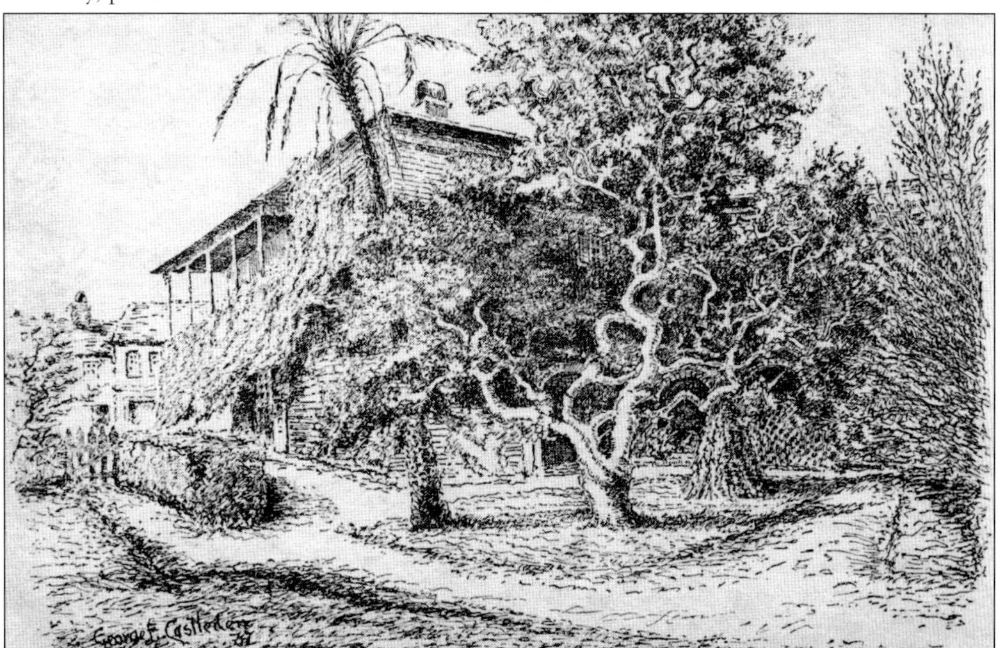

Bibliography

Bransom, Seth H. *Florida East Coast Railway*. Charleston, SC: Arcadia Publishing, 2006.

Graham, Thomas. *Flagler's St. Augustine Hotels*. Sarasota, FL: Pineapple Press, 2004.

———. *Mr. Flagler's St. Augustine*. Gainesville, FL: University of Florida Press, 2014.

Lamme, Ary J. III. *America's Historic Landscapes: Community Power and the Preservation of Four National Historic Sites*. Knoxville, TN: University of Tennessee Press, 1989.

McGoldrick, Sister Thomas Joseph. *Beyond the Call*. St. Augustine, FL: Self-published, Sister Thomas Joseph McGoldrick, 2008.

Messinger, Cheryl, and Terran McGinnis. *Marineland*. Charleston, SC: Arcadia Publishing, 2011.

Nolan, David. *The Houses of St. Augustine*. Sarasota, FL: Pineapple Press, 1995.

Parker, Susan R. "The St. Augustine Beach Hotel: A New Deal Project." *El Escribano* 42 (2005): 84–98.

Torchia, Robert W. *Lost Colony. The Artists of St. Augustine, 1930–1950*. St. Augustine, FL: The Lightner Museum, 2001.

Vigliotti, Jeannette. "A Real Senorita: Selling Spain in the 'Day in Old Spain' Festival." *El Escribano* 51–52 (2014–2015): 71–81.

About the Organization

The St. Augustine Historical Society is the oldest continuously operating museum and historical society in Florida. Beginning in 1881 as an informal group that met in private homes to discuss topics of historical and scientific interest, the society formally organized on New Year's Day 1883. In 1899, the society purchased a colonial house and its contents, known as the Vedder Museum, but these holdings were lost in a disastrous fire in 1914. Undaunted, the society struck a deal with the US Department of War to manage the abandoned Fort Marion, a tenure which lasted until 1935, when the fort became the Castillo de San Marcos National Monument.

In 1918, the society purchased two colonial buildings, the Tovar House and the González-Alvarez House, the latter of which had been exhibited to visitors since 1892 as the Oldest House (see images on page 84). In 1970, the González-Alvarez House was designated a National Historic Landmark by the US secretary of the interior. Today, these buildings form the nucleus of the Oldest House Museum Complex. In 1924, the society passed another milestone when it constructed the Webb Building, the first structure in Florida designed as a museum. The Webb Building today houses the Manucy Museum of St. Augustine history. In addition, the society is a steward of the Fernández-Llambias House, another National Historic Landmark. In the 1920s, the organization lobbied successfully for federal restoration of the 18th-century blockhouse Fort Matanzas.

During the 1950s, the society embarked on an ambitious program in preparation for the city's quadricentennial in 1965. Projects included a major restoration of the Oldest House and a complete redesign of the museum exhibits in the Webb Building. The society also restored four colonial houses, purchased several historic sites to create public parks, and built six houses in the "St. Augustine Style." In addition to its museum operations, the society has built the state's best private collection of documents, maps, photographs, and printed sources relating to the history of St. Augustine and early Florida. These collections are accessible to the public at the society's research library, located in the historic Seguí-Kirby Smith House, the birthplace of Confederate general Edmund Kirby-Smith. The society has long published books, pamphlets, and periodicals, which are available on its website, www.oldesthouse.org. The St. Augustine Historical Society continues to play an important role in the preservation and interpretation of the unique heritage of the nation's oldest city.